THE LAST ITALIAN

PORTRAIT OF A PEOPLE

GERMANY

Zurich • AUSTRIA

Bolzano •   Trieste •

SWITZERLAND

Padova •   Venice •

Lugano •   Verona •
                                      Ferrara •
Milan •   Parma •
Geneva •   Po River   Bologna •   Rimini •

Turin •   Genoa •   la Spezia •   • Florence
                                  Pisa •   Perugia •
FRANCE   • Livorno   Siena •

Nice •   Bastia •   ELBA

Mediterranean Sea   CORSICA   Ajaccio •

Sassari •
SARDINIA

Italy

AND SURROUNDINGS

Cagliari •

A DESTINATIONS BOOK

THE LAST ITALIAN

PORTRAIT OF A PEOPLE

WILLIAM MURRAY

INTRODUCTION BY JAN MORRIS

PRENTICE
HALL
PRESS

NEW YORK   LONDON   TORONTO   SYDNEY   TOKYO   SINGAPORE

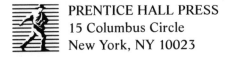 PRENTICE HALL PRESS
15 Columbus Circle
New York, NY 10023

Some of the material in this book has previously appeared in slightly different form in the following publications: "Cronaca di Roma," "The Chains of Hope," "Horseman, Come Back," "Forza, Italia!," "The Spoils of Sperlonga," "The Agony of Cassino," in *The New Yorker*; "The Queen of the Bogs" in *The Traveler*; "The Model and the Playboy" in *Cosmopolitan*; and "The Last Italian" in *California* magazine.

PRENTICE HALL PRESS and colophons are registered trademarks of Simon & Schuster, Inc.

Library of Congress Cataloging-in-Publication Data is available

ISBN 0-13-508227-7

Design by Robert Bull Design

Manufactured in the United States of America

10 9 8 7 6 5 4 3 2 1

First Edition

This book is dedicated to my mother, Natalia Danesi Murray, who gave me a great gift—an Italian heritage.

CONTENTS

FOREWORD

NOT TOO LONG ago I was browsing in my local bookstore through a number of travel guides to Italy and wondering what country the authors of these volumes were writing about. With one or two exceptions, most seemed to be describing an Italy I didn't know—a fairytale land of unpolluted beaches, unspoiled countrysides, inexpensive hotels and restaurants, great museums, superbly preserved cultural sites, and efficient public services. I found myself wanting to know if the authors of these books had recently spent any time in some of the places they were describing and actually taken part in the daily life of their inhabitants. They seemed to me to be perpetuating a highly romanticized view of a nation that had, in fact, ceased to exist nearly fifty years ago, with the advent of the Second World War and the social and industrial revolution that succeeded it.

I don't mean to imply that Italy is today devoid of the pleasures and benefits so glowingly delineated in the average guidebook—far from it—but I do mean to say that it is a far more complex and difficult place even to visit than the casual tourist is being led to believe. In essence, what Italy has done for the past four decades, since the end of the war and the adoption of a parliamentary democracy mostly dominated by the right-of-center Christian Democrats, is opt totally for an American-style capitalism that has transformed it from a largely agrarian society of small landowners, artisans, artists, and independent entrepreneurs to a heavily industrialized nation dominated, like our own, by banks and corporations in alliance with compliant politicians. This policy has brought a large measure of prosperity and created an entirely new middle class of property owners with a strongly vested interest in maintaining the system that has enriched them. And it has changed not only the way people live, but the very face of the country they inhabit.

Italy today is afflicted by all of the ills common to the modern industrialized state—hardcore unemployment, environmental pollution, inadequate public services and health care, a growing crime rate, the rise of a subproletariat of rootless young people in the streets, the drug traffic. To outsiders, the most visible sign of these woes is the growing squalor of the scene before them. In the cities, ancient buildings, monuments, and classic ruins rot in the polluted air or are shielded behind scaffoldings for restoration and preservation; around the so-called historic centers sprawl ugly housing developments and industrial slums; in the countrysides, woods and fields are disfigured by factories and trash dumps, once scenic coastlines have disappeared behind cement walls of villas, hotels, and apartment houses. As the late Peter Nichols, an English journalist who lived in Rome for many years, wrote in his introduction to *Fodor's Italy,* one of the best of the guidebooks available, "The drive from the airport, or the arrival on the outskirts by car from the motorway, necessarily takes one through ugly, unplanned suburbs, through nightmares of traffic, and dreadful moments of self-doubt arise about the wisdom of having decided to come to Italy at all."

It is not the purpose of this book, however, to discourage anyone from going to Italy. I myself go nearly every year, sometimes twice a year, and I'm never entirely at peace with myself when I'm not there. The purpose of most guidebooks, after all, is not necessarily to be reportorially truthful about a place, but to persuade tourists to visit it by pointing out only its best features; I suspect that even Dante's lower levels of the Inferno could be glowingly described and made irresistible by a peppy travel writer. What I am trying to do, on the other hand, is to protray some aspects of the Italy I know, which are not the ones to be found in the average guidebook. And I am writing about the country not merely as an outsider, but as someone who has lived there and loves it as deeply as I do my own.

Although I was born in New York City, I spent most of the first eight years of my life in Italy, Switzerland, and France. By the time my mother, a native Roman, brought me back to New York in the mid-thirties, I spoke only Italian and French and I was a little European boy who just happened to have an American father. And although I quickly became, like many immigrant children, more American than my schoolmates who had grown up here, I never entirely lost touch with my earliest background. When I went back to Italy after the war to study music, it was like coming home and it wasn't long before I was speaking Italian fluently again.

I have been going back and forth ever since, for extended visits as well as stays of a year or more, depending largely on work. In 1962, I wrote my first "Letter from Rome" for *The New Yorker*, where I have been on staff, originally as a fiction editor, since 1956, and I have now been contributing more or less regularly to the magazine and other publications from Italy and elsewhere for over thirty years. It has been a dream assignment and I can't imagine a more satisfying way for a writer to live, especially because Italy has proven to be a cornucopia providing endless nourishment to the soul and mind. In 1982, in an earlier book entitled *Italy: The Fatal Gift,* after a quotation from Lord Byron ("Italia! O Italia! thou who hast/The fatal gift of beauty"), I wrote out of my Roman background and about many of the sights, sounds, and people—especially the people—that make Italy such a fascinating place.

In this volume, I am picking up pretty much where I left off eight years ago. Some of the material has appeared in *The New Yorker* and elsewhere, in somewhat different form, and some is original. It is essentially a collection of pieces about a variety of Italian events and topics that at first glance might seem to be unconnected, but I would like to think that there is an underlying, unifying thread here that transcends mere geography. It is not by accident that I have called the book *The Last Italian,* the title of its closing chapter, which is about an old Roman surviving his era and living out his last days far from home, in the streets of San Francisco.

With all the changes that have occurred during the past few decades in Italy, largely as a result of the country's heedless materialistic onrush into a future dictated largely by the silicon chip and venture capital, one constant has remained—the Italian character, in all its infinite variety. What seems consistently to emerge from the pages I write about Italy are aspects of this character—brilliant, artistic, theatrical, inventive, energetic, irreverent, irresponsible, witty, cynical, and spectacularly improvisational. Italians, one must constantly bear in mind, are survivors, who have come together to form an independent nation for not much more than a century. As a result, they have always been quick to subvert authority and to salvage from defeat and oppression whatever opportunities have presented themselves. Often this has meant having to leave home, taking with them and preserving wherever they went the basic attitudes and characteristics that distinguished them as Italians.

Italy, therefore, is not simply a geographical entity, but an ethos—a point of view I hope is confirmed by what I have written in these pages. Everywhere I go I carry a bit of her around with me and I tend to look upon the activities of mankind in general with a point of view I like to think of as quintessentially Italian. "Is there any other country in Europe where the character of the people seems to have been so little affected by political and technological change?" W. H. Auden asked, in the introduction he wrote some years ago to an edition of Goethe's *Italian Journey.* I doubt it and I think it's the main reason that we all keep going back.

—William Murray

INTRODUCTION
BY JAN MORRIS

IT WAS IN 1849 that Count Metternich described Italy as being "merely a geographical expression," but his apothegm still has point today. Italy has been a united nation for 120 years, but the people of its different provinces still vary widely in style, temperament, and physique, honor a relatively pragmatic kind of patriotism, and are more immune than most of us to the homogenizing effects of politics and technology. Their country seems to me less the Republic of Italy, even now, than just a place where the Italians live—or even more grandly, a place where *people* live, Italians so often appearing to possess some particular arcana of universal humanity. During the World Cup Soccer tournament of 1990 I was not alone in rooting for the Italian team simply as representative of us all.

It is very proper then that William Murray, who was born of an Italian mother, lived part of his childhood in Italy and has spent three decades writing about the country, should give this book a grandly generous form. Not for him the narrowing of vision that goes with political or social theory, still less with tourist literature. He is writing about a real place, a place of many beauties but of much ugliness too, which has been as familiar with war and crime as it has been with art and saintliness. This is a work not about the appearances or even the reputation of Italy, but about the straight contemporary truth of it.

INTRODUCTION

Perhaps only an author of mixed Italian and foreign blood could really do such a thing—and especially one who has watched Italy undergo the astonishing changes that have occurred since the Second World War, transforming the country for better or for worse from a picturesque survival of an older Europe into an unusually forceful example of industrial capitalism. William Murray is at ease both with rural and with city Italians. He has an eye for the corrupt and the absurd, as well as for the splendid. He can interpret for us the twin languages of earthiness and spirituality that are vernaculars of Italy, homeland both to the College of Cardinals and the underground Black Economy. Not least, he can write with a touching empathy about the last Italian of his title—the archetypal Italian emigrant, living out his life in a San Francisco retirement home but still at least as Italian as the relatives he left at home so long before.

Perhaps I am being romantic, when I see in the Italians some enlarged or clarified mirror image of us all, with all our failings and all our virtues. Perhaps I am only wishing, as so many of us do, that I could be more like an Italian myself. Whatever the truth, *The Last Italian* makes one realize once more that somehow or other the people of the peninsula—even when they are dying in California—have held themselves closer than most of us to the elementals of life, death, humor, and love, not to mention profit and good food.

THE LAST ITALIAN

PORTRAIT OF A PEOPLE

ROMANS
FROM ROME

It is good to trust, but it is better not to trust.

—old Roman proverb

CHAPTER
ONE

CRONACA DI ROMA

THE EARLY MORNING sounds of the street in Rome where Andrea d'Angelo works are as familiar to his ears as the voices of his wife and children. There are, first of all, the intonations of the people in the quarter, quintessentially Roman in character—calls of greeting and instruction, jokes, friendly insults, warnings to small children on their way to school, imprecations against the fates, the weather, the authorities, the deities who are supposed to watch over daily events but too often fail to do so. These very human utterances, couched most often in the harsh, nasal, shattered accents of larynxes nurtured largely on wine, pasta, bread, and cheese, and aged by overuse to a fine, mellow tone of bellowed insouciance, rise like a chorus from the cobblestones outside Andrea's establishment, a *trattoria* called Il Grappolo d'Oro.

From the moment Andrea arrives to begin his working day inside the Grappolo, which is located on the Piazza della Cancelleria, in one of the oldest quarters of the *centro storico,* these voices never entirely cease, even in midafternoon, when many Romans take a *pisolino,* an hour's rest, to digest their food and refresh themselves for an assault on the second half of the day; always, somewhere, someone will be calling, either to summon a child to duty or to bewail the failure of some project or simply to assert the validity of a claim to someone else's attention. "A-a-a-ah, Mario-o-oh, what are you doing? . . . A-o-o-oh! You think I'm stupid? . . . E-e-eh! But who's this here? Come

3

here, beauty! . . . A vision! A miracle! Listen, Elena, now I'll tell you!
Cretina! . . . Hurry up, *stupido,* we're dying of hunger here! . . . *Mah!*
They can kill you, what do you care? . . . Listen to him, will you? A
mountain of lies, not a word of truth . . . A-o-o-oh, but what's happening? But what is this, the end of the world? . . ." The shouted senti-
ments punctuate Andrea's day, but so familiarly that most of the time
he doesn't even hear them. They merely act as an acoustical background to cushion the rhythm of his labors. Without them, he would
undoubtedly begin to question his presence there, perhaps even the reality of his existence.

The voices are not the only sounds from the street. There are, of
course, all the familiar other noises of the quarter at work—windows
and doors opening and closing, shutters banging, objects falling or being dragged across the cobblestones, chairs scraping over pavements,
the screech of iron screens raised and lowered by the local shopkeepers as they open and close their establishments in concert with the
passing hours. All these are sounds Andrea has heard all of his working days, not only in this street, but in all of the streets and piazzas he
has labored in for the past forty-three years, ever since he first came to
the city.

If he doesn't hear them as well now, if he fails to individualize
them at all anymore, it is not only familiarity that has dulled his senses.
The tapestry of small, human voices and familiar activities that once
compiled the whole of Andrea's aural connection to his world has been
shattered by the internal-combustion engine, which has dominated the
air ever since Rome all but disappeared beneath the tidal wave of automobiles that began to wash over the peninsula in the mid-1950s and
has since all but submerged it.

The Grappolo d'Oro is located in a part of town from which traffic has not yet been banned, so that the dominant sound of the whole
quarter has become the roar of engines of all sizes and types at the service of citizens for whom the ownership of a motor vehicle has become
synonymous with material well-being. Andrea himself drives to work
every day from his home in the Tiburtina quarter, about six miles away,
and parks as close to the front door of his restaurant as he can. His car,
a tiny, white Fiat Fiorino, is only one of dozens parked in the immediate area, many of them illegally, and it now seems as natural to him to
drive to work in a great, honking mass of cars and trucks through the

4

twisting streets of old Rome as it once did to walk or to ride his bicycle when he was young and just starting out. Ordinarily, it should take no more than fifteen minutes to drive from his house to the restaurant, but often, especially in the morning rush hour, from eight to nine, it will take him at least forty minutes of agonizing bumper-to-bumper maneuvering to get there. And by the time he arrives, he often complains, his ears are accustomed only to traffic noises, his senses dulled to merely human life.

I once discussed this problem of the automobile with Andrea over a *grappa* late one night at a table in the back of the restaurant. I pointed out to him that every day the local news, the so-called *cronaca di Roma* on the inside pages of the newspapers, was dominated by accounts of accidents in which citizens had been maimed or killed by the automobile. The letters columns were full of protests about traffic abuses. People wanted to know why the municipality's tow trucks weren't more diligent in removing cars parked in hospital entrances, on narrow streets where they blocked the passage of buses, on sidewalks, even on the steps of churches. Why, readers of the *cronaca* insisted, should the huge air-conditioned sightseeing buses full of tourists be allowed to obscure the city's most famous monuments? How were people supposed to get in and out of their front doors or their places of business without having to scramble like mountain goats over vehicles jammed side by side in every available, if often illegal, space?

I reminded Andrea that walking had been one of the traditional pleasures of daily life in Rome. He and I had arrived in the city within a year and a half of each other, he in late 1945 and I in the spring of 1947, when Italy had barely begun to recover from the hardships of the war years and the German and Allied occupations. There were trolley cars in service, including a line, the *circolare,* that encircled the inner city, bounded in part by the Aurelian Wall, and there were electric buses, linked umbillically to overhead power lines, that snaked through various sections, although the current failed often and was periodically shut off for hours at a time. A few gasoline-powered monsters roared along the Corso and other main arteries, but the best way to get around the *centro* then was by hopping on and off the *camioncini,* rickety jitneys, some of them powered by sputtering motorcycle engines, whose owners had improvised and appropriated various routes through the city, thus making it possible to get from one quarter to another. Otherwise people travelled on foot or by bicycle. Few citizens had private cars and these disappeared at night, hidden away behind locked gates and high walls. Public transport stopped soon after nightfall, taxis were very scarce, and by eleven P.M. the city had emptied itself of vehicles. The great piazzas and monuments and ruins basked serenely under dim street lamps and I remember long evenings of late-night conversations with friends at various outdoor cafés, after which we would stroll home through silent streets, the only noise the sound of our footsteps on the cobblestones. I now recall that period of my life as an enchanted time.

"And what were you doing then?" Andrea asked.

I had spent part of my childhood in Rome, I informed him, and I had come back to live in Italy after the war, mainly to study music. I wanted to become an opera singer.

"Ah, then you were not working," he said.

"I was studying."

He nodded, as if trying to imagine what my life had been like compared to his own. "Luckily, I did not have to walk far," he said. "And then for a while I had a bicycle."

I began to understand that the prospect of walking anywhere or riding in a crowded bus would obviously not seem attractive to a man who had spent most of his life on his feet. The complaints and debates raging in the *cronaca* left Andrea indifferent. "It is a small but comfortable car and I can listen to the radio," he said. "I also use it to shop for the restaurant." The automobile, I realized, was not a source of inconvenience and needless expense to him; it had, in addition, become a symbol of his achievement and his status in society.

ANDREA HAS lived in the Tiburtina for thirty years. The quarter is named after the old Roman road the Emperor Hadrian used to get back and forth from his famous villa at Tivoli. Andrea settled there because it is also the road that leads to his home town of Amatrice, a rural center in the hills of upper Lazio, almost on the border of the mountainous region of the Abruzzi.

For some reason, most of the best cooks in Rome come either

from Umbria, the province north of the city, or the Abruzzi, and Andrea's father was also a chef. Amatrice is full of good cooks and has given its name to one of Italy's better pasta dishes, spaghetti or *bucatini all'amatriciana* (or, in corrupted form, *alla matriciana*). The town also has a so-called dancing tower, which oscillates a foot and a half or more when its powerful bells ring out the hours, and the hills surrounding it were, according to legend, once populated by witches, who could be observed on Saturday nights holding diabolical meetings and cavorting about the countryside. Otherwise, Amatrice has not much to recommend it, according to Andrea. It is a sleepy, provincial center with little industry and, as in most areas of the south, much unemployment.

Although Andrea had relatives in Amatrice, for many years he seldom returned there, except for occasional holiday visits. He had no car and it wasn't easy then to get back and forth by bus or train. Also, he was working very long hours and had little time off. When he moved to the Tiburtina, however, it comforted him to feel that he was living in a part of Rome that could be said to be on the way back to his place of origin. Also, when he first moved there, much of the quarter was still open countryside and not like living in a big city at all. Parts of the area were even without light and water, and it was full of squatters, fugitives from the poverty of the provinces who had come to Rome to find work and couldn't afford to live anywhere else. "When my husband brought me to live here in 1934, it was terrible," one old woman recently recalled in the *cronaca* of a Roman daily. "The tears ran every other minute. People said to me, 'You'll see, you'll get used to it.' In fact, I did get used to it, I've become a fighter."

By the time Andrea and his bride Marcella settled in the Tiburtina, the quarter had begun to explode with the blocks of large apartment houses, thrown up here and there practically overnight, that distinguished the unbridled building boom of the late fifties. The Tiburtina flowered into a postwar *borgata,* an outlying residential area in which the red, pink, and yellow palazzi seemed to be tumbled on top of one another without reason and in violation of all zoning laws requiring adequate public space, roads, schools, and parks. To the writer Pier Paolo Pasolini, who wrote about the Tiburtina at the time in his novel *Una Vita Violenta,* the whole quarter "looked really like Jerusalem, with that mass of slabs, one on top of the other, aligned over the fields, against the old quarries and glaring in the full light of the sun. . . ."

About twenty-five thousand people now live in the Tiburtina, with a population density that is one of the highest in the city. Andrea and Marcella, a Roman girl whom he met while working in a restaurant, own an apartment in one of the newer palazzi, with adequate air and light and enough room to have raised their two children, Maria, twenty-eight, and Paolo, twenty-two, in comfort. By the time they settled in the Tiburtina, the worst of Andrea's early struggles to survive in Rome were over and they were relatively well off. For others in the quarter, the memories of life there in the early years are bitter; it was a place to escape from. "It is still a ghetto and it's difficult to get yourself out of it," commented a young woman who grew up there and recently moved away. "It's a mark that remains stuck to you all your life."

UNTIL I met Andrea, I had never known anyone who lived in a *borgata*. Part of my childhood had been spent in the streets and parks of the *centro storico,* where my Roman relatives and ancestors on my mother's side of the family had lived all of their lives. My earliest memories of Rome were of various houses and apartments, all of them with gardens and terraces from where one could look out over the city, with its scores of church cupolas and hillsides peppered with private villas and stands of umbrella pines. Always, I remember, the focus of my gaze, especially from the rooftop terrace of my grandmother's apartment, would be the dome of St. Peter's, which seemed to soar hugely out of the earth, as if summoned to appear by the force of longing it represented. I could never have imagined living in Rome and not being within sight of it, or, for that matter, within easy distance of the Castel Sant'Angelo, the Campidoglio, the Colosseum, the various ancient forums, and all the other famous ruins that had become neighborhood landmarks to me.

Later, when I went back to Rome as an aspiring tenor, after a gap of fourteen years during which I lived mainly in New York, it would never have occurred to me to settle anywhere but in the *centro.* A few of my relatives, including my aunts Lea and Franca, my mother's younger sisters, had by then moved into newer neighborhoods, where the streets were wider and lined by the sort of comfortable middle-class apartment houses I had become used to in Manhattan. I couldn't understand why they had done so. The very heart of old Rome was where I wanted to be and during that period of nearly five years, when I remained uninterruptedly in the city, I lived in various rooms or shared cramped quarters somewhere in the ancient *rioni* on both sides of the Tiber. Wherever I happened to be, it was always within easy walking distance of the Rome I knew and loved best, a triangular cobweb of streets and alleys, piazzas, baroque churches, Renaissance palazzi, and ancient stone houses anchored by the Piazza del Popolo, Santa Maria in Trastevere, and the Colosseum. And for the past thirty-five years, during which I've managed almost always to spend at least several weeks and occasionally months at a time in the city, I've followed the same pattern, whether staying with relatives and friends or in one of the small hotels in the area between the Spanish Steps and the Pantheon.

I only became aware of the *borgate* in the late 1950s, as a social phenomenon. Italy was in the midst of a tremendous industrial boom and the *borgate,* in all their hideousness and squalor, at least represented a break from the old stratified order of things. Italians of the new middle class, acquiring their first cars, refrigerators, and television sets, not only couldn't find adequate housing in the older sections of their cities but often actually preferred living in these new neighborhoods, where the plumbing worked and the air was cleaner and the countryside was only minutes away. If none of the people I had grown up with and cared about happened to live in the *borgate,* this was only because they simply hadn't had to fight their way up from the bottom.

During the 1960s, my Aunt Franca and her husband occupied a large, rambling flat at one end of the Campo de'Fiori, a piazza in the middle of the old papal city through which travellers passed on their way to the Vatican and which today is still the site of a daily open-air market that can trace its origins back to the days of the ancient Roman Republic. It is also very near a number of other famous locations and landmarks, such as the Palazzo Farnese, the Piazza Navona, and the Palazzo della Cancelleria, once the home of the papal chancellery and still housing several ecclesiastical courts. From time to time, I would eat out in the area, which teems with small restaurants, wine bars and cafés, and it was thus that I happened to discover the Grappolo d'Oro.

The Palazzo della Cancelleria, built in the late fifteenth century and long regarded as one of the most beautiful Renaissance palaces in the city, quite naturally dominates its surroundings. In fact, it occupies one whole side, the head, of the T-shaped piazza named after it. The Grappolo d'Oro is located in an ancient, thick-walled apartment building on the stem of the T. The ground-floor premises are flanked at the corners by stores selling leather goods and automobile spare parts. Directly across the way is another very old building with a barbershop and a beauty parlor fronting on the street. The stem, one block long, is one of the oldest thoroughfares in Rome, only a short block away from the Campo de'Fiori.

When Andrea and his two partners, Carlo Maggi and Alvaro Renzi, took over the Grappolo in 1966, it was a local *osteria* in which the old men of the neighborhood came to play cards, drink Frascati, and munch on local, typical Roman dishes—*panetelle*, pizza, *panini*, veal stews, tripe. They sat at plain wooden tables in the dark, talked, joked, and stayed for hours. "When we came," Carlo explained not long ago, "we cleaned everybody out, like cowboys and Indians." The intention of the new partners was to convert the *osteria* into more than just a neighborhood hangout. "We wished to raise it to a more acceptable level, a true *trattoria* that would draw clients from all parts of the city, as well as the foreigners."

The location was an excellent one, next door to many of Rome's best-known tourist stamping grounds, and the premises themselves were promising. They consisted of two good-sized main rooms under handsomely beamed ceilings, with a kitchen at the back and an enormous cellar for storage below. In addition, during the warm months, it would be possible to put half a dozen tables on the cobblestones outside, where eaters could gaze at the austerely elegant marble facade of the Cancelleria.

The three partners had known each other for years. Andrea and Carlo, who comes from L'Aquila in the Abruzzi, met when they were both eighteen and working as waiters in a small restaurant off the Piazza Barberini, in the commercial center of Rome. They had both begun at thirteen as dishwashers, then worked their way up from one job to another in places all over the city. Soon after they met, they had begun to talk about having their own restaurant one day, but at the time the dream seemed a distant one. In fact, two years later, Carlo emigrated to Venezuela, where he spent the next decade, still working in restaurants and saving as much money as possible in order to return.

Meanwhile, Andrea continued his career in Rome. By the time Carlo came back from South America in 1962, he had become the manager of another *trattoria* and had also met Renzi, who was a few years older and equally experienced in the business. The three men now decided to pool their resources and to look for their own place. By that time Andrea had worked, in one capacity or another, in about sixty different restaurants and there was very little he didn't know about the day-to-day workings of the business. It was the only real education he had ever had. "I left school in the fifth grade, when I was thirteen and a half," he recently reminisced. "It was 1945, the war was just over, and there was more hunger than schools. My family sent me to the city to learn the business." He slept at first in a room with five other young men also in search of work or just starting out. "It was difficult," he continued, "always with very long hours and almost no time to do anything else."

Whenever he talks about it now, it is as if he had never had any choice in the matter and he cannot imagine his or anyone else's children wanting to go into the profession today as a career. "No one likes it," he has said. "The hours are long, your life is sacrificed to it." What little time he does have to himself is spent with his family. His daughter Maria is married, has a child and works part-time as a bookkeeper. She and her husband, who is employed as a technical director for a large international manufacturing concern, occupy an apartment on the same floor of their building. His son Paolo recently completed his military service, which is obligatory in Italy, and has gone back to school; he is still living at home. "This means Marcella can go on keeping an eye on all of us," Andrea said not long ago. "There is an old proverb in Italy: 'I am the boss, but the person who commands is my wife.'"

FROM THE moment I walked into the Grappolo d'Oro, sometime during the summer of 1968, it became one of my favorite hangouts. It was then a typical, very modest Roman *trattoria*, with paper tablecloths and bare walls, but the atmosphere was friendly and the food simple but superb. It was also cheap and had been discovered by tourists wandering about the area, taking in the sights. They came early and sat outside in the warm weather, munching on pasta and drinking white wine from the *castelli* in the Alban Hills. At nine o'clock, when the Italians started to arrive, the Grappolo would begin to fill up and by ten there would be bunches of people standing about, sometimes in the aisles, waiting to be seated. The word on good, reasonably priced food goes out very quickly in Rome and restaurants like the Grappolo soon acquire a large hard core of devotees, who eat there regularly, at least once or twice a week.

My earliest memories of Rome, in fact, are inextricably enmeshed with recollections of wonderful meals. The women in my family were all fine cooks and I grew up, even in New York, eating daily the sort of food only the finest Italian restaurants here can occasionally approximate. When I went back to Rome after the war, it seemed perfectly natural to me to be eating inexpensively in establishments such as the Grappolo d'Oro, where every dish was prepared to provide not merely nourishment but pleasure. The term "fast food" had not even been coined and the Italians I knew considered American cooking to be an atrocity, comparable to the bland cuisine of the English, a race famous throughout the peninsula for its insensitivity to all aspects of material well-being. A meal in Rome, even in the middle of a working day, was an experience to be savored and lingered over and never took less than two or three hours, after which one went home for a snooze behind closed shutters before going back to work. At night, long after the tourists had departed for their hotels and *pensioni,* the Grappolo would remain busy, sometimes until nearly midnight, with tables of diners reluctant to abandon the source of such contentment and still nibbling on cheeses, fruit and *dolci,* sipping Frascati, sweet *vino santo* or a liqueur. And after, the talk would be about food—discussions about the quality of the fish, the tenderness of the veal, the freshness of the mozzarella (I have a friend who won't eat a mozzarella more than six hours old), the success or failure of a particular recipe, all carried on with the intensity of a political debate. Good cooking in a Roman *trattoria* is not merely a necessity, but a philosophical imperative.

Nevertheless, it is unusual to hear anyone in Rome speak well of a particular restaurant. Even the regulars at a favorite haunt will seldom praise it. A couple of years ago, after an absence of several months, I was discussing the Grappolo with a Roman crony of mine.

We had just finished eating there with a party of friends and I had expressed satisfaction that standards had not been lowered while I was away. My friend disagreed. "It's not the same," he said, and proceeded to complain that a pasta serving he had recently ordered had not been cooked *al dente* and that twice in the past two weeks his favorite dish, *penne all'arrabiata,* had not been spicy enough. He also commented that he had been finding less variety in the offerings on the *antipasto* table. I observed that he must have been eating there regularly, as often as two or three times a week. He shrugged. "What do you expect? It's not what it was, but it's not bad," he said. I stopped worrying. Not bad is a term of encomium in Rome.

ONCE A week, either on Tuesday or Friday, Andrea has to get up before five o'clock in the morning and drive to the great wholesale and produce market of Rome, which is located in the Testaccio, not far from Porta San Paolo and the Aurelian Wall, to the west of the inner city. (He and Carlo take turns at this chore, as did Renzi, until his death in an automobile accident ten years ago.) There he spends several hours buying much of the food the Grappolo will serve during the next few days. The scene is chaotic and the haggling over prices foul-mouthed and nerve-wracking. Andrea does not allow any of it to affect him personally; it is simply another reality of his life that he has learned to accept and make the best of. "I don't fight with anyone," he explained one morning, after an exchange of insults with a fishmonger that had seemed potentially lethal. "We play-fight, we pretend. Otherwise it is a waste of time, yours and theirs."

Who would want to fight with Andrea? He has essentially a sweet, gentle temperament, reflected in a readiness to smile and joke, but his body exudes brute strength. He is about five-feet-ten, with brown curly hair and dark brown eyes, and he looks older than his fifty-five years, but his arms and shoulders are massive, his head thrust forward as if he could launch himself like a battering ram at whatever might choose to challenge him or stand in his way. Carlo, too, has the arms and shoulders of a weight lifter. Once, a few years ago, a party of visiting German journalists caused considerable trouble in the restaurant. The men had drunk too much wine and had become involved in an altercation with a table of Americans behind them. Voices were raised, chairs scraped back, the decks cleared for action. The appearance from the kitchen of Carlo and Andrea—quiet, benign-looking, but obviously ready to intervene—quickly smoothed matters over. No actual outbreak of violence has ever marred the premises of the Grappolo.

Rome, as a whole, has never been a violent city. Thieves break into houses, steal automobiles, snatch purses, and lift wallets. Bandits hold up jewelry stores and theater box offices. Drug addicts and pushers infest the streets, piazzas, and parks of certain areas, most notably in Trastevere and the poorer quarters. Murders, however, are rare, each one an event worthy of headlines and, especially if the occasion involves jilted lovers, follow-up stories in the *cronaca,* perhaps even cautionary editorials on the lamentable decay in public morals. Rape, however, is rarer still and kidnapping for ransom, a favorite crime in the south, has all but ceased entirely.

During the 1970s, the so-called Years of Lead, Rome, like every other large Italian city, was the site of numerous atrocities perpetrated by the Red Brigades and other terrorist groups. Then there were the frequent riots in the streets and piazzas, largely caused by confrontations between gangs of hoodlums of the Left and Right. The shopkeepers and restaurant owners simply pulled their iron shutters down and rode out the disturbances. It's undoubtedly a comment of sorts regarding the Roman attitude toward food that no popular eating place was ever invaded and smashed up. It is also a well-known fact that in Rome rallies, marches, and riots never seem to take place at mealtimes.

Nevertheless, Andrea and Carlo have occasionally felt obliged to shut down whenever some sort of demonstration lapped too close to their door. The Piazza Navona and the Campo de'Fiori are frequently the sites of large political and protest rallies, and the action sometimes overflows into the area of the Cancelleria. Today, most of the trouble comes from gangs of teenagers and young people, most of them unemployed, who roar past on motorcycles or settle in large, noisy groups in various favorite haunts, such as Piazza Farnese, Piazza Navona, and around the Pantheon. They are considered to be a rabble of delinquents by many of their elders, even though they are mostly harmless. The public telephone in the Grappolo, like many all over town, carries a permanent out-of-order sign, even though it works perfectly. "We don't want the hippies in here," is Andrea's explanation.

On a recent warm, sunny morning, Andrea arrived at the Grappolo d'Oro at his usual hour of nine o'clock. Carlo, a bachelor who lives in an apartment around the corner from the restaurant, had preceded him by a few minutes and had already opened up the premises; he had been cleaning the ice chest to the left of the front door where the day's fresh fish would be displayed. The chairs were piled up on the tables and a tall, thin young man with dark hair and thick glasses was sweeping up. In the back, the two cooks were already at work over steaming kettles and saucepans, their round, soft, pale faces beaded with sweat; they both suffer from sinusitis, the occupational hazard of Roman cooks, who work usually in damp, hot kitchens from which they emerge either into dust and heat or the chill air of the cooler months. They are neither of them happy men, though they are the best paid of all restaurant employees, with individual earnings of about three thousand dollars a month. Andrea, especially, keeps close tabs on them and can, in a pinch, fill in himself. "If after forty-three years, I couldn't cook . . ." he once said, ending the sentence with the eloquent shrug of a man who has seen many chefs, the prima donnas of the trade, come and go.

There are not so many jobs, even for good cooks, that the turnover these days is great. In addition to these two and the young man sweeping up, the Grappolo employs only two other people, the waiters, one of whom is Andrea's nephew. (On weekends, Paolo sometimes helps out.) Andrea and Carlo have often talked about hiring others, especially during the summer months, when they could use more help to serve the customers eating outside. They have never been able to afford it. "In Italy, everything is bureaucracy," Andrea explained. "From the moment you give work to someone, you are at the mercy of the government—taxes, social security, medical insurance. Worst of all, it is almost impossible to fire anyone. You must pay a liquidation, which can amount in some cases to millions of lire." This system, he maintained, was making it impossible for the young to find work, because there is no such thing in Italy as temporary employment. "People can be hired and paid, illegally, in cash only," Andrea continued, "but it is dangerous. What if they denounce you to the labor unions or the tax officials?" There were about a hundred and fifty thousand young people out of work in Rome at the time and the situation was worse elsewhere, especially in the south. "There is work, always, for those who really want to work," Andrea has always insisted, "but certainly it is not easy."

In addition to the daily grind around the premises, almost every day Carlo and Andrea have to buy additional supplies in the Campo de'Fiori, especially at the height of the tourist season, when business is better than usual. They are both familiar figures to the vendors behind their stalls of fresh fish, vegetables, cheese, and meats, and they move about the piazza buying kilos of lettuce, asparagus, eggplant, and beans from the Roman countryside, strawberries from Terracina, peppers and oranges from Sicily, with a nod, a hand gesture, a quick exchange of amiable insults. ("This one screws me all the time," Carlo said one day, when I was trailing him about the piazza. He was referring to a leathery-looking, beaming, middle-aged woman, who was hovering protectively over mountains of lettuce and artichokes. "U-u-uh," she replied, a hand slapping at the air in protest, "he makes my ear whistle with his lies.") No one tries to con them into buying produce that is not quite fresh or fish more than a day old or a chicken a bit too scrawny, because it would be a waste of time. These men can tell at a glance what is worth the money and what isn't; their living depends on it. "We've been doing this so long, it's like breathing," Carlo said.

Inside the Grappolo itself, the early part of the morning is spent preparing the day's vegetables and fruit at a long, wooden table Andrea calls "the torture rack." The work is done with a long, thin, very sharp knife Andrea calls his eleventh finger, which has, he points out, "already ruined the other ten." Both his hands and Carlo's are blunt-fingered, calloused, scarred, stained dark from the leaves and juices of raw plants. The two men work in silence, with the casual, swift expertise of dancers at the barre.

They shear away the outer leaves of the artichokes, peel the stems and punch in the chokes with a thumb jab. They trim the strawberries, then soak them in wine and vinegar. They cut off the thick ends of the asparagus stems, scrape the sand away, then tie them into bundles for the pot. They slice up the mushrooms, chopping down on them as briskly and efficiently as a machine, making a sound like the hammering of carpet tacks into soft wood. On an average day at this time of year, the Grappolo will serve between ten and fifteen kilos of pasta, thirty to forty artichokes, three kilos of asparagus, a couple of dozen popular fish—turbot, dentex, flounder, gilthead, bass. Every day between sixty and eighty mostly contented people will come, eat, leave, unaware of the effort being made, the price being paid, and why should they care? It's not their business, after all; they have their own affairs to trouble them.

THE CONSTANTLY rising cost of everything is the chief affliction Italians complain about endlessly, but it is not the only one. Rome, like every other major city in the world, has become not only expensive but a difficult place to live comfortably. In addition to the impossible traffic and inadequate public transportation system, which is periodically crippled by strikes and slowdowns, everyone agrees that the air in the *centro storico,* with its narrow cobblestoned streets and alleys hemmed in by ancient palazzi, has become almost unbreathable. And the noise levels at all hours of the day and night are among the highest in the world. "Living in Rome today is like being compelled to attend an endless rock concert," an American resident of many years remarked during my last visit. "We're all going deaf, which may not be a bad thing."

Trattorie like the Grappolo d'Oro flourish as small oases in this chaotic maelstrom of daily living. Romans have always liked to eat out and a meal in any restaurant is a social occasion. It is also no more expensive to eat out than in; one of the peculiarities of life in this city is that it often costs more to shop for one's groceries than to have them prepared and served up in a public establishment. This is because there is a huge disparity between the prices paid at the wholesale level in the general markets and those the public confronts in the retail stores, which are subject to all sorts of taxes not imposed upon the owners of restaurants. "Even when private citizens pull in their belts," a Roman dealer in salamis and cold cuts declared in the *cronaca* not long ago, "the public powers land violently heavy blows."

When I was living in Rome some years ago with my wife and small children, we made a determined attempt to eat at home regularly, mainly because we felt that eating out as often as we had been was not conducive to a healthy family life. We were soon disabused of

17

that notion. My wife was spending half of every day shopping (this was before the advent of the *supermercato,* a relatively recent phenomenon in Rome) and it was costing us more to eat at home than out. Also, my children loved the noisy conviviality of the Roman *trattorie* we liked to frequent and enjoyed being fussed over by the waiters, all of whom seemed to be capable of ecstasy at the mere sight of hungry children. We soon resumed our former routine of going out several times a week to one favorite spot or another and the experience turned my children into connoisseurs of good cooking and incipient gourmands.

It was during this period that my wife and I also paid a courtesy call on an old friend of my family's, whom I'll call Count Fabio Traversi. He was an elegant old Roman aristocrat, who lived in a gloomy apartment on the Aventine hill. He received us with kindly, old-fashioned courtesy. A tiny, wizened Sardinian maid, who, he informed us, had been with him for thirty-five years, served tea and cookies on an elaborate silver service that was clearly a family heirloom. The talk, as it often does in Rome, soon settled on the subject of rising costs and food, as well as the increasing scarcity of good cooks to ease one's way through life. Three of them had recently come and gone in the Count's service and he now found it necessary to eat out more frequently. It was too expensive to employ a cook, he told us, what with all the new labor laws, the unions, taxes, and social benefits one had to deal with.

I tried to strike a positive note. After all, I argued, Italy was in the middle of an economic boom. Working people now had a chance not only to earn well, but to acquire material goods they had never dreamed of owning before. They also had a right to be protected by all the new social programs the postwar democratic governments had instituted after the fall of Fascism.

The Count sighed. "Ah, *caro* Bill, you are so right," he said, "but you see, wherever social justice occurs, there life becomes a little less gracious."

B Y N O O N the Grappolo d'Oro begins to look pleasing to the eye. The straight-backed, cane-seated wooden chairs have been set in place and clean white tablecloths lie over dark red undercloths; short-stemmed wine glasses gleam in the soft light. The day's offering of fresh fish shines on its bed of bright green yucca leaves. On the walls hang landscapes and still lifes by the Roman painter Franco Mazzilli, a friend, who also designed the frieze of vines and grape clusters, executed in dark wooden panels, that ring the walls. Beyond the three rows of tables in the main room is the buffet counter, now being heaped high with cold hors d'oeuvres—serving plates of spicy salami, artichokes *alla Romana,* vegetable *frittate,* sweet-and-sour onions, beans, shellfish, eggplant cooked in several different ways, mushrooms, asparagus, chicory, beet greens, spinach, eggs mayonnaise, fresh sardines, bowls of fruit. Shelves crowded with wine bottles rise above them, framing the entrance to the kitchen.

On a small blackboard set above the buffet and facing the room, Andrea chalks in the day's menu: *spaghetti con vongole, risotto alla pescatora, ravioli ricotta e spinaci, tortellini al sugo, pesce alla griglia, abbacchio alla cacciatora, zucchini ripiene di carne, vitella al forno, bocconcini di tacchino, trippa alla Romana, cervelli burro e piselli, bracciole di maiale, corattela d'abbachio, rogno vitello trifolato, fegato di vitella.* Despite the fact that about a third of the *trattoria*'s clientele are foreign-born, mostly Americans and English, no attempt is made to translate any of these terms. Andrea feels that the language of food is international. "The table is sacred," he says, implying that the integrity of what the Grappolo d'Oro offers cannot be compromised to suit the transient needs of the itinerant, unlettered diner.

It is this attitude that has made Italians in general, but especially in Rome and to the south, intolerant of foreign cooking. They feel no need to sample any other cuisine but their own and not until the late sixties did the French, Chinese, and Japanese begin to open establishments all over town. Even today, these places are frequented mainly by foreigners, only occasionally by the Romans themselves. During one of my first visits some years ago to a newly opened Chinese restaurant on the roof of a building just off the Via Veneto, I asked our waiter about several of the dishes listed on the menu. He was a middle-aged Roman dressed in a mandarin costume with a little round hat perched on his head like a soup plate. He looked at me in horror. "How do I know?" he said. "You don't think I eat this stuff?"

Andrea himself has never eaten in a Chinese restaurant. Nor does he have the time to enjoy his own cooking. He, Carlo, and their staff have lunch together every day at eleven-thirty. They eat quickly and in silence. All that these people have had to say to each other has long since been said. By noon, a very early hour for the luncheon crowd in Rome, the *trattoria* is ready for its first clients, who at that time of day will almost certainly be tourists. Andrea stands ready by the buffet table, a napkin over his left arm. He is like an actor in a long-running play, no longer really interested in the action but ready to assume his part, every speech and every move of the role so deeply ingrained in him that he could not possibly miss a cue, a line, or a piece of business, even if he wanted to. "I am tied here," he once said, "by need and the weight of years."

O NE O F the great pleasures of coming back to Rome year after year is the expectation of finding things unchanged, the people and locales one loves still in place. For many years I never had to buy a new address book, because the one I'd first acquired in 1947 remained serviceable. Foreigners came and went, but my Roman friends and relatives mostly stayed put. Only during the past few years, with the loosening of old rent-control laws and the soaring of real-estate values in the *centro,* have I noticed many changes. Still, it's a comfort to return and to find so much of the city itself as it was when I last left it and has been, in some cases, for centuries. The great monuments and piazzas and ancient, winding streets still retain their character and their comforting, reassuring identities, even when all but overwhelmed by the metallic clatter of the automobile. And for me, as the years have passed, one of my favorite points of reference has become the Grappolo d'Oro, to which I now return, happy to find it as fixed as the paving stones of the city itself.

Historical commemorations are common in Rome, and every spring, beginning in May, the city begins to celebrate its own existence. One section after another comes alive with some special manifestation designed to lure shoppers, tourists, and the merely curious. Along the Via dei Coronari, only a few blocks from the Cancelleria, the merchants of antiques and objets d'art stay open for a week until midnight, their shops illuminated by torches set into the walls above them on both sides of the narrow street, closed to traffic by temporary barriers in the form of large flower pots. On the Via Giulia, one of the oldest and most beautiful thoroughfares in the city, threading its way between the delicate baroque facades of small churches and the impressive outlines of medieval palazzi, the municipal government sponsors a series of free evening concerts, about a hundred and fifty in all, ranging from jazz to classical music. Later there will be acrobats and other circus acts in Piazza Farnese, theater in the parks and other piazzas, open-air concerts in the Campidoglio—the so-called Roman Summer that has become an annual feature of life here.

Andrea has never had the inclination or the time to take part in any of these celebrations. At night, when his working day is over, his only thought is to get home. The drive back to the Tiburtina at that hour, between midnight and one o'clock, takes him only about fifteen minutes; there is almost no traffic and he can count on being in bed by one-thirty or two A.M. The pattern of his life is physically punishing and never varies. He suffers from high blood pressure, a sore back, and aching feet. On Sundays, the only day of the week the Grappolo is closed, he would prefer just to sit around the house until dinner time. "My family would like to go to the movies and sometimes we go out, but what I really want to do is sleep," he said recently.

He never eats at home and Marcella is not expected to cook for him. A few years ago, after his father died, Andrea inherited a small stone house in the hills of Amatrice and has since converted it into a modest country retreat. If he's not too tired, he and the entire family will drive up there and spend the day during the warmer months. In August, the *trattoria* will shut down for two weeks, and he and Marcella will take a vacation. Like millions of other Italians, they used to head either for the mountains or the seashore, but now they retreat to their refuge in Amatrice. "The air is clean and it is peaceful," he says.

Andrea has never attended a concert, visited any of the city's famous sights, and takes no part in its cultural life. His task, as he sees it, is to provide good food at reasonable prices so that he can go on earning enough money to support himself and his family. He does not feel in the least deprived nor is he envious of what he feels he cannot have. By every current economic standard, he is living better than the great majority of his fellow citizens. "Let the politicians talk," he said not long ago. "They love to talk, that is what they do best. For me it is all rhetoric. Life is hard and work is all. All the rest is dreams."

CHAPTER
TWO

THE CHAINS OF HOPE

THE FIRST PEOPLE to protest publicly a few years ago against the continued presence of drug pushers in their part of the city, the Don Bosco quarter in the Tuscolano area, to the southeast of the Aurelian Wall, were a handful of middle-aged citizens, among whom was the mother of a fourteen-year-old heroin addict. Armed with broom handles and other improvised weapons, the group suddenly showed up at midday on a Monday in late November in the so-called little gardens, a triangular, treeless open space off the Via Ponzio Comizio, and surprised two well-known local dealers, a couple of young men lounging about a park bench and waiting for clients. With shouted threats and blows, the little band routed the pushers and warned them not to come back.

The incident triggered a major revolt. By evening, the "damned triangle," as it is more familiarly known to the inhabitants of the zone, was invaded by hundreds of residents, spurred by the event to demonstrate their own rage and sense of frustration at a situation they have been compelled to put up with for years. "Here we live watching who shoots up, who dies, who steals," one man observed. "It's impossible to live here anymore." By nightfall the protest had become formalized. Lists of names had been collected, attempts had begun to organize regular patrols of the area, a hastily assembled delegation of mothers was being put together to call at the local police station, and there was much talk of forming a permanent "Committee of Struggle" to oversee all these efforts.

What had inspired the protest was the news of the death a day earlier of a young man named Giuliano Boldrini, who had expired of hepatitis in Udine, where he had been doing his obligatory military service. According to the people of the quarter, he had been an addict for years. "He was a Roman, he lived here on the Via Comizio. He was a wonderful kid, a friend," one acquaintance recalled. "Then he also ended up in drugs and now he, too, is dead." "I'm a drug addict, but I want to quit, I can't go on any longer," another young man told a visiting reporter. "Here in Don Bosco, in the little gardens, it's become the market for all of south Rome. This has become the stronghold of the drug scene."

The Don Bosco is a typical postwar Roman *borgata,* a hastily constructed residential quarter of dreary, slablike apartment buildings lined up like giant dominoes along narrow, dusty streets devoid of adequate public services, schools, hospitals, piazzas, parks, even churches. Thrown up during the boom years of the 1950s and sixties, the *borgate* violated with impunity most of the city's zoning laws and building codes and enriched the private speculators who constructed them, often with the connivance of the politicians and bureaucrats who were supposed to oversee and enforce the laws. They have rapidly degenerated into a crime-ridden outer ring of slums in which hundreds of thousands of Romans are compelled to live, only a few miles from the famous historical heart of the city, but as remote from it as if inhabiting an entirely different civilization. "The Third World begins in the *borgate,* " a Roman architect once told me. Essentially, it is a world of poverty and despair, from which the young have increasingly sought to escape through drugs. "Today, we found the strength of desperation to demonstrate, but inside our rage has gone on for years," an old man of about seventy commented to a visitor. "Because of the drugs this quarter has become violent. There's death in the air."

Unlike most other spontaneous outbursts of public exasperation, the furor in the Don Bosco did not fade away. Aided by the publicity given the event by most of the city's newspapers, the residents continued to demonstrate and their example was quickly followed by protesters in other parts of the city. Groups of volunteers patrolled the little gardens and slogans scrawled on building walls warned the pushers to stay away permanently or risk being assaulted. "They'll stay away, all right, for a while," a boy of fourteen declared. "It's become too hot for them."

The heat inevitably attracted the attention of the city's political establishment. Six days after the initial demonstration, Mayor Ugo Vetere, a Communist whose votes came largely from the *borgate,* showed up in the little gardens at four P.M., accompanied by several members of his administration and a swarm of policemen. They were met by about a thousand residents, many of whom had grievances to air and demands to make, and who were undeterred by a cold, overcast sky and the rain that started to fall soon after the mayor arrived. "Look at all the cops there are today," one participant observed. "It's the first time I've seen them here."

Mayor Vetere, a gray-haired, dark-browed, affable man with an easy colloquial style, listened to various specific pleas for help—more police, more street lights, permanent headquarters for the Committee of Struggle, financial support, and many other similar requests—and delivered himself of the usual political homilies concerning the need for more jobs for the young and a more efficient administration of existing public services. He also assured the crowd that its demands would be granted, though he didn't explain specifically how or when such help could be expected. "I feel I am with you," he concluded, raising his voice to be heard through the falling rain. "You are an important example for Rome and also for the rest of Italy. I am on your side, as always, all the way." His words were punctuated by the loud sobbing of Boldrini's mother, who, with her husband and daughter, were in the front ranks of the assembly.

It was after six o'clock by the time the mayor left and the meeting began to break up, but many lingered to tell the reporters present their various stories. In all of them the quarter was depicted as an open marketplace where dealers in narcotics swarmed and bags of heroin were sold like potatoes. "No one ever helps us and it's been going on for years," one pale, bone-thin young man confessed. "I've been shooting up for ten years. Every morning I have to make the rounds of all the hospitals to get a dose of methadone, which they never give me. So what do I do? I shoot up."

No one who has lived in Rome for any length of time in recent years can remain oblivious of the drug traffic, which has become a national plague. Heroin, marijuana, and hashish can be purchased openly in many streets and piazzas all over the city, and any streetwise teenager knows what the going price is for anything, from a simple joint to a hit of the hard stuff. A well-known open-air café in Piazza Santa Maria in Trastevere has drilled holes in its coffee spoons to keep them from being stolen and locks its restroom doors to prevent anyone from shooting up on the premises. Used syringes can be found any day in most parks, often jabbed into the trees, and along the banks of the Tiber. Drugs are even hustled in the elementary schools and a good many Italian families have had some experience with the drug scene, since it has become almost impossible to shield one's children from contact with the users, who need to push narcotics on others in order to feed their own habits. Even heavy drugs are relatively cheap in Italy (the going price for a gram of heroin, enough to keep the average addict going for one day, in the streets of Rome not long ago was a hundred and sixty thousand lire, about ninety dollars at the prevalent rate of exchange), but still expensive enough to ensure that most addicts can only stay alive through a life of crime.

People die every month from overdoses and the authorities seize hundreds of pounds of heroin and other substances. "Rome has now torn away from Milan the title of drug capital," a local official named Salvatore Margherito declared at a press conference. He also pointed out that it had been difficult to sequester much cocaine, the narcotic now most in demand, because, unlike heroin, it was a "party drug" and not readily available on the street. Although precise figures on the total number of addicts are, for obvious reasons, hard to come by, it has been established that perhaps as many as two hundred thousand Italians are hooked on heroin and cocaine, while several hundred thousand others frequently smoke hash and marijuana. Italy, with a population one-fourth that of the United States, has an estimated half as many confirmed drug users, a figure that shocks a great many people here, who have never thought of the Peninsula as a crime-ridden haven for the underground narcotics trade. That most of these users are under thirty makes the situation all the more alarming.

According to a spokesman for the United States Drug Enforcement Administration (DEA), which maintains a well-staffed office in Rome and works closely with the Italian law-enforcement agencies trying now to cope with the situation, Italy has long been a transit area for the clandestine shipment of narcotics from all over the world into the United States, primarily through Sicily. (It has been estimated that about 60 percent of all the heroin smuggled into the United States transited through Italy.) Not much of this product was destined for local consumption, since the profits to be made abroad were so much greater. After the smashing of the notorious French Connection in Marseilles in the late 1960s, however, and a number of other successful international police operations that have resulted in arrests and confiscations all over the world, some of the morphine-based narcotics imported into Italy, primarily from the so-called Golden Triangle area in southwest Asia, began to filter into the streets of the Peninsula itself. During the early eighties, the Italian police uncovered a dozen laboratories for the processing of heroin, mostly in Sicily. During the same period, over five hundred people were arrested in connection with the drug trade, but the crackdown came too late and has since not interfered very much with the ready availability of drugs to anyone with the money to pay for them. "The heroin is still coming into the country from either Pakistan or Bangkok," I was told at the DEA headquarters. "And we've been so occupied with heroin that we've sort of ignored the cocaine situation, which is very much on the increase. Obviously there are major problems here."

The problems are compounded by Italy's relative inexperience in dealing with the medical as well as social aspects of drug addiction. About twenty-two thousand addicts are currently undergoing therapeutic treatment in public hospitals and clinics all over the country, as well as the nation's 215 residential communities, whose inmates, all of whom have volunteered for treatment, receive little in the way of psychiatric counseling and are weaned away from junk mainly by the substitution of methadone, a less potent synthetic narcotic that eases the craving for heroin and removes the victim from a life of desperation in the streets, but is itself addictive. Furthermore, the habitual use of an illegal drug is not in itself a crime under Italian law and the user who volunteers for treatment can take himself off the program at any time and go back to his former life, which many of them soon do.

Although most Italians, in or out of public life, have long known in a general sort of way that there is a serious and growing problem here, and that the organs of the state have failed to come to grips with it, the specifics of drug addiction, its consequences and how to deal with them, have mostly remained a nasty little secret shared only by the victims and their relatives and friends. It became a national public event at last with a trial that took place several years ago in Rimini and focused attention on what was becoming a major catastrophe. The trial and the events surrounding it quickly became a symbol for the frustration and horror most citizens felt over the seeming inability of the authorities even to understand the dimensions of the problem, much less begin to cope with it. "What the trial also illuminates," a reporter on the scene observed in the *Corriere della Sera*, "and on which public opinion and the government must reflect, is, above all, the panorama of failures. . . ."

RIMINI IS a wealthy provincial resort town on the Adriatic coast north of Rome. It is surrounded by rich farmland and has a permanent population of roughly a hundred and thirty-five thousand, dozens of flourishing industries, and about thirty-five hundred hotels and *pensioni* to accommodate the hundreds of thousands of vacationers and tourists who flock to its beaches in the summer. With this prosperity has come the drug problem. There are an estimated several thousand users in the region, only a small minority of whom have sought treatment or have enrolled themselves in one of the forty-two communities in the area.

One of the most successful of the latter was San Patrignano, a self-supporting cooperative of 540 ex-addicts of all ages, who lived and worked together on a large property a few miles out of town. Originally a private farmstead of grapevines and orchards, San Patrignano rambled over 1.8 million square meters and included dormitories, a main dining room, apartments for married couples, a pool and other recreational facilities. The community farmed, maintained a large dairy, and raised pigs and sheep, as well as racehorses and purebred cats. There were thirty-six different trades one could practice or learn and everyone was expected to contribute. The members could leave to go to school or to sell their products, but while on the premises their lives were meticulously regimented and the rules were strict. They had to get up at 7:30 A.M., take a shower, spend at least eight hours a day in study or productive work of some kind, and take turns at such chores as cleaning up and waiting on tables. They were permitted to smoke up to ten cigarettes a day, but alcohol and coffee were forbidden. They were not allowed any money of their own and could not accept presents or donations, except for personal clothing supplied by members of their families. In short, they lived quasi-monastic lives of self-denial and hard work, subject to the collective will of the community.

Nevertheless, visitors to San Patrignano over the years had consistently reported favorably on the program there and the success the community had in reclaiming even the most desperately addicted young people, all of whom had harrowing stories to tell, from lives broken and wasted by a total dependence on drugs. Not the least of the benefits available to the inmates was free medical care, either furnished by volunteer doctors and dentists or paid for by the community, a crucial need, since 90 percent of the new arrivals at San Patrignano suffered from some form of venereal infection and all were either ill or physically rundown. "In San Patrignano I saw a factory where things and men were being built," the minister of justice, Mino Martinazzoli, declared, after a tour of the premises the previous fall.

Few people unconnected to the drug scene had even heard of San Patrignano, until the police, alerted by a young woman named Maria Rosa Cesarini, suddenly raided the premises in late October and found six young people locked up and chained in various rooms, one of them a converted pigeon coop. Vincenzo Muccioli, the founder and leader of the community, was arrested and jailed for thirty-six days, before being released to await trial on a number of charges, the most serious of which was unlawful imprisonment. A series of subsequent raids, some of them nocturnal, by other state agencies, including treasury and labor officials, found other violations and some community members were arrested on old charges dating back to their lives of street crime. Muccioli's methods were subsequently denounced by a court-appointed committee of experts, as well as the official press organs of the Communist Party and the Bishop of Rimini, Giovanni Locatelli. Muccioli himself was depicted in a number of accounts of his career as an ignorant, dictatorial, self-enraptured personality, who dabbled in seances and saw himself as an infallible, Christlike savior.

Muccioli, however, immediately had plenty of defenders, including most of the inmates of San Patrignano and their relatives and friends. They were quick to point out that the procedures used, including forcible restraint, were the only ones that worked with confirmed addicts and that everyone had been informed of them and had agreed to abide by them before being accepted into the community. "We don't unlawfully lock up anyone," Muccioli later informed the court trying his case. "The young people arrive at San Patrignano by their own free choice or have been entrusted to us by magistrates. They ask us to save them and we tell them all what the rules are." He also pointed out that several of the people liberated by the police had immediately fled back to a life of drug-induced crime, while those arrested for old offenses and removed from the community's care would undoubtedly ultimately suffer the same fate. His contention was given immediate weight by the death of one of his more desperate cases, a young man named Leonardo Bargiotti, who died, a presumed suicide, under a train only a few hours after his release during the original raid. According to Muccioli and others, much of his time had to be spent either preventing people from leaving or persuading them to come back. "The addict is a person capable of understanding," he declared in defense of his methods, "but not of willing."

By the time the trial finally got under way five years later, with the state pressing charges of fraud and unlawful imprisonment of eighteen inmates against Muccioli and thirteen other community members, the whole country had become aware of San Patrignano and its founder. Muccioli's face, in fact, had become as familiar as that of any media star and to almost everyone except his prosecutors he had become a national hero. When a large sack of rusty chains was dramatically produced in court by the prosecution as evidence against the defendants, a woman present named Maria Castellani, the mother of one of the victims, was moved to tears of joy. "I would have kissed those chains," she declared to the press, "because for my son they were the beginning of salvation." Her attitude, it has since turned out, is the one shared by most of those who have followed the case and since commented about it.

Muccioli himself, a tall, heavyset, robust-looking man with thick, graying curly hair, dark eyes, and a dashing black mustache, proved to be his own best advocate. He was born in 1934, had been married for twenty-three years and had two sons. He inherited the original property at San Patrignano and he and his wife owned a hotel in Rimini, where he became increasingly aware of the growing drug problem in the streets. By 1977, in Piazza Tre Martiri, in the heart of town, he no-ticed that the groups of stoned youngsters who gathered there every day were becoming increasingly numerous. "And the people passed among them with indifference," he recalled. He sold the hotel and founded his community, which early in 1979 began to accept its first volunteers. In addition to his own resources, he was helped by contri-butions and especially the wholehearted financial support of a forty-eight-year-old Sardinian oilman and industrialist named Gianmarco Moratti, who had met Muccioli in 1978 and become a devoted parti-san of his cause. (He and his wife spent their vacations living in a trailer at San Patrignano and prior to the trial they had refused to give interviews, because, in Moratti's words, "my father has always taught me that the worst profiteering is to get publicity from the troubles of others.")

Muccioli was a persuasive, disarming talker and quick to admit his own failings. One of the major criticisms originally levelled against him was his lack of education or any formal training for the work he had undertaken, to which he once typically replied, "But I am pro-foundly ignorant, absolutely uncultured. I've never liked to read." He added, however, that he had a commonsense approach to learning and a retentive memory. His defense of his methods at San Patrignano was based on the acquired conviction that drug addiction could not be cured chemically, medically, or psychotherapeutically, but only through "solidarity and friendship" and "iron controls." "If I see a kid in crisis, I talk to him, I walk with him, sometimes that's enough," he told a weekly columnist named Gianpaolo Pansa. "But if I see him al-ready gone in his head, if I realize that he's thinking about the piazza where he'll fine heroin again, I can't let him go. I'd be failing the com-mitment I made to him when he came in."

Soon after the trial began, it became obvious even to Muccioli's denigrators that, in view of the circumstances, the case against him seemed an outrageous miscarriage of justice, a glaring example of an uncomprehending, unqualified bureaucracy ponderously committed to applying an outdated penal code to a set of circumstances and a so-cial dilemma with which it was unequipped to cope. Witness after wit-ness, including many of those who had originally testified against Muccioli, withdrew their accusations or greatly modified them. His original accuser, Maria Rosa Cesarini, a soft-spoken, worn-looking woman in her late twenties, admitted that she had been an addict for three years before going to San Patrignano. She stated that she had been consistently well treated there and never subjected to physical violence. Although she insisted that she felt this had in no way entitled Muccioli to lock her up for sixteen days to keep her from escaping, she also confessed that she had run away six times before and that she had immediately gone back on heroin, become a pusher and killed someone in a car crash, for which she had served time in prison. She said that she was now free of drugs, married to another ex-addict and employed in a parish church. She professed to have found God and to bearing no ill will toward Muccioli and his associates. By the time she had finished her testimony and walked silently back into obscurity, it seemed incredible to many of those present in the courtroom that the cumbersome legal apparatus of the state should have been set in motion by such a witness.

As the case proceeded, with dozens of other witnesses, including a number of public figures, coming from all over the country to Muccioli's support and with most of the press on his side, the government prosecutors found themselves almost alone in their unpleasant chore. After several Communist Party officials and prominent members testified on behalf of San Patrignano (one hero of the Partisan Resistance in the Second World War declared he would return his decorations and medals to the government, if Muccioli were found guilty), the party press ceased its denunciations of Muccioli and his methods and adopted a tone of guarded neutrality. Several weeks into the trials, the bishop of Rimini, who had previously refused a number of invitations to visit San Patrignano, suddenly showed up there, had himself photographed with Muccioli and declared himself a great admirer of the community.

It seemed as if for the first time the entire country had been made aware of a terrible national calamity ignored until then by everyone not directly affected by it. This alone, in the view of most observers, could not in any way justify the ordeal to which Muccioli was being subjected. "I feel myself a worm for having written so many words on drugs without ever having lifted a finger to save one addict," Signor Pansa wrote in the weekly *Espresso*. "Muccioli has given salvation to many. This Italy, which in the past seven years has seen nearly fifteen hundred of its young people die of heroin, ought to honor him, make him a knight of the republic, bring him into the schools to speak. And instead, no. This state puts him on trial. What shame!"

Muccioli was eventually found guilty of several minor charges, given a token sentence and allowed to reopen his facility.

CHAPTER
THREE

HORSEMAN,
COME BACK

FOR A NUMBER of years now, the visitors who come to Rome to tour the city's celebrated archaeological sites have frequently found themselves confronted by monuments all but hidden from view by scaffolding and protective panels, or are faced by an empty space instead of the famous statue or artifact they have come to see. This unhappy situation is due to the fact that for the past decade most of the city's great treasures have had to undergo emergency restoration in order to safeguard them from the accelerating destructive effects of a polluted environment. Many of these locations had been neglected for so long, as in the case of the Colosseum, the Pantheon, and most of the ancient forums, that they had begun quite literally to fall to pieces, not only from the corrosive chemicals spewed into the atmosphere by automobiles and industries, but also in part from the daily vibrations caused by the heavy traffic through the streets surrounding them. Fortunately, not all of the rescue work has been carried out simultaneously, so that it has always been possible to visit at least a majority of these sites without being disappointed. Then, too, Rome is such a cornucopia of antique wonders that one could not hope in any one trip to glimpse more than a tiny fraction of the marvels from the past on permanent display. An old friend of mine, who lives in a rooftop apartment overlooking a section of the Trajan Forum, maintains that he has never been able to take a walk through any part of the *centro storico* without seeing something—a fragment of a statue, a piece of an old column, a bit of an old wall, a portion of a temple embedded into a later structure—he hadn't noticed before. "One life isn't enough for Rome," he said.

The Romans themselves are so used to living daily in the middle of their open-air museum that they rarely complain either about being deprived of a familiar view or being shut off from visiting a cherished monument. In fact, the overabundance of wonders can become an inconvenience, especially when it conflicts with a public need. It is impossible, for instance, to dig anywhere in Rome without uncovering an archaeological relic of some kind, after which all work has to stop until experts from the Commissione delle Belle Arti show up to evaluate the find and decide whether to allow the job to proceed as scheduled or call in their own crews to unearth what may become another prize to add to the heap already on hand. It took the city twenty years to complete its postwar subway system partly because the excavations burrowed into layers of extinct civilizations, producing additional tons of valuable artifacts. The circumstance was romantically immortalized by Federico Fellini in his movie *Roma,* but the construction delays angered those who had moved out of the crowded *centro* and had counted on the proposed transportation system to whisk them swiftly to and from work. Similarly, the recently announced intention of tearing up the Via dei Fori Imperiali, a main traffic artery that links the Colosseum to Piazza Venezia, in order to dig under it and convert the whole area into a single huge archaeological park, has annoyed those who use the avenue daily and would be compelled to detour through the narrow side streets. "Rome is a living city, not only a museum for the dead," a woman who lives on the Colle Oppio, near the Colosseum, recently told a visitor. "I don't like the idea that I am living in a ruin."

The struggle for space between the needs of the living and the dead is an ongoing one in Rome and no one seems to have come up with a solution. The municipal government has recently been making use of some of the more famous monuments, such as the Circus Maximus and the Colosseum, for contemporary cultural events, concerts, and exhibitions of various kinds, and modern art shows have been held in the Castel Sant'Angelo and the Capitoline Museum. The venture has been severely criticized by some as a misuse of the city's patrimony. "After decades of neglect by the state and the municipality, Rome does not have the necessary exposition spaces," a cultural critic named Antonio Cederna observed in *L'Espresso* not long ago, "and so the contemporary art shows (De Chirico, Warhol, Klimt, Schiele, etc.) are put on in the museums of the Campidoglio, hiding Tiziano, Lotto, Caravaggio, Rubens, Guercino, or in Castel Sant'Angelo, which ought instead to become the museum of itself."

Cederna goes on to point out that quite a few famous palazzi and monuments are currently being occupied by groups of people who don't belong in them and who exploit them for dubious purposes. The seventeenth-century Villa Doria Pamphili, for example, spectacularly situated in a public park on the Janiculum overlooking all of Rome, was recently taken over for six months by the European Community, with probable consequent damage to what the writer calls "its architectural and environmental integrity." The baroque Palazzo Barberini is also the seat of an officers' club that gives parties and puts on private functions in rooms that ought to be entirely devoted to housing the National Gallery of Ancient Art, with its three thousand pictures dating back to the thirteenth century. The seventy-seven rooms of the Torlonia Museum, with its six hundred sculptures, one of the most important private collections of such masterpieces, have been converted into small private apartments and the statues relegated to a couple of basement rooms.

What many experts feel to be the most typical and painful case of neglect is the fate of the so-called Antiquarium Comunale, which has been looking for a permanent home for over forty years. It consists of about sixty thousand objects in bronze, terracotta, iron, ceramic, ivory, glass, and marble, now packed into boxes and crates and stored in various warehouses and cellars all over the city. Among these pieces are table utensils, toilet articles, surgical instruments, agricultural tools, weights and measures, toys, dolls, oil lamps, writing materials, jewels, funerary equipment, votive offerings, slave collars, even tickets and passes to theatrical events—all the appurtenances and bric-a-brac of daily life in ancient Rome, dating back to the very earliest historical periods. Much of it was unearthed during the furious digging and construction that took place in the late nineteenth century, shortly after Rome had become the capital of a united Italy, and for a while part of the collection was on display in a museum that has since been abandoned. From time to time, some parts of the Antiquarium are included in various special exhibitions mounted by the Capitoline Museum, but most of it continues to languish unseen in the city's storerooms. One of the country's many talents,

Cederna sarcastically observes, is a sort of "archaeology in reverse, which reburies what has been brought to light from the past."

A notable exception to the general indifference, or perhaps resignation, with which most Romans regard the remnants of their community's past glory is the equestrian statue of Emperor Marcus Aurelius, which until a few years ago had stood at the entrance to the Campidoglio, on the pedestal designed for it nearly five centuries ago by Michelangelo. After two thousand years, the Marcus Aurelius, the only equestrian bronze to have survived the millennia, has become, along with the Colosseum and the statue in the Capitoline Museum of the Roman she-wolf suckling Romulus and Remus, the very symbol of the city itself. When the giant figure of the great emperor—bearded, curly-haired, and riding forward, hands outstretched as if in benediction—had to be removed for restoration and preservation, the event was sadly commented upon in the press, mainly as another cruel manifestation of the damage inflicted on the past by the heedless demands of a modern industrial society.

Since then the statue has been housed in the ground-floor main hall of the Istituto Centrale del Restauro, where it first underwent literally thousands of scientific tests and examinations to determine its condition and what could be done to repair it, then was subjected to a painstaking process of restoration. Some months ago, the institute was opened for several weeks to the general public, so that people could drop in to see the relic and find out for themselves how it was getting along and what still needed to be done to it. The main problem still under discussion was what would be done to protect it from future decay.

When it was first announced in 1981 that the monument was "sick" and in urgent need of attention, there was a considerable controversy over its eventual fate. A number of experts and art historians contended that it would be too risky to return it to the Campidoglio, where it would once more be exposed to the exhaust fumes of the traffic below and possible vandalism. (Several years ago, a terrorist bomb severely damaged the façades of the Renaissance buildings behind it.) It was proposed to substitute a copy for the original, which would then be put on permanent exhibit somewhere, perhaps safely behind the walls of the Capitoline Museum, or perhaps to install an entirely different sculpture for it, something modern and more in tune with the times. The public reaction to the debate in the press revealed an overwhelming sentiment in favor of eventually bringing the famous statue back to its familiar spot. An ancient proverb predicts that the city will survive as long as the Colosseum stands, but for many people Rome will not be Rome again until Marcus Aurelius is back on his horse above the city over which he ruled.

CHAPTER
FOUR

FORZA, ITALIA!

THE QUINTESSENTIAL ROMAN attitude to public events is skepticism, which is undoubtedly why I couldn't find anyone at Le Capannelle, the city's thoroughbred racetrack, on Italian Derby day, a few years ago, who thought that any of the local horses in the race had a chance to win. The prevailing attitude was best expressed by the ruddy-faced, middle-aged hard knocker I consulted soon after entering the grounds. "One thing is certain," he declared, in a voice like a cracked tuba, "when the foreigners are here, the Italians are always betrayed."

Though the tuba may have been sounding a historical truth, his attitude seemed unfounded to me. Of the eleven three-year-old thoroughbreds entered in this edition, the one hundredth running of the Derby Italiano on Sunday, May 8, the day after our own Kentucky Derby, none of the three foreign colts, two English and one French, seemed to have outstanding credentials. The favorite, on the strength of a couple of recent wins against mediocre company in Paris, figured to be the French entry, Tintern Abbey, probably because he was trained by François Boutin, who won this race the last three years it was limited to Italian-breds. Neither of the English invaders, High Cannon and Brogan, seemed to have any credentials at all. They had won races at Thirsk and Bath respectively, small provincial tracks partly obscured by shrubbery. Brogan, however, was trained by Ian Balding, who also coaches equines for the Queen of England, admittedly an intimidating factor in Italian racing circles. "They wouldn't spend all this money, would they, only to put in an appearance here?" was the way a young Roman standing next to me at the paddock railing put it before the first race. "These English are cretins in life, but not with horses."

This acid diffidence in the face of the foreigner is understandable. The sport of thoroughbred horse racing is, after all, an English invention and all derbies everywhere take their name from Edward Smith Stanley, twelfth Count of Derby, who staged the first one, at Epsom Downs in 1780. The formula, pitting the season's best three-year-olds against each other in the spring over a distance of ground, has proved so successful that it has been imitated everywhere the so-called improvement of the breed flourishes; there are now over a hundred derbies worldwide. Romans, of course, have been betting on horses at least since the chariot races in the Circus Maximus, when the English were still in caves and painting themselves blue, but in matters involving the modern thoroughbred the Anglo-Saxons have set all the standards and imperiously laid down all the rules.

For a long time they also won most of the races. This probably accounts for the fact that until three years ago the Italians limited access to their own derby to homebreds, a way, perhaps, of keeping local interest up and the loot *in casa,* a tactic adopted with roaring success for centuries by the Roman Curia. Then, in 1981, to increase the prestige of the race, it was thrown open to anyone with a four-footed purebred hopeful in his stall. To no one's surprise, the English captured these last two renewals, which led to renewed cries for the closing of the frontiers. Luckily for international *pubbliche relazioni,* the outcry went unheeded. "Horse racing is an exquisite expression of competition and so it must remain," an official of the Italian Jockey Club recently declared, pointing out quite accurately that no one could take a derby won by a second-rate horse seriously. Garrido, the last Italian winner, in 1980, went on to cover himself in mediocrity.

And yet, over the years, Italy has produced some fine animals, including the undefeated Nearco, who won this derby in 1938, and went on to become a top sire in England, of all countries, and Ribot, also undefeated in sixteen races and the dominant horse of a generation ago. More recently, pickings have been leaner, but such Italian horses as Appiani, Hogarth, Orange Bay, and Sirlad have done well abroad, if not spectacularly, and the tactic of opening up an important race, it was felt, could only help in the long gallop.

The Italian Derby has always been run at Le Capannelle, ever since its debut in 1884, when the first four finishers were fillies. Since then the event has grown in importance until it has become synonymous with the history of the Italian thoroughbred. The official international seal of approval came in 1961, when Queen Elizabeth herself showed up as a spectator. The finish of the race that year was marred by a claim of foul, which led Her Majesty to declare that it would all become clear to them when they could see the replay on the telly. Everyone reportedly smiled and pretended not to understand English, since closed-circuit TV cameras had not yet been installed and would not be for another two decades.

Horse racing in Italy has traditionally been the private domain of a few very wealthy titled families, mainly in Rome and Milan (one stable, the Dormello-Olgiata, has won nearly a third of these derbies), and until very recently no attempt has been made to lure the paying public to the grounds or to cater to its needs. The average daily attendance at Le Capannelle is about three thousand and the betting handle well under two hundred thousand dollars. This hasn't prevented the racing associations from offering sizable purses, mainly because the funds depend from the Ministry of Agriculture, which, of course, draws its sustenance from the national budget and, therefore, ultimately drains the taxpayers.

This year's derby, only the fourth of eight races on the card, offered a total of 220 million lire (about a hundred fifty thousand dollars) in prizes, including three gold cups, to owners and breeders, with a guaranteed 100 million lire to the winner. To help pay for all this, the private company that leases the grounds from the Rome city government was looking forward to an attendance of about ten thousand and a betting handle of half a million dollars, out of which it would cut about 17 percent. Clearly, the whole enterprise is administered in the highest postwar Italian tradition of massive deficit financing.

Beginning sometime in the Middle Ages, the nobles used to race their horses through the streets of Rome, from Piazza del Popolo down the Corso to what is today Piazza Venezia. The habit was tolerated but frowned on by the papal governments, probably because the pontiffs, in their heavy vestments and conical miters, never felt comfortable in the saddle. Under pressure, the city's sports were eventually persuaded to transfer their still unofficial meets to the open countryside about eight miles south of the Campidoglio, along the Via Appia halfway toward the Alban Hills. Already on the premises were a couple of *capanne,* huts where an enterprising local named Ser Giovanni sold coffee to travellers. The new track took its name from his humble establishment and hosted its first official meet in 1881.

The basic topography has not changed much since then. Le Capannelle is still essentially a huge, flat field of about three hundred acres containing a stable area for nine hundred horses, two training tracks, an inner dirt course, a steeplechase layout, and two main turf courses, the Pista Grande and the Pista Piccola. There are stands of umbrella pines and a fragment of an ancient aqueduct behind which the horses periodically disappear. Sprint races are run out of a chute on the straightaway and the stretch from the turn of the Pista Grande to the finish line is four and a half furlongs long. The total circumference of the Pista Grande is a mile and five-eighths, the horses run clockwise, and the emphasis, as elsewhere in Europe, is on stamina and tactics rather than on sheer speed. The Italian Derby, like most real derbies, is run at a distance of twenty-four hundred meters, about a mile and a half, which is generally considered the classic test of quality.

I hadn't been to the Italian Derby since it had been internationalized and I spent most of the time prior to the race wandering happily about the premises. Although the management had made a number of practical improvements—more TV monitors, computerized betting machines, many more grandstand seats, more bars, a glassed-in restaurant over the stretch serving execrable food—the emphasis was still on holiday informality. The three main buildings, terraced sandstone blocks disguised as fin de siècle palazzi, loomed above an expanse of hedged-in green where entire families had gathered to picnic, drink Frascati, and kick soccer balls. The accredited bookmakers, mostly fat, cold-eyed men in rumpled business suits, still operated inside their kiosks, where they chalked up the changing odds primarily to suit their own narrow views of the universe. Old men and women sat over small portable stands hawking fresh olives, *fave,* nuts, dried seeds, and slices of fresh coconut. The hard-core three thousand punters were all present, as were many other people for whom *il derby* had obviously become simply an annual social event. The women's fashions this year leaned either to maximum informality—blue jeans, cotton tops, jumpsuits, minis—or ruthless materialistic display, featuring expanses of slaughtered animals and snarls of gold chains.

The racing establishment asserted itself mainly inside the saddling paddock and the walking ring, where the atmosphere exuded entrenched money—expensively tailored suits and dresses, ties, even hats, the old-boy network on full display. Through this elegant crowd the horses and their grooms moved at first almost like intruders, tolerated guests at an ancient ritual. Up to twenty minutes before post time for the big race, I had almost forgotten what I had come to see.

This was corrected by the appearance of the jockeys in their eye-popping silks and white breeches, and ultimately by the animals themselves—sleek, tightly muscled, beautiful, and dumb. Tintern Abbey looked especially impressive. He belonged to P. S. Niarchos, whose father once owned all the merchant ships Onassis didn't, and was trained by Boutin, the French magician. Furthermore, his regular jockey was Cash Asmussen, a nice-looking transplanted American kid with an apple-pie smile. He had been a leading rider in New York, but had flopped in Southern California, where his lethargy out of the starting gate had often landed him in trouble on the tight turns of those mile tracks. He had never been a favorite of mine, but his mount was being sent off at about even money and I began to feel a chauvinistic twinge of compassion on his behalf. He had not ridden in Rome before and failure to win on a heavy favorite here is usually rewarded by loud whistles and raucously obscene speculations on one's ancestry. Occasionally, losing jockeys require a police escort back to the safety of their quarters.

The hopes of most Romans rested on a big, leggy gray colt named Celio Rufo, who had won two of his three local races despite bolting to the outer hedge and was trained and ridden by a hometown favorite. I also liked the looks of My Top, a lightly raced import from Milan who had recently won a graded stakes race there at a mile and a quarter and was trained by Alduino Botti, a relative newcomer who last year won with 52 of his 116 entries at Le Capannelle, an extraordinary winning percentage anywhere. His jockey, however, was listed as one P. S. Perlanti, nicknamed Peo, a tiny mustached man whose chief claim to attention seemed to be that he had the shortest legs and longest arms of any rider in Italy. His home track was Pisa and in Rome this year he had won only one of ten efforts, not a reassuring figure. Betting on him to beat Asmussen seemed equivalent to wagering on one of the Nibelungen to do in Siegfried. None of the other Italian entries seemed to have much of a chance, so I wound up risking a few lire on Celio Rufo.

I should have remembered what eventually happened to Siegfried. When the race went off, Tintern Abbey was full of run, but Asmussen choked him back to third. A rabbit named Balkny, My Top's stablemate, went out to set a fast pace. When the field finally emerged from behind the trees, the ruin and a motorized TV camera crew speeding along the infield and effectively blocking the view of everyone not in the top rows of seats, it still looked like Tintern Abbey's race; he was clearly waiting for the speed to die and would easily romp home.

At the head of the stretch, however, just as the speed wilted, the Abbey crumbled. It should have been Celio Rufo's moment, but, "troubled by mysterious phantoms," as one commentator was to describe it later, he lugged to the inside this time and disappeared. A quarter of a mile from home, the English horses were running one–two, with Brogan looking like a sure winner. My Top, however, suddenly exploded out of the middle of the pack to the outside and, with Peo Perlanti perched like a tiny Valkyrie on his shoulders, swept past Brogan to win by two lengths in excellent time.

Horse and rider were escorted to the paddock for the award ceremonies by a shouting, cheering throng that eventually hoisted the grinning Peo to its shoulders and paraded him around the ring. Asmussen, returning for the weigh-in, received a rousing chorus of insults, mainly regarding his legitimacy, and quickly vanished into the jockey room. The owner of My Top, a husky-looking, middle-aged meatpacker named Emilio Balzarini, made a speech in which he declared, to much applause, that Italians always got there, perhaps a little later than others because they had less money. He had bought My Top for about fourteen thousand dollars, the most profitable ever of his meat imports.

No one was ungracious enough to point out that My Top was an English-bred; it was enough to know that he had been raised and trained in Italy. It remained for one of the visiting British, however, to deliver an unkind cut. "You see, in England my horse could never have finished second in a Group I race," Ian Balding informed an interviewer. "In Italy, he succeeded and this, of course, makes me very happy." The empire lives.

LEGACIES

CHAPTER
FIVE

THE SPOILS
OF SPERLONGA

LEONE PEZZUCO WAS nineteen years old when he was drafted into the Italian army in early 1940. One of seven children (four boys and three girls), he lived with his family in a one-room apartment on the second floor of an old house on the corner of the Piazza della Repubblica, the main square of an ancient fishing village called Sperlonga, which is located on the Mediterranean coast of Italy about seventy-five miles south of Rome. Leone slept at the foot of his parents' bed. He did not own a pair of shoes and he had long since dropped out of school to go to work in the fields between Sperlonga and the neighboring town of Fondi. The big farms were mostly owned by rich landlords, some of whom lived in Rome and Naples, and Leone's status was that of an unskilled day laborer. He could count on working about two hundred and fifty days a year, for which he received minimum wages, barely enough, he recalls, to keep himself clothed and fed. As an unskilled, barely literate worker, he had nothing to look forward to except a lifetime of tilling someone else's fields, the only occupation available to him and one guaranteed to keep him permanently impoverished.

Leone's military service coincided with Italy's entry into the Second World War as an ally of Nazi Germany, and for the next five years he served as an antiaircraft gunner in and around Naples, which was heavily bombed during the closing months of the war. In the early spring of 1944, after Italy's surrender, the German takeover and the

51

Allied invasion of the peninsula, Leone left his unit and decided to go home. The Allied advance up the boot had been stopped by the Germans at Monte Cassino, a few miles inland and south of Sperlonga, and German troops occupied the countryside through which Leone had to pass. He hid during the day in fields and abandoned farm buildings and took several nights to walk home, a distance of about seventy miles. Sperlonga was eventually liberated on May 15, 1944, by American troops moving up the coast after the fall of Cassino, by which time Leone had already gone back to work on the land.

He had also married a cheerful local girl named Anita, who worked as a seamstress. They moved into a tiny one-room apartment of their own and were looking forward to raising a family, even though their economic future seemed circumscribed, not only by Leone's lack of education and skills, but by a centuries-old class system based on property and rank. Sperlonga was a poor town, in which most of the valuable property, as well as the good farmland in the surrounding area, was owned by a handful of so-called *signorotti,* petty noblemen, who had inherited it and had a strongly vested interest in maintaining the status quo. During the Fascist years, little had been done to better the lot of the poor and the assumption on the part of most Sperlongani, even with the coming of democracy, was that little would change. Fifty percent of the workers in Leone's category were illiterate, a situation considered entirely normal by the local population. "One did not go to school, because the school [and] instruction were considered a 'right' of the 'gentlemen,' " a local historian named Vincenzo Guglietta wrote in his book, *Sperlonga, Storia e Leggenda.* Any attempt by a member of the working classes to acquire an education was considered a shameful act of subversion, "a grave insult" to a system founded upon the exclusion of the poor from any prospect of self-improvement.

"In 1946, I was a peasant working on the land," Leone once recalled. "Then I heard that they were hiring men to work on the new aqueduct to bring running water to the town. I got a job with the water board and taught myself to be a plumber." He worked for the municipal water board for thirty years, during which time he also helped to install a sewer system, not only in the old town but for the sprawling housing developments being built all along the coast to the north, between Sperlonga and Terracina, about twelve miles away. He was the only person who knew exactly where every foot of pipe had been laid and his services became much in demand among the private contractors who, beginning in the 1950s, were building summer houses for the new bourgeoisie created by the economic boom of the fifties and sixties.

Shortly after he began to work for the water board, Leone became aware that a new town was rapidly being created just to the north of Sperlonga, along the beach. Like most of the ancient villages of Italy, Sperlonga huddled on a rocky promontory, this one thrust out like a stubby finger into the Mediterranean. During the Middle Ages, the inhabitants of these southern towns had all taken refuge at night within their fortified walls, where they benefitted from a relative degree of safety from bandits, pirates, and the mercenary armies of quarreling princes. The coastal areas and the plains had remained largely uninhabited for centuries. Now, with the coming of *il boom*, Italians, who had never before been able to build themselves vacation homes or considered moving out of their cramped quarters in the medieval *centri storici*, began to move into more spacious, modern houses on flat land. A whole new city calling itself Sperlonga Mare was rising below along the waterfront.

The building boom everywhere was largely unplanned and uncontrolled. Leone realized that not only was there an immediate shortage of public facilities—schools, churches, playgrounds, parks, markets—but even of shops selling basic necessities. He decided to open a general store and persuaded Anita to run it, even though they both had doubts it could succeed. "People were used to shopping in the old town," he explained to me not long ago. "But on our very first day we had so many customers that Anita's feet swelled up to twice their normal size and we had to stay open until after nine o'clock."

Today, Leone Pezzuco is a rich man. He has retired from the water board and only occasionally works as a plumber, usually for friends or friends of friends, but he and Anita still run their store, which is open during the warm vacation months and sells hardware, dry goods, and beach equipment to the tourists who flock into the area. He and Anita have themselves moved out of old Sperlonga into a large, whitewashed villa they built on the slope of the hill just above the shoreline. His two daughters have graduated from college. They have both married and have children of their own. One is a biologist, the other an accountant, and they live nearby with their husbands. Every summer they all move into the villa and the family is reunited during August, Italy's traditional vacation month. Every winter, Leone and Anita close up the store and travel. They have been all over the world and this year they plan to spend two months in Miami before going to Venezuela. When I once asked Leone if he had mastered any foreign languages, he laughed and said, "I don't even speak good Sperlongano." A tall man with a long nose and thinning brown hair, Leone likes to laugh and clearly enjoys his affluence. "Before my time, all Sperlongani were either peasants or fishermen," he said. "My generation was lucky. We were given the opportunity to become somebody and some of us profited."

I have known Anita and Leone ever since I first visited Sperlonga in the mid-1960s. A few years earlier, my mother had bought the ruins of a building at the southern edge of town and built herself a small house with picture windows and a large rooftop terrace overlooking the beach and the open sea. Other relatives and friends of ours have built or bought vacation homes in Sperlonga, and every year my wife and I spend at least several weeks here. Like many other small towns up and down the coasts of Italy, Sperlonga has become a fashionable resort, with a flourishing economy based largely on the presence of *forestieri,* outsiders, and a growing influx of summer tourists, who now swarm into the area by train and bus. The changes this traffic has brought to Sperlonga have been enormous and Leone's story is by no means an isolated one. Many Sperlongani have been enriched by the phenomenon, which in one generation has greatly altered a way of life that had persisted for centuries. The generation gap between the older Sperlongani and their progeny is consequently a vast one, as attested to by Leone's remark to me one summer day, while we were comparing notes on our children. "My daughters grew up wanting cars, motorcycles, TVs, and stereo sets," he commented. "I made them work to earn what they wanted and made them pay me back when they graduated from school and I loaned them the money for their cars. They thought life was what it is on television, where even the poor have everything. I thank God every day that I don't have a son, because I would be serving a hundred-year sentence for murder. No one wants to work for anything anymore."

The complaint, of course, is a familiar one, and not only in Italy.

In Sperlonga, however, it seems to have a certain validity, if only because the contrast here between the past and present is so dramatic. It is readily discernible in almost every aspect of local life, even in the way members of the same family dress on various occasions. I recently attended a Sunday morning service in the local church, a new building on the edge of the *centro storico,* at which all the older women and most of the men were attired in black, all the younger people in light colors. After the ceremony, the old people walked slowly back to their homes, while their children and grandchildren scampered off to the beaches. "The old people are permanently in mourning, from the time any member of the family dies," a friend of mine who moved here from Rome recently explained to me. "Their children do not mourn. The old people do not go to the beach, their children have grown up at the beach. In thirty years, Sperlonga has leapt one hundred years ahead."

The old people seem, in a way, to be in mourning for a life that is vanishing and those of us who came to Sperlonga from the outside are also in mourning for that life. Every year we see a slow corruption or a disappearance of what it was that brought us to this village in the first place. "But I know that I am wrong," my friend continued. "Life, even in a place like Sperlonga, is not a picture postcard, all folklore and mandolins. The Sperlongani want what everyone wants—money, cars, big houses, material possessions. When we outsiders came, they saw how we lived and they are imitating us. It is not possible to blame them."

THE FIRST *forestiere* to buy a house in Sperlonga was an architect from Rome named Alberto Boccianti. He, his wife, and two other couples had first visited the area in the spring of 1940, just as Italy was preparing to go to war. The men sailed down the coast from the Circeo, an island resort a few miles north of Terracina, while the women proceeded on bicycles. Due to unfavorable winds, it took Signor Boccianti's party seven hours to complete the trip, but eventually they arrived after dark at the Fontana Beach, just north of the town. They found a small *trattoria* with a few rooms to let, where they ate and slept. The next morning, which happened to be Easter Sunday, they climbed up a flight of steep steps to the village, not knowing what they would find. "No one would talk to us," Boccianti recently recalled. "There was a Mass being said by an old priest in an ancient church hidden in a maze of narrow alleys. We walked all over the village and people looked at us as if we had dropped from the moon."

From a distance and the beach below, Sperlonga had seemed an enchanted place. The stone houses, an off-white stained by years of wind, sun, and rain, clustered together on their rock against a brilliant blue background of sea and sky. The scene looked unreal to the architect, as if an artist had dreamed it up as an illustration for a children's book. The beaches to the north and south were almost completely deserted, except for a few fishermen's huts and the little *trattoria* where they had spent the night. Before leaving, they swam in the sea and picnicked on the beach in perfect isolation. "My wife and I decided then that one day we would come back," Boccianti said. "Because of the war and my work, it was over six years before we did return. But once you have seen Sperlonga, it is impossible to forget it."

This impression is one shared by a majority of those who have visited the village over the centuries. "The aspect of the town is strange and unusual," a clerical visitor reported to his ecclesiastical superior in Rome toward the end of the nineteenth century. "Except for a bit of piazza at the entrance, all the rest is divided by very narrow little streets, about one in ten of which is flat, all the rest being very steep or made up of steps that are very tiring to climb. Then a road runs around the city internally, passing through and under the houses, with countless arches and obscure passageways, while others divide the circle, descending from top to bottom. The houses in the interior are dark and admit little air, but those all around benefit from an outside view from above the beaches, the sea, the slopes of Terracina, Fondi and Itri, as well as the distant Circeo, a marvelous sight to see."

There were no handsome palazzi to be observed, according to this correspondent, but a few of the buildings, those belonging to the Cardi and Sabella families, the *signorotti* of the town, were magnificently furnished, "with paintings and diverse old objects quite pleasing to outsiders." The visitor noted, too, that the structure of the town had been dictated by the need of the inhabitants to protect themselves, especially against the depredations of the Saracen pirates who for centuries, after the fall of the Roman Empire, had raided the coasts of Italy at will.

The Sperlongani were also superstitious, he noted, and decorated the walls and roofs of their shops and houses with goat horns
against the Evil Eye. "This is a superstition quite common in the region, as it was with the ancient Romans, but which in Sperlonga seems
to be more strongly and securely enthroned." This was undoubtedly
due to the town's long history of neglect and disaster, which had created in the inhabitants a fatalism in the face of misfortune, a trust in
omens and charms of various kinds, and, above all, a wariness in dealing with all strangers.

When Alberto Boccianti and his wife showed up again in
Sperlonga during the winter of 1955 to 1956, determined to buy a
place, no one at first wanted to sell them anything. The village was still
very poor. The women of the town washed their laundry in a stream
that bubbled up from under the rocks below the southern end of the
promontory, garbage and trash were routinely disposed of by being
dumped out of windows, and there was no sewer system. The only
hope for a better future lay in developing the town's scenic resources,
but no one understood this yet. The Bocciantis were viewed with suspicion, as intruders who had some mysterious, possibly malignant purpose in mind. After weeks of searching, the architect was finally able
to buy, admittedly very cheaply, a single large room at the very top of
the peninsula that had once been used as a stall. Boccianti opened windows and built a terrace looking out over the sea in both directions. A
month after he bought it, in May of 1956, they moved in. "That first
summer was extraordinary," he remembers. "It was like living in another century. Even in the heat of mid-August, we would go down to
the beach and be alone. If there were ever more than fifteen people on
it, we would be offended."

What finally opened everyone's eyes to the future potential of
tourism in the zone were the archaeological discoveries made in connection with the construction of a coastal road linking Sperlonga to
Terracina and its neighbors to the south, Gaeta and Formia. The work
had been going on for several years when the engineer in charge of it,
Erno Bellante, a passionate amateur archaeologist, decided to dig on
his own around and inside a large cave at the southern end of the
Angolo Beach, about a mile below the village. He was convinced that
he would find not only evidences of an ancient Roman presence in the
area, but perhaps whole statues and other objects of real value.

Signor Bellante had good reason to be optimistic. The cave was called the Grotto of Tiberius, because the Roman emperor had once had a villa in the neighborhood and was known to have stayed in it on his journeys to and from his summer revels on the island of Capri, in the Bay of Naples. A late nineteenth-century print depicts several couples strolling about inside the cave, through the opening of which Sperlonga can be seen, perched on its rock. In 1880, a bearded stone head of Dionysius had been fished out of the sea very near the mouth of the cave, and in 1896 a farmer digging nearby in his vineyard had come upon two small busts of the Gracchi brothers. As late as 1935, just behind the cave, a statue in gray and white marble of a dancer was discovered. This find and the Dionysius were acquired by the Department of Monuments in Naples and put on display there, while the Gracchi busts wound up in the hands of a private collector in Rome. In addition to these major finds, the farmers in the area had for many years been coming across fragments of statues, columns, mosaics and bits of marble, which they had either thrown away, taken home, or sold.

Having obtained a permit from the Department of Antiquities in Rome, Bellante and his men began to dig inside the cave on September 10, 1957. They immediately made some important discoveries. A journalist named Arturo Fratta reported in the Neapolitan daily *Il Mattino* on the morning of October 4, 1957, that "at a depth of between thirty centimeters and a meter and a half, Bellante found the thigh, the leg and the foot of a gigantic statue, the giant's two hands, three backsides, a very beautiful head, another of a later date, three hands clutching a serpent, the head of the serpent, a hand holding the small statue of a boy, and then mosaics, decorations made of shells, arms, hands, and legs for a total of five hundred pieces. By digging, Bellante brought to light part of a pool and the pedestal of the marble group. . . ."

The engineer immediately realized the importance of his find and notified the Department of Antiquities, which on September 25 dispatched Professor Giulio Iacopi, the head of the agency, to the scene, at which time Bellante was able as well to hand him the fragments of a stone tablet bearing some writing in ancient Greek and several names of known artists and sculptors. The possibility that the diggers had unearthed the original of a famous sculpture of Laocoön and his sons fighting with the serpent sent by the gods to destroy them during the siege of Troy caused enormous excitement and was widely reported in the Italian and foreign press. Animated primarily by a desire to examine, catalogue, and reconstruct these precious fragments, Professor Iacopi ordered that they be transported immediately to Rome.

By this time, however, the Sperlongani had become alarmed. The Bocciantis, who had visited the site every day to find out what else might have turned up, informed the villagers of the decision to take all the items to Rome. The Sperlongani considered the cave and everything in it to be their own personal property and were outraged to hear that some government organization intended to steal it from them. Armed with crudely lettered, handmade signs carrying such exhortations as "We want our stones!" and with sticks, hoes, rakes, and other farm implements, a mob of several hundred Sperlongani descended on the site. For two days, on September 27 and 28, the citizens, behind an improvised barricade of boulders blocking the road, stymied any attempt by the carabinieri and the trucks sent from Rome to cart away their treasure.

The protest was sympathetically played up in the national press and the controversy eventually embroiled several government branches, including the Parliament, the Ministry of Public Education, and the Ente Provinciale del Turismo. It was decided at last to leave the relics in Sperlonga, do the necessary work of research and restoration on the spot, and build a museum near the cave to house the collection and any future finds made in the vicinity.

"I think it was this incident that not only brought the attention of the outside world to Sperlonga, but also woke the Sperlongani themselves up to the possible benefits to be derived from their inheritance," Alberto Boccianti reminisced not long ago. "Here was a place that for hundreds of years had been forgotten and ignored, then came the new road and the treasures it unearthed. Suddenly, history, which had been so cruel, smiled on it."

AN AMATEUR historian named Monsignor Nicola Ferraro speculated in a treatise he wrote in 1937 that Sperlonga owed its existence to three basic facts. The first, and perhaps most important of these, was the manufacture of a celebrated local white wine the Romans called Cecubo, much favored by the legions tramping back and forth between the capital and the Emperor Tiberius' sumptuous villa. The second fact was the presence of this villa itself, with its many outlying buildings, all within easy reach of the grotto, which had been known to the ancient Greeks. The third and most enduring fact was the opening of the Via Flacca, named after the Roman official, Lucio Valerio Flacco, who built it during the emperor's reign. Traces of this road are still visible. It was about twelve feet wide and skirted the coast between Terracina and Gaeta, passing above both the emperor's villa and the cave.

After the fall of the Roman Empire and the beginning of the barbarian invasions of Italy, the peasants and fishermen, who had been living in relative security on the land around the imperial villa, were forced to take refuge near a monastery built on the promontory by Greek monks between 554 and 568 A.D. The inhabitants gradually fortified the spot and it became what the Italians call a "closed castle," presenting to potential invaders a walled circumference, complete with a moat and drawbridge on the landward side.

According to most experts, the castle took its name from the ancient Latin word for cave, *spelonca,* which by the year 1500 had evolved into its present form. A local priest named Don Francesco Trani, however, believed the name originated in the phrase *spes longa,* the long hope, words that expressed, according to Signor Guglietta, the real moral and social situation of the inhabitants. By 1500, life in Sperlonga had become a long litany of disaster, due mainly to frequent pirate raids. It was "a life made of continual worries and anxieties, of misery and fear, drawing sustenance from the scanty yield of sea and land that [the citizens] were able to exploit with primitive means and systems."

The Saracen incursions along the Italian coast began in the early part of the ninth century and persisted for hundreds of years. The town was considered a prize not because of its wealth, certainly, but largely because of its setting, with its beaches and nearby streams of clear water. Some of the pirates eventually settled in the area and traces of their presence can still be found in the local dialect, which is unique and contains words and phrases unconnected to Latin or any of the other dialects spoken in the south.

The most disastrous and famous of the attacks on Sperlonga was undoubtedly the one carried out by a Turkish pirate nicknamed Barbarossa (Red Beard), who commanded the fleet of the Ottoman Sultan Suleiman II. His main purpose was to abduct a famous beauty, Giulia Gonzaga, the countess of Fondi and Traetto, whom the Sultan wanted to add to his harem. Barbarossa showed up with a large fleet off the coast early on the morning of August 8, 1534, and disembarked two thousand armed men on the Angolo Beach below the town, while the fleet proceeded up toward Terracina on a secondary raid. The Sperlongani took refuge behind their walls, but were unable to put up much of a resistance against the invaders, who first sacked the fishing port, then broke into the town itself. Only fifty-one inhabitants survived, the rest having either been killed or taken as slaves.

Barbarossa's force then turned inland toward Fondi, a larger and much richer town about ten miles away. The main prize he was after, however, the Countess Giulia Gonzaga, described by a contemporary chronicler as "intelligent, cultured and of singular beauty," managed to escape. Tipped off by a fugitive from the attack on Sperlonga, the beautiful Giulia reportedly fled nearly naked out of a window and hid in the nearby woods, while the pirates sacked and burned the town. Barbarossa's ships also attacked and devastated Terracina, but he was repulsed at Itri, a town a few miles south of Fondi, where the citizens, alerted in time, put up a furious defense from inside their strongly fortified *castello*.

Even though Barbarossa's ruinous raid was by no means the last one, Sperlonga somehow survived, even if it never prospered. A fiscal report on the village by Neapolitan tax officials in 1690 reveals that the population was 705, of whom only three families could be considered well off, while about a dozen others were able to scrape along adequately. "All the other inhabitants practice fishing, carrying on agriculture and work as coachmen, taking their fish to sell in all the nearby places and also into the Roman state." Almost everyone was poor and the town depended, as it had for many years, on work it could scrape up from its neighbors. The description is astonishingly similar in tone to all the ones made from time to time over the next two hundred years. The one constant in Sperlonga was poverty.

The main trouble was that, after the fall of the empire, Sperlonga was cut off from its neighbors. The main Roman road south, the Via

Appia, reached the coast at Terracina, then turned inland again toward Fondi and Itri, before reaching the sea once more at Gaeta. The Via Flacca had been abandoned and Sperlonga's only link, except by sea, to the rest of Italy was by a narrow road, little more than a footpath, to Fondi. Not until 1871 was a project approved to build a real road between the two towns and work was not completed on it until 1889.

The isolation and sufferings of the village over the centuries, and its dependence upon the powerful noble families who ruled in Fondi, formed the character of the town. They created, according to Signor Guglietta, "an inferiority complex, induced it to submit always to everything, with a dismaying passivity. . . ." This attitude affected everyone and everything in Sperlonga, prolonging a feudal state of mind that resisted any attempt from whatever quarter to better the lot of the citizens and to free them from the past.

That liberation finally came about as a result of the new two-lane highway from Terracina. Also named the Via Flacca, it follows roughly the route of the old Roman road, then proceeds through a series of tunnels toward Gaeta and Formia. It was opened to traffic on February 9, 1958, after six years of work, and it immediately put Sperlonga on the map. It still took close to three hours to drive down from Rome, but property prices soon began to soar, as the new Italian bourgeoisie began to buy up and remodel existing houses and apartments in the *centro storico,* as well as construct villas, hotels, and *pensioni* along the northern shore. The building boom was on all over the country and it was largely uncontrolled. Even where there were zoning laws and planning boards, the real estate speculators did pretty much what they wanted. The rules were simply ignored or circumvented, while politicians and public officials conveniently looked the other way. It wasn't until some years later, long after the worst abuses had been perpetrated, that a number of scandals exploded into the public eye, involving collusion between the speculators and the guardians of the public interest. Some of these scandals helped to topple national governments and resulted in the jailing of dozens of people, mostly private businessmen and minor officials. Not a corner of the peninsula was untouched by the boom and Sperlonga was no exception.

Much of the development of Sperlonga has been beneficial to the village. The water and sewer systems, two new schools, the Palazzo Comunale and other public buildings, the erection of a breakwater and creation of a small enclosed port, all were approved, financed, and carried out during the past two decades. Currently, there are plans for more housing projects, better roads, and additional parking facilities, measures aimed at increasing tourism and thus bringing added prosperity to the community.

Most of the criticism directed at such policies concerns the aesthetic and environmental price being paid for what amounts to a boundless dedication to progress at any cost and the negative long-range effect it will have on the quality of life in the region. "We see over the years a slow degradation," is the way it was put to me recently by a slight, bearded, intense-looking young man named Stefano D'Arcangelo, an official of the local Communist Party, who is employed in a civil-service job having to do with tourism and development. "Ideas, certainly, are not lacking, but the execution is."

A friend of mine, whom I'll call Gabriella Schiavone, has periodically, over the years, attempted to organize and rally the resident *forestieri* against this trend, admittedly without much success. "Some of us have been here for twenty years and we own property," she told me not long ago, "but it makes no difference. We are still outsiders and no one at city hall pays attention to us."

In 1962, Gabriella bought an old Sperlonga building that had once been a castle tower and converted it within into several apartments, one of which she and her family use, while renting out the others to summer residents. "What I see every year is the disappearance of the little things that were Sperlonga—chimneys, corners of buildings, stairways, balconies, terraces, windows, even the colors of the stones," she said. "For instance, the old windows were ringed in white, where the women used to wash the walls by hand. The balconies were narrow, contained within the traditional local straight iron railings. Now everything is being remodeled in the Assyro-Tyrolese style, with shutters and ornate, curlicued balustrades. The old shops in the piazza disappear, to be remodeled and reopened as *pizzerie,* ice-cream parlors, boutiques, and wine bars with names like 'New Pop' or 'Baby's.' Then there are the wire and cable lines everywhere, the television antennas, and next year the shiny new gas pipes they are planning to run along the outside walls all over. If you try to protest and to explain to these people that they are slowly ruining everything, they look at you

63

as if you are demented. 'Ah, *you* have a nice house, Signora,' they say to me, 'but you built it on our shoulders.' "

In their headlong rush to prosperity, the Sperlongani have indeed tended to ignore what it was that made their town attractive to moneyed outsiders. As the old buildings in the *centro storico* are remodeled into luxury apartment houses, they tend to lose the characteristics that made them unique and picturesque. I once arrived in the Piazza della Repubblica to find that one of the main buildings on the square had been converted into a sort of Beverly Hills Spanish mansion, with shutters, balconies, ornate iron grillwork, and painted a brilliant white. Not only did it clash with the friendly, slightly dilapidated ancient look of the rest of the piazza, but from the beach below it stuck out from its neighbors, like a neon sign mounted on a verdant hillside. I discovered that the building belonged to a Christian Democratic politician, who happened to be a member of the current administration. He was reportedly busily at work remodeling several other buildings he owned in the *centro* and every year brings new changes.

IT MAY be, of course, that something of the old Sperlonga will survive, enough to keep the *forestieri* coming back year after year. The legacy of the town's tragic past persists in its stones and nothing so dramatizes the clash between history and the future as the present-day view from Signor Boccianti's terrace. To the south, gazing toward the mouth of the grotto, the sight remains largely unspoiled, not unlike what the architect saw when he first visited the town. The Angolo Beach curves gradually toward the mouth of the cave, framed by the rocky slopes of the hills that here flow gently to the sea. Between the beach and the hill are cultivated fields of lettuce, corn, and tomato plants, with only a handful of private villas tucked back in among groves of trees and, along the beach itself, a few modest-looking establishments catering to the needs of visitors during the summer months. Ever since the archaeological discoveries around the grotto, the whole area has been under the protection of the Department of Antiquities in Rome, which prohibits private construction near the site and commercial exploitation of any kind. (The villas were built illegally a few years ago, but have been allowed to remain, a not uncommon phenomenon in a country where, as an old Roman friend of mine once put it, "There are plenty of laws, but no one enforces them.") Except during the hot months, when the beach all but disappears under long parallel rows of colored umbrellas and the seafront becomes a hive of frolicking vacationers, the aura of old Sperlonga lingers over the scene and the sense of a living past is strong.

To the north, however, the view is completely different. Sperlonga Mare has become a great jumble of apartment houses, hotels, *pensioni,* shops, restaurants, banks, and parking lots. The buildings press down to the high-tide line and every summer it seems to become more crowded, with hordes of tourists shuffling along the sidewalks and pushing in and out of the shops and restaurants. Even in the cold months, when the old town seems to be asleep and largely deserted, Sperlonga Mare remains bustlingly active. This is because most of the roughly forty-five hundred Sperlongani now live here. As the *centro storico* has been bought up by outsiders, the inhabitants have been forced to move, a phenomenon common to the rest of Italy. Many Italians, tired of the cramped quarters and the climb up into the old hill towns, have sold their ancestral homes and parlayed their new wealth into modern apartments on flat land nearer to their jobs, the new highways, and the railroad. Every hilltop *castello* in Lazio, Tuscany, and Umbria, for instance, is ringed by blocks of new apartment houses, factories, and office buildings, new towns where the real day-to-day life of these communities is lived. Only three or four hundred Sperlongani still dwell in the *centro,* which in winter can seem as forlorn and empty as a ghost town. "All of Italy begins to resemble Disneyland," Gabriella Schiavone recently said to me, "as if our past has become an amusement park to entertain the foreigners."

The past these days, however, is in danger of being abandoned completely. "There are enormous pressures to keep building," Signor D'Arcangelo informed me. "For ten years there has been a struggle between various government agencies with authority over the territory, and every now and then someone slips something past them." Some years ago, one of the most aggressive speculators managed to secure a permit to put up a luxury hotel about fifty yards from the mouth of the grotto, a project that was temporarily shelved, at least, when someone tipped off the press and a story about it was published in several local and Roman newspapers. "There is a basic lack of understanding in city hall about the tourist value of unspoiled landscapes and views," Signor D'Arcangelo said. "The landowners plead hardship, that they are forbidden by a tangle of laws from being able to earn any money from their property. The politicians and bureaucrats think that all of these problems can be solved by more roads, more hotels, more parking lots—the cement solution."

To some Sperlongani, as well as the *forestieri* who bought homes here, the flight from the past and everything it represents was best symbolized by the Tower of Truglia at the tip of the peninsula and the old church in the heart of the *centro storico.* Both structures had been empty for years and were slowly falling to pieces. The once fortified tower, from where lookouts first spotted pirate ships on the horizon, was becoming an eyesore, with gaping, empty windows and trash strewn about the grounds. It is now finally being restored and is to become a library. The old church, however, once named after St. Leo the Great, the town's patron saint, is a rotting hulk whose roof is threatening to cave in. For years groups of citizens have tried to get a permit from the ecclesiastical authorities to reopen it as a cultural or a youth center, but without success. "In the end people get tired of struggling," Signor D'Arcangelo explained, "and they turn their backs."

Another poignant symbol of this abandonment is the town cemetery, located off the Via Flacca at the entrance to Sperlonga Mare. Surrounded by a high stone wall, the graves lie in long, even rows, the stones looking shiny and new under the bright sun. There are very few tombstones indicating that anyone died before 1950; the bones of the older dead, some of whom rested in a tiny ancient cemetery inside the old church itself, have long since been dug up and consigned to a common, unmarked grave. "Only the rich are now remembered," an old Sperlongano, who still lives in the upper town, recently explained to me. "This is the cemetery of the big shots."

The daily life of Sperlonga today has thus become, as it has in so many other picturesque Italian villages, a never-ending guerrilla war between those who, like the old, the *forestieri,* and the more enlightened, educated younger citizens, see a need to preserve at least a remnant of the past, and the forces of progress at any cost, who view history in general as an encumbrance and an obstacle to material well-being. This contrast is immediately evident even to the most casual visitor. At the entrance to the old town, from the access road that curves up the hill from the Via Flacca, one enters Piazza Europa, a modern-looking square built outside the old walls and flanked by the white-stone bulk of the Palazzo Comunale, a large public parking lot, a row of modern shops, and the new church, a sterile, angled structure that could easily be mistaken for a supermarket. Beyond the Piazza Europa, a single narrow street over what used to be the castle moat leads into the Piazza della Repubblica, where the facades of most of the old houses remain pretty much as they were a thousand years ago, with drying laundry dangling from the windows and swallows darting about over the rooftops. Despite the new pizza joints and the boutiques, the sense of history here is very strong. And even in summer, when the whole town all but disappears under the crush of tourists, cars, buses, motorcycles, and gangs of vacationing teenagers armed with stereo sets and electric guitars, something of the past persists.

Among these throngs of revelers, the last of the old Sperlongani, those who have not been enriched by the boom, remain like relics of another age. The men sit placidly in their shabby clothes against the walls of the Trani Bar, a small café that has been on the piazza for over a century, gazing with mild, resigned curiosity at the comings and goings of the new invaders, while their black-robed women move through the crowd like phantoms. "When these old people have all died off," Gabriella said to me one day, "who will remember what Sperlonga was like?"

I was standing at the Trani Bar myself one summer morning, sipping a *caffè latte*, when I struck up a conversation with a middle-aged Sperlongano named Fernando De Fabritiis, who owned a small grocery store on the Via Tiberio, up the street from my mother's house. Fernando has lived in Sperlonga all of his life and likes to express his views on matters of public concern by telling jokes and stories he has known ever since he was a child. When I asked him if he thought anything could be done by the present municipal administration about the heedless overdevelopment of the area, he smiled and shook his head. "I will tell you a story," he said. "A man has a grove of pear trees, but one of these trees fails to produce, so he chops it down and he sells it to a carpenter. The carpenter carves a statue of St. Joseph out of it and gives it to the local church. The man who owned the tree goes to the church on Sunday, where everyone there is praying to the statue of St. Joseph. The man refuses to pray. He knows that piece of wood. 'It couldn't make a single pear,' he tells everybody. 'How will it produce a miracle?' "

CHAPTER
SIX

THE AGONY
OF CASSINO

THE POLISH MILITARY Cemetery in Italy, which contains the remains of the Polish soldiers who died fighting in the Italian campaign during the Second World War, is a dramatic sight. It is situated on the slope of a hill, west of the town of Cassino and directly below the Abbey of Monte Cassino, which sits on a small peak about fifteen hundred feet above sea level and dominates the surrounding valleys. The graves, lying in tightly banked, ascending rows in the shape of a huge cross, face the monastery pretty much from the same angle as the men who perished here were forced to look at it during the nearly six months—from November 24, 1943, to May 18, 1944—they spent fighting to capture it and break through the German lines.

It was the Poles who launched the final and decisive attack on the position, on May 11, 1944, and who were finally able to raise the Polish national colors above the ruins early on the morning of May 18, but at a terrible cost. About a thousand men died in this last assault—an overall casualty rate of above 40 percent—and on the final morning most of the survivors were too exhausted even to climb the last couple of hundred feet to the site, already abandoned the night before by the retreating German garrison. It is easy, in this context, to understand the degree of fear and hatred the monastery inspired among most of the Allied soldiers who fought within sight of it. Thus, the Polish cemetery seems to commemorate not only the fate of the soldiers who lie in it, but the feelings of the living men who fought in these mountains and in the narrow valleys below. The cross seems an act of defiance, even an accusation, as well as a testimony to the agony of those who died here.

I had visited Cassino once before since the end of the war and had experienced only a sense of isolation and loss, of a great, abiding grief, eloquently testified to by the presence of four major military cemeteries in the area. I had spent merely a few hours in the place, as a minor and ultimately depressing side excursion during a leisurely motor trip south from Rome to Naples along the ancient Roman roads bypassed by the postwar creation of the zippy Autostrada del Sole, and I had never stopped by the monastery itself. Completely reconstructed and recreated along its original architectural lines, after having been devastated by bombs and artillery barrages, the abbey is the mother house of the Benedictine order and was founded by St. Benedict himself around 529 A.D. It is reputed to be not only a famous Christian monument but a center of learning and culture. Viewed from below, however, it struck me forcibly as a forbidding, inaccessible place, a huge, pale, fortresslike structure perched on its peak as if in flight from the reality of human contact. It did not beckon travellers to it or seem to welcome any advance upon it, but looked to me like an abandoned Valhalla, with narrow rectangular windows set high up in the massive walls towering over terraced farmland. I had left without making the ascent to it, which at that time of year, late spring, was reportedly a slow process along a narrow, twisting mountain road crowded with tourist buses and private cars. This time, on a cold, clear but windy early November afternoon, the road was deserted and I had no trouble whisking upward around the tight bends in my noisy Fiat Panda.

The Polish cemetery is not clearly visible from the road until the very last part of the climb, when the route suddenly swings north around the mountain for one last time and emerges into the open from between clumps of trees and bushes that have obscured the memorial. I pulled over and stopped, brought up short by the sight of the memorial itself, and then I turned to the right, away from the abbey and down a long, narrow driveway into an empty parking lot. To reach the cemetery itself I had to walk past a sculpture in the shape of a broken stone column, erected in 1947 by the Casa Comunale of the city of Cassino and bearing an inscription in Italian testifying to the *"valorosi"* of the Polish army who had "fallen fighting on this bloody ground for the triumph of justice and liberty." The rest of the approach to the burial ground is up along the stem of the giant cross, outlined by tightly packed rows of fat, green cypresses. At the gate, I paused to stare upward at the tombs, with their rows of plain white crosses and Stars of David, all facing toward me and beyond to the monastery. When I turned and looked back in that direction, the building, wind-swept and isolated on its peak, for the first time seemed not merely for-bidding, but huge and hostile. I was alone and I had no desire to walk by myself up into the rest of the memorial, so, after a few minutes, dur-ing which I looked about at a series of beautiful but desolate rocky mountain ridges surrounding the site, I walked back to my car and drove up to a parking lot just below the monastery itself, comfortingly out of sight of the Polish dead.

The abbey has long been a great tourist attraction, as well as an active religious and educational center, so I wasn't surprised to find that I wasn't the only visitor, even on such a cold afternoon. There were several other cars besides mine in the lot and, as I headed up to-ward the main entrance, a group of chattering Italian teenagers emerged, escorted by a couple of cheerful-looking middle-aged priests, who had apparently just taken them on a tour of the premises. The sight made me feel less hesitant about entering the building my-self, because almost everything I had heard and read till then about the place had been connected with the war and the privations endured in the surrounding countryside by the soldiers of both sides. I wanted to experience some sense of the abbey as a haven from not only the sound of guns but the disquieting turbulence of modern life. After all, the Benedictines are best known for being educators, as well as preservers of antique texts and historical artifacts, especially those of the ancient Italic and Roman civilizations.

The part of the building, on two levels, that is accessible to the public, however, does little to dispel the uneasiness I had begun to ex-perience in the Polish cemetery. The structure, in the form of an irreg-ular rectangle, is enormous, about four hundred by five hundred and seventy feet, and is entered through a long corridor that slants upward into a large interior courtyard surrounded by a series of adjoining cloisters. Through the columned openings I caught magnificent views of the surrounding panorama, including one of the Polish memorial, but nothing on the premises provided a feeling of human warmth. The wind whistled through the open arches as I strolled about, pausing briefly to look at marble statues of St. Scolastica and Benedict himself. No flowers or plants grew in the vicinity and I saw no signs of life at the windows of the upper stories gazing down into the courtyard. Benedict, I reminded myself, had founded monasticism in western Europe and his *Regula Monachorum* had set down stern rules of behavior, based on vows of chastity, poverty, obedience, and manual labor, for his monks. (The rigorous disciplines he imposed on his followers once led a group of them to try to poison him.) The building clearly reflected the austerity of his order, if not its humanism.

It is easy to understand, however, why Benedict of Nursia, as he was known during his lifetime, should have chosen to take refuge on such a site. With the crumbling of the Roman Empire, the fertile valleys below were constantly being fought over and invaded first by various barbarian hordes, then by the contending armies of noblemen, kings, and warlike prelates. Benedict himself managed to die peacefully on his mountaintop, around 547 A.D., but in 581 the place was sacked by the Longobards and the surviving monks fled to Rome. This sort of catastrophe was to repeat itself over and over during the ensuing centuries, with the monks returning each time to rebuild and to resume their peaceful activities. With every reconstruction, the monastery assumed, understandably enough, more and more the characteristics of a fortress, taking its present shape in the early part of the seventeenth century. It was sacked one last time in 1799 by an invading French army, but had managed since then to remain inviolate, until the invasion of the Italian peninsula by the Allies in the Second World War brought the opposing forces face to face below Monte Cassino during the winter of 1943 to 1944.

On my way out of the building that afternoon, I stopped by a small gift store near the front entrance, where the monks sell postcards and souvenirs. Many of them have to do with the most recent destruction and reconstruction of the monastery, and all of the dozen or so books and publications I saw on sale were about what had happened there during that terrible time. I asked the serious young monk in charge of the shop if they sold many of the volumes having to do with the war and he told me that the subject never failed to come up, whether visitors actually bought anything or not. "You were here, too,

I imagine," he observed. "Perhaps you flew with this American." And he handed me a pamphlet with an illustrated cover depicting a rain of bombs falling on the monastery. Published by the Pubblicazioni Cassinesi di Montecassino, the official publishing arm of the order, the pamphlet is entitled "The Bombing of Monte Cassino," by Bradford A. Evans. As commanding officer of the 96th Bomb Squadron, Major Evans had commanded the mission to destroy the abbey, on February 15, 1944. He had since returned to the scene, interviewed several of the survivors and had proceeded to write his own account of the event, including in his volume photocopies of military documents pertaining to the mission, as well as a selection of before-and-after photographs of the monastery, the surrounding area, and some of the people, both soldiers and civilians, involved in the action. I discovered when I read it that night that Evans, like so many others who had participated in the battles around Cassino, had not been able to obliterate the memory of what had happened there. "From all wars, controversies are created, some to fade with time, others to linger like a cancer for years," he wrote.

I bought the pamphlet, as well as several of the other publications on sale, while assuring the young monk that although I had indeed been in the air force then and could easily have found myself over Cassino during the war, I had never left the States. I think he was disappointed. "So many of the men have returned," he said. "Not just Americans and English, but many Germans, too."

On my way back toward Cassino, I stopped on impulse at the German burial ground, which is located along a ridge of low-lying hills a couple of miles north of the town. The cemetery is in the shape of a giant horseshoe, with concentric ascending rings of graves lying beneath rows of tall cypresses and pines. It is scrupulously tended by several German organizations entrusted specifically with the care and maintenance of the nation's war memorials. It is also the largest of the ones in the zone. Twenty thousand fifty-one men, most of whom died at Cassino, are buried here, sometimes as many as three to a tomb, and at the top of the horseshoe, on flat land, are several mass graves lying beneath a tall, simple iron cross. At the time of the Italian campaign, the flower of Germany's armed forces was being chewed to pieces in a grinding war of attrition on Russian soil, which explains why so many of the names on the tombstones here are those either of men in their late thirties and forties or in their teens. A large number could not be identified at all except as EIN DEUTSCHER SOLDAT—an unknown soldier blown apart by mines, bombs, grenades, or artillery shells, and left to be gathered up and interred here, identified nationally only by scraps of clothing, equipment, or weapons found with his remains.

It's a sobering and moving experience to visit any war memorial, even more so when one happens to be alone in it, undistracted by the living. It was growing dark when I reached the top of the hill and I had very little time to look around before having to descend again, but I noted that only the very tip of the church cupola within the abbey walls was visible from here. It was a comforting sight, for a change, and as I looked at it, I was passed by a young couple in their twenties, also now about to leave. I asked them if they spoke English and if they had a relative buried here. *"I'm* English," the young woman replied, "but my boyfriend's German. His uncle, his father's younger brother, is here. Of course, he's never seen him. He was eighteen, you see."

NOTHING IS left of the original town of Cassino itself, which in 1943 was a small but prosperous community of about seventeen thousand people at the foot of its mountain. Once known as Casinum, then later as San Germano, it had been repeatedly sacked by barbarian adventurers and Saracen raiders, but had begun to thrive again in the late Middle Ages as an agricultural center and because of its favorable position on the Casilina, one of the two main roads, originally built by the ancient Romans, linking the capital to Naples. It had really begun to flourish in the late nineteenth century as a railroad hub, which by the time the Nazi and Allied armies engaged each other on the Italian mainland, made it an important strategic center, as well as one of the places the slowly retreating German forces were determined to defend as tenaciously as possible.

Much has been written about the horrors of this Italian campaign, which most military historians agree was one of the most misconceived and mismanaged, at least on the Allied side, in the history of warfare. The American Fifth and the British Eighth armies, fresh from victories in North Africa and Sicily, had landed at Salerno, near Naples, in September, 1943, and had begun slowly to fight their way north toward Rome. On a purely strategic level, no one on the Allied side had apparently bothered to worry much about the fact that throughout history no invader, beginning with Hannibal, had ever been foolish enough to attempt to conquer Italy by marching up the boot from the south.

A mere glance at a topographical map of the terrain would have deterred any sensible commander. With the single exception of the Po Valley in the north, Italy consists of an almost unbroken chain of mountain ranges, many of which extend to the coastlines, and which entirely dominate the narrow valleys along which the Allied armies proposed to advance. The Germans, at this stage of the war, were out-manned, outgunned, and almost without an air force, but they still had a formidable army and their very able generals had been ordered by Adolf Hitler himself not to give up an inch of ground anywhere. John Ellis, an English military historian whose *Cassino: The Hollow Victory* is a meticulously detailed and definitive account of the fighting there, points out that the Germans had plenty of time to select the best places to defend and to dictate the circumstances of the battle. "Their whole Italian strategy," he writes, "now hinged upon the selection of suitable defensive lines behind which to deploy most effectively their over-stretched but still determined divisions. Monte Cassino, dominating as it did the most obvious route to Rome, the old Via Casilina or Highway Six as it was now known, was an obvious linch-pin of such a line, being easily linked with the Aurunci Mountains to the south, reaching al-most to the coast, and with the Cairo massif and the Simbruini Moun-tains to the north." The valleys around Cassino were also crisscrossed by a network of linked, swift-flowing icy streams that the Allied troops would be compelled to cross while exposed to lethal fire from the de-fenders on the fortified slopes above them.

The laborious and costly Allied advance up from Salerno gave the Germans plenty of time, with the help of conscript and slave labor, to construct their so-called Gustav Line, against which the Allied troops hurled themselves in what amounted to suicidal frontal attacks. "The sufferings of these fighting troops, mainly the 'Poor Bloody In-fantry,' cannot be overstated," Ellis writes. "Only such abattoirs as Verdun and Stalingrad, Passchendaele and Iwo Jima, can justly be compared. Four major assaults were launched against the fearsome defenses that barred the way to Rome. Thousands died in these assaults and, in each interval, thousands more endured terrible privations as they shivered in their slit trenches and dugouts awaiting the order for the next attack, the next anguished scramble to prise the Germans off Monte This or Point That, the next suicidal dash into the murderous maze of pillboxes, wire and minefields that had once been some sleepy mountain village."

To compound these difficulties, the Allies were also ineptly commanded by generals who often disagreed on strategy and tactics. Mark Clark, the American commander, deeply distrusted his British nominal superior, Sir Harold Alexander, and did not always follow his orders. Both men had little respect for the other foreign troops—New Zealanders, Canadians, Indians, Poles, and French—fighting under them. These luckless contingents were smashed in frontal assaults on nearly impregnable positions, at an appalling cost in lives. Only the French were ably commanded, by General Alphonse Juin, who ultimately conceived and executed the daring flanking maneuver that finally broke through the Gustav Line and forced the Germans to retreat. He and his men received little credit for it and most often his suggestions were ignored. (After the breakthrough, he urged on his superiors a wheeling tactic that might have cut off the German retreat and prevented them from regrouping to fight again, but Clark, who had a personal photographer assigned to his staff, was obsessed with liberating Rome himself and so the Nazi divisions were allowed to escape north to prolong the campaign in the mountains around Florence through another bloody winter.) Major General Fred L. Walker, the commander of the U.S. 36th Division, which was decimated in late January in its attempt to cross the Rapido River, a poorly planned and executed maneuver in which American troops were repulsed and suffered their heaviest casualties of the war, noted in his diary, before the final assault, "I expect this attack to be a fizzle as was the one last night. The stupidity of the higher commanders seems to be never-ending."

About eighty thousand Allied soldiers were killed or wounded in these battles and the Germans lost fifty-five thousand men, a casualty total reminiscent of the trench warfare in the First World War. We ourselves lost nearly as many men in a few weeks at Cassino as we did during the first year of heavy fighting in the Vietnam War. The figures, however, fail to reflect not only the degree of suffering experienced by the troops, but what happened to the civilians living in the paths of the armies. Military historians understandably ignore this aspect of the fighting, except to note the destruction or capture of the communities involved. Not only was Cassino itself entirely levelled, but at least thirty of the surrounding villages simply ceased to exist, while another couple of dozen in the area were partially destroyed. As for the inhabitants, there are no accurate statistics about their losses and no grandiose memorials to commemorate their sacrifices. The Italians have their own Sacrario Militare at Monte Lungo, ten miles south of Cassino, where about a thousand men are entombed who fell during the so-called War of Liberation, from 1943 to 1945. The monument features an austere-looking chapel built of white marble, but is by far the most warlike of the ones in the area, with old artillery pieces flanking its entrance. A small museum across the road displays tanks, guns, and vivid illustrations of the entire Italian campaign, as well as an account of the isolated local action in which, for a week in December, 1943, units of the regular Italian army fought for the first time against their former allies. There is not a word, however, about the civilian dead and what happened to all of the people whose homes and property were destroyed.

Those who had relatives and friends in other parts of the nation safe, temporarily at least, from the fighting, took refuge with them. Many thousands, however, were forced to flee into the mountains, where they hid in caves and shepherds' huts or slept in the open, surviving sometimes for months on handouts from the local country people and by foraging about the countryside. The soldiers were usually too busy killing one another to pay much attention to them, though the Germans habitually seized any ablebodied men they could find to work on the series of fortified lines they were preparing to halt the Allied advance up the boot. (Behind the Gustav Line at Cassino, they had already established several fallback positions that ultimately served successfully to delay the Allies while the remains of the retreating Panzer divisions escaped to the north.)

The inhabitants of Cassino who were still around as the opposing forces prepared to confront each other along the Gustav Line headed either for the monastery itself or scrambled up the adjacent mountain slopes. As the fighting intensified and the Germans occupied all the strategic high points in the area, including the caves and huts that could be converted into fortified positions and storage depots, the refugees not already inside the abbey or camped around it found themselves with nowhere else to go. By mid-November, escape in any direction was made all but impossible by incessant artillery and mortar fire, as well as by a carpet of hidden minefields the Germans had laid down all around their defenses. The old men, women, and children who had tried to survive on their own wound up heading for the monastery, the one place left they hoped would remain inviolate.

They had some reason to think it might. Even though the abbey appeared visually to be a formidable strongpoint within the German lines, it had not been occupied by troops and, according to the monks themselves, was not being used even as an observation post. The Germans were dug in below it on all sides and were using several large caves in the vicinity mainly as ammunition dumps, but they had declared the building itself to be off-limits and in early December established a "non-military zone" of about three hundred yards all around it.

As for the Allies, it was well known that they had adopted an official policy of not destroying religious and cultural shrines, unless it could be clearly established that they were being used for military purposes. "We are bound to respect these monuments so far as war allows," was the key phrase in a memorandum issued to his subordinates on December 29, 1943, by Commander-in-Chief of Allied Forces, General Dwight D. Eisenhower. But he also left the decision about a building's fate up to his officers in the field. Nevertheless, with the presence of so many civilians in the immediate area and some of the monks themselves still on the premises, it seemed unlikely, if not inconceivable, that anyone would launch an attack directly on the monastery itself. It would have been construed as an act of barbarism, with unfortunate propaganda repercussions all over the world. By the time the battles at Cassino began, there were about a thousand civilians, some of them ill and many of them children, either inside the walls or in a cluster of stone farm buildings immediately below them.

THE GERMANS had been trying to get everyone, including the monks, out of the monastery since mid-October, when they informed the seventy-nine-year-old abbot, Gregorio Diamare, that the main defense line had been established through the town of Cassino and the premises would undoubtedly come under fire. General Fridolin von Senger und Etterlin, the commander of the XIV Panzer Corps and the man directly in charge of the Cassino sector, was one of those exquisitely educated professional soldiers the Germans seem able to produce in every war. Deeply cultured and a devout Catholic, he despised Hitler and the Nazi regime in general, but fought brilliantly on every front to which he was assigned. His main concern in regard to the monastery, as reflected by the attitude and actions of his junior officers, was spiriting off to safety the order's artistic and cultural patrimony. His men also offered to help with the packing and transportation north toward Rome for the entire community.

The monks chose to make use of these services, but not to abandon the abbey completely. Nor did they entirely trust the Germans. They never disclosed to them the existence on the premises of many other precious objects temporarily stored there, including 187 cases of art works from the Museum of Naples and a valuable collection of ancient Greek and Roman coins from the Numismatic Museum of Syracuse. They packed the boxes themselves and managed to keep the soldiers from knowing exactly what was in all of the large wooden crates being dispatched to Rome for safekeeping. During the two weeks it took to move everything out, a team of German photographers and cameramen recorded the event, citing it as a typical example of the civilized behavior and concern for European culture of the German armed forces, as compared to the barbarism of the Anglo-American invaders. And they also persuaded the abbot, as a concluding gracious gesture, to allow them to film a High Mass for their officers and troops held in the main chapel as the job was coming to an end.

The last two trucks left on the morning of November 3, by which time only eleven monks, including Abbot Diamare, some of the monastery's civilian employees and their families, and the refugees remained inside the walls or in the vicinity. Two weeks later, the Germans began systematically to blow up the town of Cassino and to fortify the ruins. They also worked incessantly all around the abbey, well inside the neutral zone, preparing observation posts, gun emplacements and ammunition dumps. When the abbot protested that such preparations violated the neutrality of Monte Cassino and the very conditions the Germans themselves had established for its salvation, he was assured that the matter would be taken care of and that the monks were not to trouble themselves about it.

From time to time, German officers would drop in on the monastery, either for a cup of tea or a casual tour of the grounds, and they were almost always unfailingly cordial, as well as sympathetic to the abbot's plight. The monks began to feel safe. A wartime diary kept by one of them, Don Eusebio Grossetti, records that life inside the walls went on "peacefully enough," with everyone attending to his routines and the abbot working in his study on his private archives. No one seemed too concerned about the increasing number of Allied air raids over the surrounding countryside nor the incessant booming of the guns and exploding houses below. In the evenings, the little community gathered together to observe the artillery barrages and to speculate on what might happen.

In late December, the Germans suddenly ordered all civilians out of the monastery and proceeded to enforce the command by rounding up and removing everyone they found outside the walls. Then, on January 5, they declared they would no longer respect the neutral zone and asked the monks to leave as well. They sent three trucks with Italian drivers and some military policemen to take everyone away, leaving only the monks themselves and a few people in the infirmary, who were too ill to be moved. The abbot, however, proved to be a wily negotiator. He reminded the German officers in charge of the evacuation that he had always had cordial relations with the High Command and declared that he and his monks would leave only under duress. They were allowed to remain and no further attempt was made to force them out, probably because by that time the fighting along the Gustav Line had become so heavy that no one involved in it had time to bother anymore about the fate of the abbey.

All during January, civilians hiding out on the surrounding slopes were wounded and killed, mostly by artillery and mortar shells. With no hope now of escaping in any direction and the fighting intensifying, the monastery became the only obvious place of refuge and the survivors fled to it, hiding here and there inside the walls, wherever they could find a niche. By early February, there were again about a thousand people camped on the grounds, most of them inside the walls, but even here they were not safe. The abbey had by then become a symbol of frustration and an object of hatred to the Allied troops below, whose gunners had begun to shell it regularly. The monks had warned the refugees inside not to wander near the cloisters or into the open courtyard, but even so nearly every day people were killed. Don Martino Matronola, who had assumed on January 29 the task of keeping the journal Don Eusebio had been forced to abandon due to illness, noted that "we are now impotently witnessing the gradual destruction of the abbey, with our hearts full of bitterness." He wondered if there weren't some way of notifying the Allies that they were firing on a neutral building full of innocent people, but was assured by a German medical officer visiting the infirmary that the Allies knew what they were doing and could see that no shots were coming from inside. "On the other hand," Don Martino noted a couple of days later, "if the Germans were really such praiseworthy or, better, self-styled saviors of civilization, why didn't they give up their position on Monte Cassino? One day history will provide an impartial judgment."

Early on the afternoon of February 14, several boys scrambled outside the walls to retrieve handfuls of leaflets that had been fired over the mountain slopes during the early morning by the guns of the Fifth Army. Addressed to "Italian Friends" and under the headline BE-WARE!, the fliers delivered the following message, in capital letters:

WE HAVE UNTIL NOW BEEN ESPECIALLY CAREFUL TO AVOID SHELLING THE MONTE CASSINO MONASTERY. THE GERMANS HAVE KNOWN HOW TO BENEFIT FROM THIS. BUT NOW THE FIGHTING HAS SWEPT CLOSER TO ITS SACRED PRECINCTS. THE TIME HAS COME WHEN WE MUST TRAIN OUR GUNS ON THE MONASTERY ITSELF.
WE GIVE YOU WARNING SO THAT YOU MAY SAVE YOURSELVES. WE WARN YOU URGENTLY: LEAVE THE MONASTERY. LEAVE IT AT ONCE. RESPECT THIS WARNING. IT IS FOR YOUR BENEFIT.

The Fifth Army

No one knew exactly what to expect from this message, but there was no way to get out except through the German lines and the monks had been told by German soldiers in the area that any attempt at a mass exodus would be met by gunfire. They were to await the arrival of an officer early the next day, who would presumably bring them word directly from the Vatican and tell them what to do. When an officer did show up the following morning, however, it was to assure the friars that the message was an Allied propaganda stunt and he forbade anyone from trying to leave. After he had gone, the monks resumed their morning routines and were reciting prayers in the abbot's temporary quarters, a subterranean room below the chapel, when the first bombs began to fall, at about nine-thirty.

"The thick walls of our refuge with everything in it, shook in a terrifying way," Don Martino recalled. "Smoke and dust entered through the narrow windows. . . ." A young woman named Oslavia Pignatelli, who had taken refuge with her parents and another family in the post office (now the gift shop) told Major Evans many years later that the first twelve bombs from his squadron probably saved their lives. They had wanted to move to the lower levels of the building, but had been prevented from doing so by a set of locked doors. The opening blasts blew the doors open and allowed the refugees to escape from an area that was totally demolished later in the day.

Four hundred and forty-two tons of explosives were dropped on the monastery that day in two separate attacks by over two hundred planes. No one has ever been able to make an exact count of civilian casualties from these raids, but at least three hundred perished inside the walls, while others were killed trying to escape. It has been established that about two thousand citizens of Cassino alone died during the course of the battles that winter.

At dawn on the morning of February 16, almost all of the civilians still inside the abbey fled, leaving a total of about forty people, a few of them badly wounded, the others, except for the monks themselves, mostly women, children, and old people. The Allies continued to shell the building as if it had already become a fortress, while the survivors were still trying to figure out a way to leave. "By now we have persuaded ourselves that there is nothing to be hoped from men," Don Martino wrote that evening.

Finally, early the next morning, the courageous abbot led the survivors out on foot and the little column made its way down the north side of the mountain, under occasional bursts of artillery fire, until it reached a medical waystation not far from the Casilina. In the afternoon, a German ambulance took the monks away toward Rome, as bombs were once again raining down on the abbey, and the next day the religious community was joyfully reunited in the capital. But not before the abbot, at the insistence of General von Senger und Etterlin, had been pressured into signing a statement declaring that the monastery had never been used by the Germans for military purposes. Don Martino, for one, was not fooled. "The German Command wanted to free itself with clean hands of the abbot and the monks in order to take possession of the ruins of the monastery for warlike purposes," he noted later.

The bombing of the abbey, in fact, turned out to be enormously useful to the Germans. The walls of the main building were a hundred and fifty feet high and ten feet thick; they resisted remarkably well, providing in their partly ruined state just the sort of secure fortifications behind which troops could fire at will on their attackers. Since the building's neutrality had clearly been violated, there was no reason any longer not to make use of it and for the next three months Nazi troops poured down a lethal fire upon the wretched men below.

The bombing had been originally requested by the commander of an Indian division, whose men were about to be used in still another of the series of suicidal frontal attacks that characterized the Allied offensives at this time. It may have worked briefly as a morale-booster, but it exacted a fearful toll later. Only Clark, in one of his few moments of military prescience, opposed it, but he was overruled. As for the enlisted men, who suffered the most, their attitude remained one of undiminished loathing. "I don't know how a monastery can be evil," a British soldier declared later, in defense of the operation, "but it was looking at you. It was all-devouring, if you like—a sun-bleached color, grim. It had a terrible hold on us soldiers."

APART FROM the war memorials in the vicinity, there is little to remind anyone today of the horrors experienced here during that winter of 1943 to 1944. The town of Cassino has been completely rebuilt and has resumed its traditional role of a bustling commercial and agricultural hub, now of about twenty thousand people. Since 1967, with the creation of an industrial zone on the outskirts, it has also become a manufacturing center of such importance that there has been talk of making the city the capital of a new province. To an outsider's eye, it looks like any of a hundred other new towns or suburbs, with its two main streets, the Via de Nicola and the Corso della Repubblica, full of cars and trucks and its shops crowded with buyers.

Italy, however, is a country full of dramatic contrasts between its past and its postwar industrial development. Nearly every population center, even the smallest village, retains an ancient core of old buildings, many of them dating back to Roman times and usually protected by law from overdevelopment. These neighborhoods look much the same as they have since the Middle Ages and continue to impart to the nation that sense of its great past which has delighted visitors for centuries. What is unique about Cassino, as well as most of the surrounding towns and villages, is the complete absence of a *centro storico* and of any building antedating the war. The city was rebuilt in a hurry and chaotically, with almost no attention paid to esthetics or a feeling for the environment. The new buildings were plain, functional, mostly designed to imitate the cold austerity of the architecture favored by Benito Mussolini and his Fascist government, with its dreams of vanished glory. The result is a sprawl of colorless, boxlike constructions of the kind seen in public-housing projects, and almost unrelieved by gardens, parks, or friendly cobblestoned piazzas. There is nothing in downtown Cassino, or in the surrounding villages, to hold a visitor for a minute beyond a need to eat or stop at a gas station.

The people of Cassino, not surprisingly, are reluctant to recall the past. The few who will talk about the war remember it mainly as a time of anguished waiting, in which their lives seemed to be suspended in a void. "I left before the Allies arrived," a woman I met in a bookstore told me. She was in her late seventies and owned a nearby pharmacy. "My husband had been wounded in North Africa and had stayed home after the Armistice. With our two children, we went to be with relatives in the Abruzzi, near Anticoli Corrado. Every day we expected the Allies to come, but the shepherds would return from the hills only with news of bombardments, the sound of distant guns. We had no word of anything that was happening at Cassino. It was only after we went back that we understood what had happened."

There is little in the people's daily lives to remind them of the war. Central Cassino has no statues or monuments or even commemorative plaques—merely the small black-and-white road signs indicating the way to the various military cemeteries. "Only the tourists go there," a woman behind a bar in the middle of town informed me. "No one cares anymore. The young do not know about it and the old speak of it only to each other. It is finished now."

Nothing in the area recalls the American involvement in the battle, either; the nearest American cemetery is at Nettuno, near Anzio, about sixty miles from Cassino. Nor are the French, whose final attack was crucial, remembered except as objects of terror. *I Marocchini,* as the Italian civilian population called all the French troops, most of whom were from North Africa, were accused of looting every village they liberated and raping as many of the inhabitants as they could get their hands on. "Men, women, children, it didn't matter to them," the proprietor of a Cassino restaurant where I had lunch told me. "They had no stake in the war. To them it was an adventure."

I drove southeast about twelve miles to the town of Venafro. It sits in a valley through which the French had fought on their way up to Cassino and in which their dead are now buried. It is the most desolate of the war memorials I visited, partly because it is so isolated from the others, and also because very few relatives of the North African soldiers buried there ever visit the graves. About three-fourths of the 3,414 men entombed here are Muslims, but they all lie under similar headstones that declare each one *"Mort pour la France"* and, as a separate commemorative plaque proclaims, *"Gloriously Fallen, 1943–44."* I was given a spontaneous tour of the cemetery by three young Italians, who take care of it, and whom I found huddled about a small electric stove in a stone cabin where they store their tools. They seemed delighted to have an outsider to talk to and were eager to point out to me how immaculately and lovingly the graves were seen to, laid out in long rows across a grassy expanse of flat, treeless land. "It's a shame so few people come," one of them said. "It is as if all these men died for nothing." I was left with an almost overpowering feeling that perhaps the woman behind the bar in Cassino had been right—that no one cared, and soon no one would remember.

Later I visited the British memorial, which also rests on flat land, about a mile outside Cassino. Four thousand two hundred and sixty-five men are buried here, among them some whose identity is KNOWN ONLY TO GOD. They lie in even rows of graves under modest tombstones and surrounded by a line of umbrella pines. There are also monuments paying tribute to men buried elsewhere, whose graves have been lost, and to an estimated four thousand British soldiers whose bodies were never found. The cemetery is lovingly tended by Italian caretakers, who have planted along the rows of tombs various herbs and red rosebushes, some of them still in bloom during my visit. The place seemed the most human of the memorials I saw, partly because many of the stones bear inscriptions, occasionally in verse. One of them summed up my own feelings about the region and what I had learned during my stay. HE GAVE OF HIS BEST, HIS UNFINISHED LIFE, read the inscription for T. Brown, of the King's Regiment, who was killed on May 12, 1944, at the age of thirty.

On the south side of the cemetery, under a simple stone bower furnished with a marble bench, I found the register of the dead and a large black notebook, in which visitors are asked to write their names and addresses and to make comments. Most of the people who had passed through recently were British, as was to be expected, but, to my surprise, I noticed quite a few Italian names. The day before my arrival, a group of ten or twelve young people from Cassino had come there, obviously for the first time, and had clearly been moved by their visit. "This must never happen again," one young man had commented. His friends had limited themselves to a single phrase. "Love and peace," they had written, over and over, the words marching eloquently down one side of the page, as if nothing else could atone for what had happened there.

CHAPTER
SEVEN

THE VENETIAN MASK

VENICE HAS ALWAYS loved a good show. In fact, hardly a week passes now, even during the cold and clammy off-season months from the end of October to late March, without some sort of public celebration in honor of a saint or a notable historical event. Among the grander and best-known examples are the Feast of the Redentore, held on the third Sunday in July to commemorate the end of a plague in 1575 that in two years wiped out a third of the population, and the *Regatta Storica,* which dates back to 1300 A.D. and features a highly competitive seven-and-a-half kilometer boat race that awards expensive prizes, usually won by professional gondoliers. Then there are the coarser revelries associated with the annual Film Festival and the very entertaining public flaps over the mountings of the Biennale, the modern art show that has never failed to generate enough controversy to keep the critics and participants vitriolically at odds with each other in the press for the full twenty-four months between showings. Sandwiched between these major happenings are a great host of lesser manifestations, usually featuring lights, costumes, and music, all rooted in some past occurrence and punctiliously authenticated by the historians of the relentlessly imaginative Ente del Turismo.

The basic idea, of course, is to keep the tourists, with their travellers' checks and credit cards, coming, and not just during the traditional season. About ten years ago, the city administration sponsored a relaunching of the winter carnival, with the appropriate rhetoric to authenticate the proceedings and imbue them with the unique Venetian patina of authenticity. "Everywhere they call it 'carnival,' but everywhere it's different," wrote the anonymous author of the official pamphlet announcing the undertaking. "The carnival is more a 'state of being' than a 'doing.' For this reason, the carnival is the mask, behind which each person conceals his appearance, but through which he reveals himself." Masks have always been a feature of Venice's carnival season, particularly during the last two centuries of the city's decadence, when the upper classes and wealthy foreign visitors disported themselves wantonly behind them, and the canals and *calli* of the Serenissima swarmed with the most expensive courtesans in Europe.

Until the mayor's initiative, the carnival had lapsed into a squalid travesty of itself, featuring small groups of grotesquely made-up children disporting themselves in the larger *campi* and which the poor used as a begging expedition. In 1980, the refurbished proceedings, which lasted for five days, promoted what amounted to an open-air costume ball in Piazza San Marco and a number of cultural manifestations, all connected in some way, however tangential, to the historicity of the Venetian carnival.

Since then, the enterprise has become almost too much of a success. It now lasts eleven days, includes dozens of lectures, concerts, plays, ballets, operas, and art shows, and nightly converts Piazza San Marco into a huge discotheque for as many as forty thousand elaborately costumed and masked revellers. The last Saturday of the celebration lures an estimated one hundred and fifty thousand Italian and foreign visitors into the city, nearly twice the resident population. It has, in other words, become another in the seemingly endless series of public to-dos designed, according to the more cynical observers of the local scene, to keep the tourist cash flowing and at a time of year when Venice is shrouded in cold fogs and has for decades hibernated behind the closed shutters of her hotels and crumbling palazzi.

Despite the cavillers, with their by now familiar complaint that Venice is in more danger of being submerged by tourists than by the capricious waters of her lagoon, there is no doubt that the carnival, like every other festival here, is enjoyed by a majority of the citizens, many of whom take an active part in the proceedings. (One of the secondary benefits has been a revival of the ancient art of the *mascararo*, the designing and making of the sort of elaborate masks that used to be worn for the occasion by the aristocrats of the republic and which are now on sale year-round in many shops as expensive, original souvenirs.) And although the basic thrust of the enterprise is, indeed, to make money, this consideration doesn't seem either to embarrass the Venetians or to diminish their own pleasure in participating. "We can't complain, because, after all, mass tourism was invented by us," a Venetian acquaintance informed me one day. "As for the masks, people used to come to Venice under false identities partly in order not to be stripped of their wealth. We are an island people and islanders have always been pirates."

It is only mildly ironic in this context that the diversion which now arouses the greatest local enthusiasm is the only one almost completely divorced from moneymaking and which cannot trace its origins back to any specific historical event or religious date. The *vogalonga*, or "long row," was dreamed up in 1974 as a lark by a group of young men, most of whom belonged to one or another of the city's rowing clubs. One of the men, Paolo Rosa Salva, had recently completed his military service in the Alpine troops, who put on a "long march" on skis as part of their training exercises, and he suggested a similar enterprise to his friends. On St. Martin's Day, November 11, nine boats set off for a row across the lagoon and down the length of the Lido to the village of Malamocco, where prizes of salads and chickens were awarded to every participant. "It was not a competition," Rosa Salva recently recalled. "It was a sort of rediscovery of the lagoon."

They had so much fun that they decided to publicize the event and see if they couldn't involve the city in some sort of similar annual affair. The whole history of Venice is inseparably connected to the existence of the lagoon, they reasoned, but in recent years the citizens seemed to have lost touch with this quintessential local aspect of life. "People were going less and less into the lagoon," a journalist for the Venetian daily *Il Gazzettino* recently observed. "The traditional boats were disappearing, replaced by more convenient ones made of plastic." Rosa Salva and his friends saw the *vogalonga* as an opportunity to reawaken enthusiasm for a traditional Venetian pastime, and also as a way of protesting against the increasing presence of speedboats and other noisy motorized forms of transportation in the waters.

To their surprise, the idea caught fire. With the full cooperation of the municipal and maritime authorities, and the enthusiastic support of *Il Gazzettino,* the first official *vogalonga* was held on May 8, 1975. There had been worries expressed over how many people would actually participate and whether the amateur oarsmen would be able to negotiate a punishing thirty-kilometer route, but these were soon dispelled. Five hundred and forty-three pioneer rowers in all kinds of vessels showed up early in the morning at the broad mouth of the Grand Canal, between the Riva degli Schiavoni and the island of San Giorgio, and milled happily about awaiting the start. "It was like seeing one of those eighteenth-century prints, with the basin full of wooden boats," an American resident recently recalled. "When the cannon on San Giorgio went off—boom!—everyone began to row like mad. It was the greatest thing I ever saw."

The *vogalonga* was an immediate and huge success. Thirty-six hundred rowers in 1,197 boats took part in the second edition, held on May 28, 1976, and in 1979 over five thousand participants in more than seventeen hundred boats tackled the by now traditional thirty-two kilometer route, which is in the shape of a bulbous eight, from the basin of San Marco around Sant' Elena to Murano, Mazzorbo, Burano, Sant'Erasmo, and back up the Rio Cannaregio to the Grand Canal. Usually, no more than half the boats complete the course, but no one keeps tabs and no one cares. The *vogalonga* is not a race and it has never been privately sponsored or commercialized. Anyone can row in it, including enthusiasts from other parts of the country and foreigners, more and more of whom are showing up every year. Each rower, whether he finishes the full course or not, receives a "diploma of participation" and a commemorative medal. "The whole point, after all, is to have a good time," my American friend remarked. "It's a celebration, not a contest."

The *vogalonga* I attended a few years ago was no exception. Despite the prospect of a cold and rainy day (according to the forecasters, it had been the worst spring since 1763), 3,389 boats took part. I showed up at the Riva degli Schiavoni at about eight A.M., an hour before the official starting time, to find dozens of entries already festively milling about in every direction under an ominously gray sky, while recorded Vivaldi blared from loudspeakers mounted in Piazza San Marco.

I counted twenty-two different kinds of vessels, from one-man kayaks and *sandolini* to sleek racing shells and cumbersome rowboats manned by muscular teams of uniformed and helmeted oarsmen, and including, of course, a large sprinkling of gondolas. Several of the latter were crewed by women, who received the loudest cheers from a great crowd of watchers massed along the banks to witness their departure and whose boats were the gayest, some adorned with flowers from stem to stern. At nine o'clock, precisely on the hour, the rowers raised their oars in salute and took off, as the crowd cheered and the cannon on San Giorgio boomed, blowing a white puff of smoke over the extraordinary scene. All around me people were shouting and waving, and, like my American friend, I found myself beaming from the sheer exhilaration induced by the spectacle.

Along with thousands of others, I strolled leisurely across town and found a post just below the Ponte delle Guglie, a bridge over the Rio Cannaregio under which the finishers would have to pass. They began to show up shortly after eleven o'clock and straggled in for several hours—sweaty, exhausted, and triumphant—to the clapping and loud *"bravi"* of the rest of us, packed in like anchovies along the winding banks of the canals, the parapets of the bridges, and the windows and balconies of the palazzi. All of Venice seemed to be present, while, luckily, the rain held off and the sun even managed to break through for a couple of hours.

Among the arrivals were boats I had singled out earlier, as well as many extraordinary ones I hadn't noticed before. My personal favorite was a slow-moving black gondola rowed by a husband-and-wife team in their seventies. The woman, bent with age, was perched on the prow and gazing fiercely straight ahead, with a great hooked beak of a nose that I recognized from a score of Venetian paintings and that reminded me of some warrior doge storming the ramparts of a beleagured city. She and her husband rowed slowly and in perfect, graceful synchronization. A number of us were happily in tears, without quite at the moment knowing why, and it didn't matter in the least that she and her consort had almost certainly rowed no more than a small portion of the route.

I discussed the matter later with Count Girolamo Marcello, a middle-aged Venetian nobleman, who can trace his lineage back to the eighth century, and he maintained that Venice "is only sensations, impressions." The *vogalonga* stirs up ancient emotions of pride and long-

91

ing deep enough, the count maintained, to make even the most reclusive of the city's surviving aristocrats want to share in the goings-on. When I asked him whether he, too, had participated in the long row, however, he shook his head and smiled. He preferred to watch, he informed me, from a private office inside the Palazzo Ducale. "The Marcellos have never rowed," he explained apologetically. "They have always been in command of the ships."

THE LAGOON has been the central preoccupation of Venetian life for about fifteen hundred years, but never more so than in the past two decades, when the city has been increasingly and repeatedly flooded by *acque alte,* or "high waters." Venice rests an average of about thirty inches above sea level on quite literally millions of rock-hard wooden piles driven like stakes over the centuries into the mud. The lagoon itself, which is about thirty-five miles long and never more than seven miles wide, is a crescent-shaped, 210-square-mile shallow body of water full of mud shoals and sandbanks, peppered with partly submerged islands, crisscrossed by narrow, treacherous channels and subject to often capricious currents. From the very beginning, the *acque alte* have been a feature of life here, especially in the late fall and winter, when the warm African sirocco blows hard enough from the south to push the relatively shallow upper portion of the Adriatic toward its banks. The water pours into the lagoon through the three channel entrances past the Lido, the long sandy reef that protects the city from the open sea, and at high tide surges over the *fondamenta,* floods the canals and bubbles up through the drains of Piazza San Marco and the *campi.* Throughout history Venice has suffered periodic flooding, but never for very long, and the phenomenon was always regarded as the relatively small price the Serenissima had to pay to remain virtually impregnable to attack, thus guaranteeing her independence. *Acqua alta* even became a metaphor for freedom, as in 1848, when Venice rose against the Austrians, briefly restored the republic and sang a song warning the Hapsburgs that "the water is rising around the doors, it will be hard to sponge it away."

Much has been written in recent years, however, about the high waters that now threaten the very survival of the city. During the first fifty years after official records began to be kept, in 1876, Venice was flooded an average of twice a year. During the 1930s, however, the numbers rose, until during the fifties the city was being innundated an average of sixteen times annually. Today, that figure has more than doubled, and it does not include the many other days of the year when Piazza San Marco and its surrounding area, the lowest lying quarter of the city, lie under at least several inches of water for hours at a time. An official *acqua alta* is gauged at three and a half feet above sea level, a height that will flood most of the *centro storico*. When it continues to rise, quite often to four feet and occasionally to five and six feet, the damage to the more ancient buildings and vulnerable art treasures, as well as to basic public services, can be devastating, as in the famous flood of 1966, when the water rose to a level of nearly six and a half feet above sea level and caused havoc.

Except for the worst manifestations, the Venetians usually seem to be able to cope quite well with this contingency. In the lower-lying portions, they have pretty much abandoned their ground floors, the shopkeepers have improvised waterproof barriers at their front doors and raised their merchandise to higher shelves, and everyone sloshes cheerfully about in rubber boots or tiptoes gingerly along over the raised wooden walkways that crisscross the more frequently flooded areas. Still, no on denies that the problem is a major one. The *acque alte* now afflict the city all year-round. When I was there in May, for instance, a time of year once considered immune, the sirens warning of an impending high water went off twice, the first time at midnight, May 21, which roused people from their beds and sent many of them hurrying to their places of business to take protective measures.

This particular *acqua alta* submerged 70 percent of the city. From my third-story window in San Polo, near the Rialto, I watched the water ooze up over the bank of the canal at the end of my *calle* and silently invade the whole narrow alley, burying it under slimy, refuse-strewn liquid. The harm even such a relatively minor flooding can cause is considerable. "The humidity that creeps up the walls," a reporter recently noted in the weekly *Panorama*. "And the grim, threatening, irresistible, treacherous, cursed water. High water that invades *campi, fondamenti, calli,* hidden gardens, shops, the ground floors of inhabited houses." The walls of many buildings, the writer pointed out, have been permanently marked with dates testifying to the unenviable high-water levels reached during the more damaging episodes, and on others the effect can be traced by the salty encrustations and corrosions the receding waters leave behind. There is little doubt in anyone's mind that, unless some remedy is found, Venice will eventually crumble away and sink permanently beneath the polluted waters of her lagoon.

The trouble can be traced back to the years immediately after the First World War, when a number of private industries began to build factories at Porto Marghera, a few kilometers west of Venice, on marshland drained and reclaimed from the water. The original idea seemed sound, since Venice had ceased to exist as an important seaport, and it was necessary to create jobs for thousands of people unable to earn a living from tourism; the Veneto in general, a backward agricultural province, had become one of the poorest areas in Italy.

Unfortunately, the cure turned out to be worse than the disease. The development of the industrial zones along the coast, which became frenzied during the late fifties and sixties, lured more and more people into the once quiet residential suburb of Mestre, which became a huge urban sprawl of housing developments, where two hundred and fifty thousand people now live. Every year the population of Venice itself has decreased, however, so that today only about eighty thousand citizens still make their homes here. "The fact is that the industrial zone of Venice no longer has anything Venetian about it," Indro Montanelli, the author of a series of articles on the problem, commented in the *Corriere della Sera* in the late sixties. "Not labor, because this is provided not by Venice, but by the land that the peasants have, here as well, abandoned en masse to transform themselves into workers. Not capital, because the firms which have established themselves here have their home bases in Milan and Turin, from where most of their executives and technicians come. . . . What should have been the lung of Venice has become an outpost of the Lombard–Piedmontese economy that squeezes and crushes Venice."

The industries on the mainland require adequate space, and the filled-in land they occupy has greatly reduced the drainage area of the lagoon, causing the tides to back up. Their need for fresh water, which they at first pumped exclusively from underground artesian wells, lowered ground levels. They caused the access channels from the open sea to be dredged in some places to twice their normal depth and excavated an entirely new one to accommodate the larger oil tankers that needed to reach the refineries, measures that tended to increase both the weight and the volume of the currents flowing daily in and out through the approaches to the city. They discharged chemicals and untreated waste directly into the lagoon, which altered its delicate ecological balance and ravaged the local fishing industry. (The clouds of gnats that now fill the sky during the summer months are a direct result of the reduced number of fish, which feed on the larvae.) They belched pollutants into the air that have caused marbles, bronzes, even the tough white Istrian stone of which much of the city is built to decay and rot. And as the years have passed, despite repeated acknowledgments from some of the perpetrators and from many persons in positions of authority that there *is* a problem and that something eventually will have to be done; despite the implementation of a few corrective measures (the artesian wells have been shut down and several water purification plants are under construction on the mainland); despite the passage of a special law in 1973 to save Venice and a proposed outlay of over a billion dollars, about a quarter of it already appropriated by the Italian Parliament, to achieve this laudable aim— nothing has been finally decided, no comprehensive program has been put into action, and no basic agreement has even been reached as to how to proceed.

The plan currently in vogue, and the one favored by industry, is to construct huge water gates at the three main entrances to the lagoon, which could be shut against the high tides. This is opposed by most ecologists, as well as many other experts, who claim it won't work, but will simply shift the full weight of the sea elsewhere, perhaps over the Lido itself, while preventing the tides from carrying out their necessary cleansing and renewing functions inside the lagoon. What does seem clear to everyone, however, even the most sanguine optimists, is that the thousand-year-old successful relationship between man and his environment in the Venetian lagoon has been effectively destroyed. According to a local expert named Marino Potenza, in a recent booklet entitled *Il Mare Era Più Lontano* (The Sea Was Farther Away), the lagoon now revenges itself by swallowing up the city at will, just as easily as the torrents of words devoted to the subject drown out the calls for immediate action. "They hold meetings, studies, seminars, and a tide of paper ends up overwhelming the question," Signor Potenza observes. "A lagoon of chatter, someone called it. But the focal point of the problem is still far off and perhaps it isn't even being approached from the right direction."

The main reason it has been so difficult in Venice to agree on a way to save the city is that the Serenissima is no longer mistress of her own fate. Administratively, Venice includes both Porto Marghera and Mestre, the ugly stepchildren, with their acres of docks, smoke-belching factories, refineries, chemical plants, and hideous apartment complexes. The interests of the mainland residents are necessarily linked to their jobs, and their main concern in recent years has been the financial ups and downs of the Italian economy. Despite some recent signs of improvement, the local plants and the port are still operating at far less than capacity and workers are periodically laid off. In such a climate of potential despair, it is largely useless to talk as if the only major concern of the area's inhabitants should be the elimination of the *acque alte,* the restoration of the lagoon and the preservation of Venice as an open-air museum for foreign tourists. Whatever the solutions decided upon to save Venice, the interests of the industrial workers and their families will have to be taken into account, a consideration that is always uppermost in the mind of every local politician, in or out of office. When an attempt was made, in 1979, to separate the Serenissima as a political entity from Marghera and Mestre by holding a referendum, the move was opposed by all of the political parties and was handily defeated.

Tourism, however, is the city's leading industry and would seem to offer the best hope for the future. The sheer number of visitors is astonishing. During the summer months, they pour into the *centro storico* at the rate of between twenty and thirty thousand a day. They pack the ferries and the bridges, swarm over the Rialto and down the Merceria, move in a sludgelike mass through the narrow *calli,* bunch up in line for gondolas and speedboats, elbow each other in the stores and at the trinket counters, squat exhausted in whatever shade they can find in Piazza San Marco and along the banks of the canals. Most of them come for no more than a day or two, many without hotel reservations and carrying all of their belongings on their backs. They spend close to a billion and half dollars a year and without them Venice would have been reduced by now to a ghost city inhabited by the very old and the canal rats.

Nevertheless, this so-called mass tourism causes difficulties of its own. The campers don't spend enough money, according to the municipal authorities, to pay for the damage they cause, in contributing to the pollution of the waters, the garbage in the streets, the wear and tear on public transport, pavements, and monuments. Several years ago, the problem became so acute that the mayor proposed closing the city to anyone without a room reservation and selling a limited number of daily admission tickets to everyone else. The measure was fiercely opposed by most of his colleagues in the governing coalition, as well as by the tourist bureau, but it was applauded by many Venetians. "Everyone understood my proposal very well," the mayor declared. "Certainly it's an idea and we have to discuss it together." He suggested closing the causeway linking Venice to the mainland to all auto traffic, converting the railway into a mass transit system, with new terminals north and south of the present single facility, and building youth hostels and other campgrounds to absorb the great mass of visitors. He also suggested converting the Arsenal, now a mostly unused military base that occupies one-sixth of the land area of the *centro storico,* into a center for campers and visitors seeking cheap lodgings. "But above all," he continued, "I want to make Venice understood to the tourists. It's not possible they should arrive as barbarians and not even go and see one museum."

This emphasis on what the mayor and his supporters called "quality tourism" led to charges that the administration would like to build a dike of money around Venice and convert the Serenissima into a sort of rich man's Disneyland, admission limited to an elite with enough credit cards to foot the bills. The battle lines on this issue, as on so many others, have been drawn for decades and everyone seems to have his own views on the subject. "We've studied these problems for a hundred years," the owner of a bookstore in San Marco told me one day, "and we do nothing." When I quoted him to another Venetian acquaintance of mine, however, the latter disagreed. "It is not that we do nothing," he said. "If we wish to go forward, however, we have to study our past, because we have had all of these problems before. If we become exasperated, it is because outsiders cannot understand, they are not Venetians. And that is irritating to us."

There is even comfort to be derived, I discovered, from the political gridlock that has immobilized every rescue effort. "Ecology con-

ciousness has been much raised in the past few years," Paolo Rosa
Salva informed me one morning, in the local office of Italia Nostra.
"Now there are several magazines specializing in the ecology and they
are widely read. So the fact that nothing has been done is good, in a
way, because at least nothing terrible has been done."

It does seem to outsiders to take the Venetians a very long time to
make decisions and to agree to act on anything. The treasures of the
Ca' d'Oro, an outstanding example of fifteenth-century Venetian architecture containing a priceless collection of paintings by Mantegna,
Guardi, the Bellinis, Titian, and other great masters, were barred to
public view for fifteen years because of haggling over bureaucratic
procedures and scrambling about for the necessary funds to complete
the work. Another recently opened exhibit inside the Palazzo Ducale,
for example, also took several years to prepare, even though it pro-
vides such a fascinating glimpse into the secret backstage life of the republic that it is possible to wonder what could have taken the
authorities so long to get around to mounting it.

Now open to inspection is the hidden warren of small rooms and
prison cells, linked by narrow corridors, steep staircases and secret entrances, where the real day-to-day business of the Serenissima was
transacted. The formal affairs of state were conducted in the open—in
the ducal quarters, the luxurious reception rooms, and the Great
Council Chamber familiar to millions of casual visitors—but the dazzling facade hid a humbler and darker reality. Here are the private offices of the secretaries, lawyers, prosecutors, registrars, notaries, and
other civil servants; the archives, the kitchens, the storerooms, the
arms; the frighteningly intimate chambers where the Council of Ten
and the three robed judges of the Holy Inquisition debated the fates of
their charges; the torture room, where the wretched suspects were
painfully interrogated; the tiny rooftop cells called the Leads, freezing
in winter and stifling in summer, where the more eminent prisoners,
including Giacomo Casanova, were housed. And throughout, scattered casually over the walls and ceilings of the main halls, can be seen
frescoes by Veronese and others, as well as a pair of tremendous trip-
tychs, painted between 1500 and 1505 by Hieronymous Bosch. The
tour, by reservation only and limited to groups of no more than twenty-
five at a time, has been brilliantly conceived and painstakingly docu-

mented; it is an absolutely essential experience to anyone more than casually interested in the terrifying humdrum realities of history.

Not long ago, the Italian publishing house of Longanesi re-printed, forty years after its first appearance, a book entitled *Agenti Segreti a Venezia, 1705–1797* (Secret Agents in Venice), edited by Giovanni Comisso, a scholar who had come across the material while visiting the State Archives of Venice, during the winter of 1940. What he found were the detailed reports and comments submitted by local spies and paid informers of the republic during the last century of its existence. They provided a complete picture, Comisso noted, of "Venetian life in the seventeen-hundreds, with so many tiny and gossipy particulars as to supply what amounted to a photographic documentation, even in color, of life during that period."

The book, with its depiction of a decadent police state and its host of lickspittles, soon ran into trouble with the Fascist censors, but it has been reissued several times and has now become a minor classic of its kind. This is because the people recruited by the state inquisitors to keep tabs on their fellow citizens were not professionals, but simply local hangers-on, most of whom had nothing better to do with their time than gossip colorfully and viciously about their neighbors. One of them, for a time, was Giacomo Casanova, who, at the end of his life— old, tired, and starving—humbly offered his paid services. His reports are characterized by an excess of unctuous moralizing on the scandalous behavior of his compatriots, but apparently the Venetian magistrates read them with a distrustful eye. Casanova was himself simultaneously spied upon and the pages devoted to his activities reveal him as an impenitent heretic, still devoted to seduction and the gaming tables.

The Serenissima recruited her informers from every stratum of society in every quarter of the city and nothing escaped their vigilant senses. No detail, no incident, no compromising phrase went unnoted. Every major and minor transgression is reported, with illuminating comments on appearance, behavior, expressions, tones of voice, gestures, postures, circumstances, all the details to make up a series of the sort of delicious genre pictures painted by Pietro Longhi. As the years passed and the republic sank further and further into inertia, decadence, and squalor, with the Jacobin winds already blowing coldly through the *calli* and Napoleon looming larger in the background of the city's long, last *carnevale,* the inquisitive, brilliant, witty, malicious, fascinating Venetians kept right on sticking their noses into each other's business and talking, talking, talking. Luckily for the rest of us, they have never stopped.

NEAPOLITAN
CONNECTIONS

CHAPTER
EIGHT

THE OLD CAT

NAPLES TODAY IS an assault on the senses. From the heights of Posillipo, the residential northern arm of the bay, or the still relatively verdant slopes of Vesuvius to the south, the city looks much the same as it always has—a great chaotic jumble of ancient *palazzi*, tenements, villas with small private gardens, churches, famous monuments such as the Palazzo Reale and the Castel Nuovo, shipyards, docks, marinas, piazzas, the long tree-shaded waterfront stretch of the Villa Comunale, the row of luxury hotels nestling next to each other along the esplanade of Santa Lucia, each familiar sight a jigsaw piece in the huge sprawl of the city around its magnificent natural harbor. From such a distance, on a typically sunny day, nothing seems to have changed. Like an elegant old invalid, somewhat overdressed for the occasion in the glorious rags and tatters of a colorful past, Naples seems to bask in its history, content, as always, simply to survive. As seen through the haze that shimmers off the deep blue water of the gulf, the city seems as reassuringly eternal as the familiar local songs that for centuries have celebrated its immortality.

When I first beheld this sight again, after an absence of nearly seven years, my first reaction was one of elation, because I spent part of my childhood here and I have family roots in this area that go back many generations. Every time I have returned to Naples in the past, almost always after an absence of several years, my first glimpse of the city, usually from above or from the water, has never failed to move me, and this time was no exception. What was different from other occasions was the feeling I had, as soon as I began my descent by car into the heart of the *centro storico,* that something drastic had happened, that just below the surface of life here some profound change had taken place from which the elegant old invalid might not recover.

At first I thought my uneasiness might be due to the sheer noise and the polluted air, both largely caused by the incredible traffic that swoops along the avenues, clogs the side streets, washes over the main piazzas, obliterates sidewalks, makes a mockery of traffic signals and pedestrian rights of way. The Neapolitans ignore all attempts to channel the flow of their automobiles; they drive through stop signs, over barriers, in bus and trolley lanes, the wrong way on one-way streets, and through the narrowest alleys, always in a frenzy of honking horns and revved-up engines, with swarms of motorcycles and scooters weaving precariously through the bumper-to-bumper mass with the fearless bravado of Hollywood stuntmen. The right-hand pass, the sudden turn from the wrong lane, the last-second lunge through a red light, the conquest of an illegal parking space—all are considered routine aspects of driving here. An hour in the streets of Naples is a nerve-shattering experience, comparable, perhaps, to a day spent in the New York subway system. "The situation is agonizing," the mayor of Naples, Maurizio Valenzi, declared in a newspaper interview a few days after I arrived. He went on to point out that the city's overworked traffic cops had pretty much simply given up, especially after the earthquake of the previous fall, when some two hundred streets had to be closed permanently due to the danger of cave-ins and collapsing buildings. "The Neapolitans, in flight during the earthquake, are still fleeing today," the mayor continued. "And the chaos can only spread."

By the time I read these words I had begun to understand the extent of what had been happening there since that terrible Sunday evening of November 23, 1980, when, at exactly 7:35 P.M., the earth of Campania and Basilicata, two of Italy's poorest regions, began to shake. The first and most severe tremor, with its epicenter under Mount Marzano in the interior of Campania, about fifty miles southeast of Naples, lasted seventy seconds and affected an area about two hundred kilometers long by about sixty kilometers wide. It was succeeded by a series of aftershocks that devastated over a hundred communities in an area inhabited by about 1.5 million people. As reported at the time, worst hit were the hilltop villages nearest the epicenter—Laviano, Calabritto, Caposele, Conza, Teora, Sant'Angelo dei Lombardi—towns that quite literally ceased to exist. But the destruction was almost equally awesome elsewhere in the area, with over half the buildings in most of these communities reduced to rubble or rendered uninhabitable. Although no exact count of the dead has ever been made, it has been estimated that about five thousand people died, five times as many as perished in the earthquake in Friuli and the Veneto in 1976.

As such disasters go in Italy, this seismic event was by no means the most catastrophic in the history of the volcanic peninsula (an estimated hundred and twenty thousand people, for example, perished in Sicily and Calabria during the Messina quake of 1908), but it was bad enough and could not have come at a worse time for this part of the country. The area consists mainly of small farms and vineyards scattered among the barren slopes of rocky mountains dotted with tiny villages linked to each other mostly by narrow, twisting dirt roads. It has for centuries been a land ignored and neglected by the central governments in Naples and Rome, and from which the younger men now emigrate in search of work, either in the industrialized northern cities or the richer countries of Western Europe. Thus, the earthquake served to exacerbate and to focus attention once again on the dual problem that for many decades has afflicted the Mezzogiorno, as the southern part of the country is called: what to do about such underpopulated, depressed areas, where even in the best of times the living is precarious, and the overpopulated coastal cities like Naples, which lack any means to provide permanent employment for their slum dwellers, at least a quarter of whom are always without work.

The incalculable damage done by the earthquake, so immediately and dramatically evident in the interior, took much longer to manifest itself in Naples, where the tremors were less severe in intensity, very few buildings actually collapsed and only a few people died. Nevertheless, what is known locally as a "cold quake," the term for a seismic episode without a plethora of corpses and only a few cave-ins, soon threatened to bring about a complete dissolution of a social structure that had for many years survived by its wits and all sorts of peculiar expediencies on the edge of an abyss. Before this last cold quake, for instance, about a quarter of the city's buildings had already been estimated as unsafe for human habitation, though people went right on living in them. Nothing had been done in the past half-century to repair or rebuild those crumbling *palazzi* and decrepit, dank tenements where most of the city's poor live. The postwar frenzy of building that, mostly in the twenty years between 1950 and 1970, threw up hundreds of ugly structures, many of them in violation of the zoning and building codes, did nothing to alleviate this situation. It buried the outskirts of Naples in concrete blocks and enriched the builders and their cronies, the politicians in power, but left the heart of the old city intact in its perilous squalor.

Already badly damaged and weakened by the aerial bombardments of 1943, during the Allied campaign up the Italian boot in the Second World War, and several previous cold quakes, most notably one in 1962, the old houses of Naples were badly mauled, occasionally cracked open by the tremors. Within a week of the original shock, an estimated fifty thousand people had been rendered homeless, an event that threw into startling relief the age-old crisis of this city and activated the forces of despair that now threaten its very existence. "The earthquake was like a dog that catches an old cat in its mouth," is the way a bookstore owner on the Via Roma, the main commercial avenue, explained it to me. "It took us in its teeth and shook us gently a few times and dropped us on the ground. And now we can't get up again."

The visual evidence of the earthquake's effect was readily apparent to anyone who wanted to see it. Off the Via Roma, many of the buildings crowded along the cobweb of narrow streets and alleys, the celebrated *vicoli* of the old Spanish Quarters, were propped up by wooden pillars and huge scaffoldings of iron girders that shut off light and air but served at least to keep the shakier structures from collapsing altogether, while across most of the streets three-foot-high concrete walls allowing only for the passage of pedestrians had been thrown up to bar motorized traffic, with its dangerous vibrations. Printed signs warning of possible cave-ins and falling debris marked the entrance to many areas, not only here but elsewhere in the *centro*.

One of the great pleasures of a visit to Naples used to be a stroll down Spaccanapoli, or "Split Naples," the local generic term for the succession of narrow avenues that divides the *centro storico* roughly in half and is flanked by the decaying monuments and great baroque palazzi of the Spanish aristocracy that flourished here during the era of the Bourbon monarchy. Although this part of Naples also includes a dense network of refuse-strewn side streets and often fetid *vicoletti*, the sort of neighborhoods where about a quarter of the city's roughly 1.5 million people live, often in the abject squalor one associates only with Asian slums, the scene, even to the most disapprovingly Anglo-Saxon eye, has never been without its purely picturesque qualities. And along Spaccanapoli itself, especially between Piazza del Gesù and Via del Duomo, the view has always been grand and moving, rooted in the splendors of history.

Spaccanapoli, like the Spanish Quarters, had become a ruin. In addition to the metal gridirons across many of the side streets, about half of the great palazzi themselves had to be propped up and were disfigured by scaffolding and supporting beams. On the Via del Duomo itself, the cathedral had been closed to visitors while it underwent repairs, and even San Gennaro, the city's patron saint, whose dried blood, kept in a couple of ornate vials in a side chapel, still liquifies on schedule three times a year, had to perform his miracles elsewhere, most recently in the basilica of Santa Chiara. "It would take more than San Gennaro and his miracles to help here," a Venetian novelist named Piero Sanavio, who taught literature at the University of Naples, informed me, as we strolled through the quarter one afternoon. "Not only are the houses uninhabitable, but the way of life here, based on the little enterprise, the craftsmanship of the few, the so-called black work that illegally employed thousands of people in turning out the small artifacts that kept them alive—porcelains, handbags, toys, paper goods—all this has changed. What is left is despair. And violence, always now there is violence." "The earthquake also destroyed basic sectors of commercial life," Mayor Valenzi told his interviewer, "and the people, compelled by need, go against the law."

IN THE days immediately following the earthquake, the government in Rome dispatched a Christian Democratic politician named Giuseppe Zamberletti to Naples to act as "special commissioner" in charge of rescue efforts in the stricken areas. Zamberletti, a serious-minded and honest administrator with a reputation for being able to get things done, immediately proposed a mass evacuation of the homeless, most of whom were then living in tents, trailers, cars, or, in many cases, simply out in the open. He intended to put them up temporarily in requisitioned summer homes along the coast, hotels, pensions, and public buildings, such as schools and hospitals. Later, they would be moved into prefabricated houses provided by the government or private builders subsidized by it.

At first glance, the idea seemed sound enough, since he understood that the most urgent problem was to shelter people, especially the very old and the very young, after which a long-range rebuilding program could be undertaken. It was the same technique and solution he had promoted, with considerable success, in Friuli. What he failed to grasp, according to a number of local critics of his scheme, was that what had worked in the north might not work at all in the Mezzogiorno, where the social and economic circumstances of life were vastly different and conditioned by a long history of exploitation and oppression.

Although some of the children and a few of the older people were evacuated, most of the villagers in the interior refused to move. They preferred to remain near their homes and on their land, where they could continue to look after what was left of their property and, if they were farmers, their animals, which in many cases constituted the only capital they had. "The basic feeling of these people was that, unless they stayed, nothing would be done to help them," a volunteer rescue worker in Avellino commented later. "They also believed that, if they left, everything would be stolen from them, which in some cases did actually happen."

Signor Zamberletti's attitude, in the face of this opposition to his plan, remained unbending. "I am convinced," he declared several weeks after his arrival on the scene, "that in a few days, exactly as happened in Friuli, reason will prevail over sentiment and the people will move." When asked what he would do if they wouldn't go, he indicated that he had "another card to play" but would not reveal what it was. Two journalists from newspapers in Milan and Rome, Giovanni Russo and Corrado Stajano, who later collaborated on a book called *Terremoto,* about the earthquake and its aftereffects, suspected that the commissioner's secret card was the weather. The cold and snow of a mountain winter would succeed in forcing the inhabitants to leave. When that also failed to happen, however, and the peasants chose to remain, even in tents and unheated trailers, the writers reported that many northern Italians, angered by what they took to be the ingratitude and barbarous stupidity of the southerners, whom they had always regarded with contempt, became indifferent to their fate. Widely reported incidences of looting and theft that occurred during this time also disgusted the northerners and, still according to Russo and Stajano, "fed the racist feelings that revealed how, more than a hundred years after the unification of Italy, many Italians are unable to understand the historical and social roots of these criminal manifestations in the society of the south and use them to reinforce a surviving prejudice concerning the inferiority of the southerners."

In Naples itself, during those first few days after the earthquake, an overworked squad of 800 inspectors fanned out through the city to survey the damage, especially in the older quarters, after which the municipal government began to issue eviction notices. Almost twenty thousand people were put up in ninety-eight schools, another ten or twelve thousand in requisitioned hotels and pensions, a few thousand in private homes, the rest in two old passenger ships moored in the harbor, seventy railroad cars, about a hundred and twenty buses, and even in empty storage areas along the shoreline. An effort was made to requisition vacation summer and weekend homes along the coast north of the city, but here the attempt was met by the organized resistance of the owners, most of them Neapolitan middle-class families appalled at the prospect of having their hard-earned vacation spots invaded by the so-called *plebe* of the slums. They set up barricades in the streets and, in many cases, moved in themselves to prevent anyone else from occupying their refuges. (Ironically, the fiercest resistance was organized at Coppolla Pinetamare, a beachfront resort of hideous cement-block apartment houses and tawdry little villas.)

Eventually, some summer places were successfully requisitioned, but only after a cumbersome, basically unworkable bureaucratic procedure was instituted by the authorities in an effort to distinguish between "the real earthquake victims" and those people evacuated simply because their homes happened to be unlivable anyway. The distinction, insisted upon by Signor Zamberletti and his staff of outsiders, made little sense to the Neapolitan officials, who pointed out in vain that the recent disaster was not an isolated episode but merely another in a long string of calamities, always made worse by outside mismanagement. As for the local landlords, who were described as selfish and heartless in some media accounts of the episode, they, too, had their grievances. "Why hit at us?" one of them declared at the time to a local reporter. "We are working people. We acquired our homes with our savings, to enjoy the sea and nature in one of the most beautiful spots in the world. And now they want to take this away from us, too?"

In any case, all of these measures were intended to be temporary, the first phase of a broader, long-range solution to the whole problem of housing in Naples. The second phase, to be completed within a period of eight to ten months, was to put up enough prefabricated buildings in designated open spaces, if possible within the city limits, where some thirty thousand people could be accommodated for up to three or four years, until more permanent public housing could be constructed and the damaged sections of the *centro storico* rebuilt.

By that mid-July, almost eight months after the earthquake, very little had actually been done. An emergency reconstruction law to aid the victims had finally been approved by the legislators in Rome, but in Naples itself debate was still raging over how the money was eventually to be spent and who was to be entrusted with this huge rebuilding and construction program, with its enormous potential for windfall profits and outright theft. Traditionally, nothing works in Naples except through an elaborate system of patronage known as *clientelismo*, with its ties to political power, and often involving subtle alliances between private industry and organized criminal bands. This aspect of the problem, as well as the apparent confusion and foot-dragging by the local authorities, had evidently alarmed Rome, where the situation was interpreted by many, especially from the north, as a typical example of southern inertia, passivity, and dishonesty. "What does the government intend to spend on Naples?" Mayor Valenzi commented, in answer to his critics. "Do we have to rebuild under earthquake-proof criteria or not? Can we expropriate the areas for the prefabricated housing or must we allow people to go on suffering in trailers? All of this has to be established by the reconstruction law, but the law delays."

When the law was finally passed and put into operation a couple of months later, the method adopted was hardly reassuring. Backed by government funding and guaranteed bank loans, and under the direct supervision of Mayor Valenzi himself, the first phase of the reconstruction process was entrusted to about a dozen private contractors, who proposed to put up thirteen thousand units (a total of about sixty thousand rooms) on empty land to be expropriated by the city. Although a few people questioned the probity of Mayor Valenzi himself, a middle-aged Communist intellectual who then headed a left-wing coalition that had been in power for more than six years without having been implicated in any major local scandal, some observers were quick to point out that this huge rebuilding program was being turned over to the sort of profit-making enterprises that for years have been submerging Naples, in the words of one critic, "in a river of cement." As Corrado Stajano had pointed out in Rome's daily *Il Messaggero* some weeks earlier, "It's clear that democratic control of local business, labor and cultural organizations is essential to avoid new hands, disguised as merciful and healing ones, again strangling a city in its death throes."

Whether Mayor Valenzi would be able to ensure a modicum of efficiency and honesty, however, was considered secondary to the increasing need of the city's so-called *terremotati* (literally, "earthquaked") to move into habitable lodgings. Many were still housed in the most primitive conditions in the temporary quarters that were originally intended to accommodate them for at most a few weeks. Even those lucky enough to have been put up in hotels and rooming houses had become impatient with the long delays of the past months. Many, in fact, had refused to wait any longer and had simply returned home. Along Spaccanapoli, where about half the buildings had been declared unsafe, people had been drifting back, making do as best they could in houses, some of them without light, heat, or water, where there was constant danger of a cave-in. "I couldn't stand it anymore," one woman told me, as she draped her drying laundry over the iron supports that propped up the wall outside her apartment windows. "I can't live in a school any longer."

On the corner of the Vico Tre Regine, in one of the most badly damaged areas of the Spanish Quarters, I came across an elderly retired couple watering the flowers growing in boxes outside their second-story window sills. They had been evacuated to a hotel in another part of town, several kilometers away, but came back home every day to water their plants and feed their pets, a cat and two caged finches, which they had not been allowed to take with them. They were alone in their darkened building, which was propped up inside and out by wooden beams and had long, ugly-looking cracks in the walls and ceiling; access to their front door was up a short flight of lopsided steps sandwiched between wooden pillars. "What are we to do?" commented the old man, whose name was Giuseppe Coraggio (the Italian word for "courage"). "We couldn't let them die. And besides, this is where I have lived for forty-two years."

In such circumstances, it was easy to understand the feeling of frustration and exasperation which eventually impelled protesters into the streets to dramatize their plight. Periodically, the *terremotati* dragged what was left of their belongings outside to improvise barricades, primarily so as to remind their fellow citizens, as well as the authorities, that for many of them the situation was desperate. One day, about fifty families still occupying a school, improvised a barricade of tables and chairs that shut off Via Salvator Rosa, a major avenue, for most of the morning and created a huge, honking traffic jam in the center of town. Another group of families, several hundred people in all, protested in Via Domenico Morelli outside their temporary quarters, a requisitioned empty building where they had been for months without running water, light, or sanitary facilities. In Via Ferrante Imparato, about fifty women and children living in a condemned building improvised a roadblock of chairs and bedding to bring attention to their plight and especially the danger to which they were exposed. To a reporter covering one of the demonstrations, a woman with three children pointed out that she and her family were forced to share three bathrooms with sixty other people and that for over two months they had been unable to get a doctor, or anyone, in fact, to check on the sanitary conditions they were being compelled to live under, which had resulted in most of the children and many of the adults coming down with ailments of one sort or another.

Even the most cursory of tours through the areas housing the *terremotati* could explain the need these people felt to protest, in whatever way they could, against what had happened to them. "You try to live for seven months like this," one man told a reporter, "you won't even feel like a human being anymore." A woman named Maria Cozzolino, who had been living for nearly a year with her husband and three children in a small cabin on board the Città di Nuoro, one of the old ships anchored in the harbor, declared, "For months now we've been told over and over that it's only a question of a little time and, instead, we're rotting here, uselessly deluding ourselves." One of the ancient afflictions of life in Naples has always been the inability of its people to believe in the possibility of a solution to their problems from any official source, whether in city hall or in Rome itself. This cynicism and lack of faith in the political establishment has rarely been contradicted by events.

ONE NIGHT, while I was in the city, a forty-three-year-old man named Giuseppe Palladino was gunned down in the streets of San Giovanni a Teduccio, a suburban slum area where five other people had previously been murdered that year. Surprised out in the open not far from his home, Palladino was killed by five pistol shots fired by a man who then drove unhurriedly away from the scene in a car containing, according to witnesses, several accomplices. No one expected the police to be able to solve the killing, mainly because Palladino himself was a convicted criminal with a long record as a mob enforcer. His death was considered merely another episode in the bloody war that had been raging for months between organized armed bands contending for territory and power. In one memorable twenty-four-hour spree, for instance, there were six other similar killings. By midsummer of that year, the death toll had risen to 115, an average of about twenty homicides a month, a statistic that made Naples by far the most violent place in the country. "An impressive record," commented a story in Milan's *Corriere della Sera,* "that raises the Campanian city to the heights of Chicago during Prohibition times."

According to historians of the genre, this latest outbreak marked the evolution of the so-called fourth Camorra, which consisted of a group of Neapolitan criminal organizations at war with each other, as well as gangs of Calabrians and Sicilians, for control of the traditional rackets, such as prostitution, contraband, and drugs. Also being contended for were the lucrative possibilities opened up by the flow of money and goods into the Mezzogiorno after the earthquake. The original Camorra, much like the Mafia in Sicily, was created in the early

113

nineteenth century as a kind of protective subgovernment, not without its romantic aspects, to redress local wrongs and keep order in a society under the heel of a foreign oppressor, in this case the Bourbon dynasty. After the unification, however, it soon degenerated into a loose alliance of purely criminal organizations that controlled much of the commerce in the city, often working hand in hand with corrupt organs of the state, while helping to keep order in the streets. The second phase began with the Allied liberation and flowered during the postwar boom years, during which the Camorra took an active part in the uncontrolled real-estate speculation that led to the "cementification" of the city. This was made possible, in fact inevitable, by a succession of dishonest municipal governments that, always for a price, issued permits that consistently ignored the zoning laws and building codes. During this era, the Camorra acquired at least a surface respectability by involving itself largely in quasilegal business ventures, often operated out of luxuriously furnished office suites and from behind benevolent-looking front organizations headed by well-known businessmen and respected public figures.

By the late 1950s, much of the purely criminal activity in the area was being run by outsiders from southern France, Corsica, Calabria, and Sicily. The Camorra, in its third phase, sided first with one group, then another, often splintering itself into contending factions, especially for control of the harbor area. This was the time of a greatly increased drug traffic, as well as the creation of entire industries based on a tremendous flow into Naples of all sorts of contraband goods, from cigarettes and liquor to transistor radios and guns. By the early eighties, the city had been divided roughly into five main zones of influence, each one under control of a separate criminal band, each with its own boss or "don," and kept at peace by a delicate network of tenuous but effective agreements founded on a mutual desire to avoid the sort of excessive violence that is liable to cause too much unwelcome public attention.

The fourth Camorra was reportedly largely the doing of an enterprising boss known as Don Raffaele Cutolo, a youthful-looking but old-style organizer who had publicly and patriotically proclaimed the rebirth of the Camorra as the upholder of traditional clan virtues and ideals, presumably in opposition to the savage, free-wheeling tactics of his competitors. Don Raffaele, with his unsmiling, long-nosed face, sometimes half-hidden by large horn-rimmed glasses, looked in some photographs like a provincial pedagogue, but he had an apparently well-merited reputation as a ruthless gang leader. Like most of his rivals, he had often been arrested and occasionally even brought to trial, but had never been found guilty of a major crime and had spent very little time in jail, though he was then languishing, while awaiting trial on a number of serious charges, in a state prison in Novara. From there he had reportedly continued to direct the operations of his followers, while also venting his opinions concerning the war he himself seemed to have been active in waging. When a magistrate named Mario Morgigni in Don Raffaele's hometown of Ottaviano, a few miles south of Naples itself, was attacked in the street by hired killers and fought them off in a gun battle that made him an instant hero, the boss expressed disapproval. "Shooting at a judge," Don Raffaele declared from his cell, "is always, and under any circumstances, a damaging provocation."

Gang wars were by no means the only source of violence in the streets of Naples. Terrorist bands, especially units of the Red Brigades, had seized on the chaos and misery in the area to step up their own activities. Having been largely scattered and immobilized in the richer industrialized cities of the north, where about a thousand of them had been arrested in the late seventies and condemned to lengthy prison terms, the *brigatisti* and others had begun concentrating their efforts in the south, and especially in Naples, with its huge population of homeless, destitute citizens, many of them young and very angry. That spring, terrorists had seized two city officials in separate raids, held them long enough to photograph them with identifying cardboard signs hung around their necks, then shot them both in the legs and left them in the street. Later, the *brigatisti* kidnapped a regional Christian Democratic councilman named Ciro Cirillo and spirited him off to a "people's prison," where they put him on trial. They also compelled him to write a series of humiliating letters pleading for his life and demanding, as the price of freedom, immediate housing for all the *terremotati*, an obviously impossible task. Cirillo was held for ninety days and then released, as a self-proclaimed gesture of magnanimity on the part of the terrorists, who were obviously able to operate freely in one of the most densely populated cities in the world.

Of much concern to average citizens, who don't see themselves as targets either of the Camorra or the Red Brigades, was the almost incredible daily outbreak of petty prime in the streets. In addition to the waves of small thefts and purse-snatchings that had become routine in most parts of the town, every quarter seemed to have its quota of small-time racketeers and extortionists. In some areas, especially the older neighborhoods, shopkeepers locked their doors and opened up only to trusted customers, while also paying a local ransom to keep from having their windows shattered. Each street corner seemed to have its illegal parking attendant, who had to be paid off to insure that one's car would not be damaged. The buzzing of mopeds behind one's back too often indicated the onrush of a team of so-called *scippatori,* youths who worked in pairs; one drives, the other snatches whatever he can—bags, earrings, necklaces, even watches—from unwary pedestrians. Other teams attacked cars halted in traffic, by reaching in through open windows or unlocked doors to grab anything in sight. Everywhere my wife and I went we were warned by strangers to be careful and it did not surprise me, after several days, to realize that we had met no other foreigners on foot, except for groups of American sailors and marines from the Sixth Fleet, on nightly shore leave in search of excitement. During our stay, despite taking every precaution, we were swooped upon three times by would-be *scippatori* and one night somebody broke into our rented Fiat, tagged with Rome plates and parked outside the front door of our hotel, to steal our spare tire. "I'm a Neapolitan," said a young policeman, whom I told about our experiences, "and I'll never leave Naples, but I'm ashamed to walk around my own city. It's not only money that's needed, it's a change of mentality."

THE YOUNG officer's assessment of the situation is one that is still widely espoused by many Neapolitans, who readily admit that daily life in their beloved city is becoming almost unbearable for nearly everyone and that too many people have abandoned hope in any possibility of a better future. A Neapolitan historian named Antonio Ghirelli has pointed out that the major difficulty here, apart from purely economic ones, has always been a conviction on the part of its inhabitants that Naples has never really been anything more than an occupied city. The plebiscite of October 21, 1860, which proclaimed a kingdom of Italy under the constitutional reign of Victor Emanuel of Savoy, he points out in the early pages of the second book of his two-volume history of the area, did not open up a happy new period for the Mezzogiorno as a whole or for Naples itself. The Spanish occupation that began in the sixteenth century was merely succeeded by a new one, that of the Piedmontese, who began by looting the Bourbon treasury, thus impoverishing the city permanently, and proceeded to administer it pretty much like a foreign colony. The pattern, obviously, was established early and persists. Traditionally, all the decisions that have deeply affected the quality of life in Naples have been made elsewhere or by outsiders working hand in hand with entrenched moneyed interests, in some cases ones inherited from Bourbon times. What the Neapolitans have done to stay alive under what has always seemed to them to be essentially a colonial system is to pretend to collaborate with it, while simultaneously corrupting, undermining, and exploiting it. When asked what he thought of his fellow citizens, Mayor Valenzi declared, "They are extreme individualists. They have no sense of the collective goal, the organized community. One's personal needs take precedence over all exigencies and over everyone else. In them we find a great fatalism, a deep skepticism; they believe in nothing. They express an anger that is more or less typical of all great metropolitan cities. It must be said that historically they have always been subjected to outside authority and that they have often been betrayed."

In the past, what has usually enabled most Neapolitans to survive, and occasionally even prosper, has been their genius for improvisation, for finding the best way around the cumbersome roadblocks thrown up by history. Even in the most terrible adversities, the people of Naples have made do, usually with charm and a sense of humor that I think of as characteristic of them. To me, Naples has always been a city full of laughter and song, no less genuine for the often calculated way these qualities manifest themselves, whether in the delightful comedies of the great playwright Eduardo De Filippo, the sentimental lyrics of its familiar songs, or merely in the humble transactions that punctuate daily life. It is still possible, for instance, to strike up a conversation anywhere in Naples that will often turn out to be illuminating, amusing and, above all, civilized. The Neapolitans have a native gift for good talk, which probably accounts for the high percentage of local citizens who have become jurists, philosophers, writers, teachers, and other skilled practitioners of the word. "Whatever else you may say about Naples, and I, for one, can't stand the place," a Roman friend of mine once told me, "I can't deny that the Neapolitans are very likable and very intelligent."

Domenico Rea, a well-known elderly novelist who has lived here most of his life, has also pointed out that Naples remains important not only as a great art center, like Florence or Siena, but also because of its spectacular natural setting. Among the traditional rewards of a visit to Naples, he once commented in the daily *Il Mattino,* was a chance to see Vesuvius or take a stroll along the promenade of Via Caracciolo, as well as "to look at the spontaneous theater" in the streets, "to assist at the comedy of the imagination." Today, he wrote, Naples has become "a bridge thrown over an inferno." He asked the reader to imagine a Spaccanapoli reclaiming its rightful place as the soul of the *centro storico* and the city as a whole once more a gay arena of cheerful sights set to the music of guitars and mandolins. "Naples would become a trap from which no one would wish to escape," he concluded. Perhaps that dream was never a reality, but the sentiment is one many Neapolitans share.

CHAPTER
NINE

THE TUNNEL
OF CHAOS

THE ORDER TO evacuate Pozzuoli, a town of about seventy thousand people on the coast of Italy, a few miles north of Naples, came in the late afternoon of October 10, 1983. By nightfall the narrow streets of the ancient city were jammed with the buses, vans, trucks, and cars assigned by the authorities to carry the inhabitants to safety. About a thousand carabinieri, police, and soldiers swarmed through the area to help and also to make sure that the order was being carried out. Not all of the citizens were being asked to leave, only those who lived in the oldest parts of town, the four *quartieri popolari* along the waterfront that had been designated during the emergency as Zone A. It had been estimated that about twenty thousand people would have to be moved right away, but eventually a total of about thirty thousand would need to be resettled somewhere. "Within the next forty-eight hours we have to provide an arrangement for all those who are living in a risky situation, even outside the most exactly defined seismic zone," Vincenzo Scotti, the minister of civil protection, had declared earlier in the day, after touring the scene. "Nevertheless, it's clear that we mustn't broaden the discussion, because in Pozzuoli itself there are realities that do not, for the moment, seem dangerous."

In Zone A, however, the reality seemed dangerous enough to have warranted equally drastic but perhaps less precipitous action earlier. Pozzuoli was being quietly shaken to pieces by what some of the residents call the earth dance, but which is better known locally as "the slow quake." Technically, the phenomenon is called bradyseism, a rising and falling of the earth caused by underground volcanic activity. Pozzuoli sits on a tufaceous promontory protruding into the Mediterranean and on the edge of the Campi Flegrei, the "fiery fields" of the ancient Greeks, who began to settle here around 530 B.C. The whole region teems with mineral springs, fountains of boiling mud, sulfur baths, mofettes, igneous rock, and other evidence of past volcanic eruption. The long-dead crater of the Solfatara, less grand than Vesuvius, its neighbor to the south, but equally ominous-looking, was identified by Virgil as the gateway to the underworld. Although it hasn't been virulently active since 1198 A.D., the legacy of its presence persists, most notably by the invisible action of the phenomenon afflicting Pozzuoli itself.

Directly under the city, about a mile and a half beneath the surface, is a huge lake of volcanic magma. When it heats up, it exerts an upward pressure that causes the ground to rise; when it cools, the surface sinks. "It's as if the city were perched on the chest of a sleeping giant," was the way it was explained to me by one of the scientists at the local brandyseism research center, established ten years earlier. "A single cough and it would be destroyed."

An actual eruption did not seem likely, and could be predicted by about two months, according to Professor Gennaro Narcisio, the geophysicist in charge of the center, but what had been happening was bad enough. In mid-July of 1982, the ground had begun to shake again and by January it had started to rise. As the tremors became more severe, due to the increasing pressure of the upward surge, they began to crack the walls, unsettle the roofs and tear staircases loose, especially in Zone A, where most of the buildings, made of stone and brick, were at least several centuries old. Although none had yet actually collapsed, a team of inspectors dispatched to the scene in midsummer by the Ministry of Civil Protection had found about fourteen hundred of the more than fifteen hundred damaged structures to be unsafe and ordered them evacuated. Since then about ten thousand people had been living nearby, mainly in public gardens and open areas along the waterfront, where they were housed in tents, trailers, and improvised shelters of one kind or another. Many had been returning to their homes, most of them propped up by beams and metal gridirons, to feed themselves and carry on at least a semblance of ordinary life during the day, but fled again at night. For the roughly two thousand people unable to cook their own meals and afraid even to visit their damaged houses, the authorities had set up field kitchens.

This was the basic situation in Pozzuoli when Signor Scotti suddenly ordered the complete evacuation of Zone A, more than three months after his inspectors had first toured the city. Some critics of the minister's tardiness in reaching this decision were unkind enough to point out that even a cursory reading of history ought to have spurred him to move earlier. The ground, after all, has been shaking ever since Pozzuoli was founded in 529 to 528 B.C. and all during the years of the city's glory, from 194 B.C. to about 50 A.D., when it was called Puteoli (the locals are still called Puteolani) and was an important Roman commercial center and naval base. After the port of Ostia was completed at the mouth of the Tiber in 54 A.D., the city's fortunes began a long, slow decline that has persisted steadily through the centuries, even though for many years it remained a spa for retired war veterans and wealthy nobles. The chronicles of all these years are peppered with accounts of volcanic eruptions and earthquakes that periodically caused the population to flee into the open and in which people occasionally died.

The violent manifestations calmed down and eventually came to an end, but for the past eight centuries the slow quake has been a fact of life in Pozzuoli. In the thirty years prior to the eruption of another neighborhood cone called Monte Nuovo in 1538, the surface of the area rose by nearly a hundred feet, before it started to sink again. The last serious episode occurred in 1969, when the ground pushed upward at the rate of two to four inches a month. Within a year, the city was cracking open and people were once more forced into the streets. By the middle of 1972, when the slow quake finally stopped as unpredictably as it had begun, some parts of town had risen nearly six feet, most spectacularly along a section of shoreline where a long-vanished Roman temple to the Egyptian god Serapis began to ascend out of the water that had submerged it centuries earlier, in a sinking phase of bradyseism, and left only the tops of three slender columns protruding above the surface of the harbor. As a result of this latest surge, and by the time Signor Scotti issued his dramatic proclamation, the temple had risen completely above water level, a delight to archaeologists and tourists, but of little comfort to the Puteolani themselves, for most of whom the slow quake has traditionally brought only discomfort and misery.

THE EMERGENCY measures taken in Pozzuoli made headlines all over Italy. In his explanations and clarifications to the press over the next couple of days, Minister Scotti also made it clear that he and his staff had everything very much under control and were moving full speed ahead. "That's enough now. We've already lost too much time," he declared. "The hour has come to take action." The evacuation had been carefully planned weeks in advance, he stated, and was being carried out with the utmost efficiency. Within six or seven months at most, an entire new "village" of five thousand prefabricated houses, "a model quarter" capable of accommodating twenty-five thousand people, would be ready on the slopes of Monte Ruscello, a lightly populated zone just north of Pozzuoli thought to be safe from any kind of seismic shock. He had already been promised by his colleagues in the cabinet that the necessary funds, about 400 billion lire (then roughly 250 million dollars), would quickly be made available, part of which would also go to remodeling the salvageable buildings in Zone A and making them quakeproof. His assurances bristled with impressive statistics not only on future plans but on what had already been accomplished: 2,920 structures inspected for damage; 843 families already resettled; 909 hotels, schools, and public buildings taken over; 1,215 tents set up; 1,555 trailers commandeered; perhaps a total of forty thousand people eventually to be moved, and so on. He also took an optimistic view of the future construction of Monte Ruscello, which would be entrusted to private contractors. "I have the greatest confidence in Italian enterprise," he said, "which will be able to execute this type of housing."

The most controversial aspect of the evacuation order, one which Signor Scotti occasionally alluded to but to which he seemed to assign less importance, had to do with where to put up all these thousands of newly homeless citizens during the time it would take to build at Monte Ruscello. Obviously, they couldn't remain in tents during the cold and rainy winter months. Under a national emergency powers act already in force, the minister pointed out, the government would be able to requisition empty flats, houses, and hotel rooms in the surrounding countryside, until such time as the refugees could be permanently installed in their new homes or be allowed to return to their original quarters. This whole part of Italy, especially along the coast, was a tourist and vacation zone, full of apartments and villas belonging to people, many of them from Rome and other large urban centers, who only used them during the summer. It was to be hoped that these owners would happily make available their so-called second homes, for which they would receive a one-year government lease and an annual rent based on the *equo canone* (the national fair-rent law) of 3 million lire, about eighteen hundred dollars. Landlords who refused to volunteer their summer places and compelled the government to requisition them would also receive a lease, but only for half the promised compensation. In addition, the Puteolani themselves could choose to make their own temporary living arrangements and, in that case, would become eligible for a monthly subsidy of 350,000 lire per family unit. But what if the owners of these empty second homes resisted the occupation order? "We will then proceed to requisition houses with the help of the army," Signor Scotti declared back in Rome, on the night of October 11.

The operation was entrusted to the minister's chief lieutenant, an administrator named Elveno Pastorelli, whose job it was first to contact the prefects and mayors of the designated areas, then make sure the government's orders were being carried out. It was anticipated that there might be some reluctance to cooperate on the part of not only the property owners but also the local politicians, whose careers depend on pleasing voters, but Pastorelli and his assistants intended to overcome any opposition by what one observer on the scene described as the only weapons available to them, "shouts and the 3 million Scotti promised."

Neither the shouting nor the money, it quickly became very clear, were going to have much effect. "They're putting spokes between our wheels," one official announced soon after she had started to work on the problem. "There's no cooperation with the local authorities." By the end of the first day after the evacuation order, only a few hundred rooms, most of them along the Campanian coast just north of Pozzuoli and belonging to middle-class Neapolitan families, had reluctantly been made available or occupied. Elsewhere, especially in the province of Latina and along the southern Pontine shoreline, a vacation zone about halfway between Rome and Naples with an estimated two hundred thousand extra rooms, almost no one had come forward to offer so much as a closet. Angelo Barbato, the Prefect of Latina, was the only officer who promised to work energetically to provide the quota of five thousand lodgings allotted to his province. "In twenty-four hours, I've requisitioned more apartments than my colleagues in Naples and Caserta," he claimed. "I understand the drama of the citizens of Pozzuoli. I've been here in Latina seven years and I know how to conduct myself." This commendable zeal, it was pointed out by several detractors, was undoubtedly due to the fact that he had already been transferred, as of December 1, to Padua, where he would not have to answer to the local landlords for the expropriation of their property.

It turned out, however, that, even as plans were being made to evacuate Pozzuoli, and well before Minister Scotti's public pronouncements on the crisis, teams of carabinieri, police, and firemen had been quietly taking a census of the empty space available, not only near the city, but all the way to Terracina, about seventy-five miles to the north. Actual requisitioning had begun two days before the evacuation notice, when about fifteen hundred soldiers and policemen fanned out along the coast as far up as Minturno, an ancient Roman town with picturesque ruins and an ugly modern residential suburb called Scauri. There, on the night of October 8, the officers seized ninety-five apartments along the waterfront in an operation several witnesses described as a "blitz" and, in some cases, by a means that came to be known as "the pig's foot."

Several of the victims of this procedure described to a reporter what had happened. "We had six apartments, one for us and five we rented in the summer," said a Roman named Franco Poccia. "At ten o'clock at night the carabinieri arrived, submachine guns in hand. The dogs were barking madly. 'Open up or we'll kill the animals,' they told us. They came in, they requisitioned the whole little palazzo. So they could leave us the apartment in which my father has been living since he retired, they went to check the icebox for butter and fruit, and to see if the trash sack was full." "A friend of mine telephoned me," testified Giovanni Malatesta, a resident of Caserta. " 'Look, they're requisitioning your house.' When I arrived, they had already kicked in the front door and changed the lock on the gate. It's an old family house. We live in two of the apartments, in summer. The other two we rent out. They took them all."

Another witness, who preferred to remain anonymous, explained that the officers had first tried to persuade the local carpenters and locksmiths to open the flats, but all had refused, "a little gesture of solidarity. So then the firemen intervened," he continued. "Some forced the front doors, others lowered themselves toward the windows from the rooftops. The owners arrived. Some shouted, others, instead, asked lucidly for explanations. Unfortunately, the orders were clear and nothing could be done about it." "True, we had to act in a hurry," Gaetano Colletta, the vice-prefect in charge of this operation, answered in defense of his methods, "but we couldn't do otherwise. It was logical that first we had to requisition apartments along the waterfront. Villas, even at the fair-rent rates, are too costly for a family of refugees."

Once inside, the officers reportedly made a meticulous inventory of the contents of each apartment, including furnishings, pictures, and down to the last glass and ashtray. This was being done, it was explained, to avoid the errors of previous requisitions, most notably the one in 1980, when thousands of Neapolitans, fleeing from their own earthquake damage, had had to be temporarily put up in empty hotels and summer houses. "Three years ago," declared Francesco Rosillo, the mayor of Minturno, "the refugees, even though there were fewer of them, left the houses in pitiful conditions. Crumbling walls, broken furniture. And none of the owners were ever reimbursed. Maybe that's what shatters the solidarity we feel for people living through very hard times."

The mayor, in fact, a Christian Democrat who had been in office barely a month, had already resigned in protest. He had also sent telegrams to various ministers and prefectures in which he predicted public disorder and asked for a suspension of all requisitioning until an exact count could be made of what lodgings were available, most of which, he declared, would be freely offered by public-spirited citizens responding to the official calls for help. Locally, however, he expressed misgivings. "Unfortunately," he admitted to a reporter, "no one believes in the promised payment of 3 million or the one guaranteeing indemnity for any damages."

The forebodings turned out to be well founded. The government temporarily suspended the requisitions, but by the morning of October 12, in Scauri itself, only seven houses had been volunteered by their owners. Now, with the evacuation in Pozzuoli presumably in its final stages or well under way, the operation would have to resume. "If necessary," the prefect of Latina confirmed, "we'll go up to Gaeta, Sperlonga, Fondi, and Terracina."

Oddly, the great tidal wave of fleeing Puteolani had so far failed to materialize. The first three families to be resettled away from the immediate surroundings of Pozzuoli arrived in Minturno during the afternoon of October 11. These pioneers, as they were called in excited media accounts of the event, having been unable to find shelter in the resort developments along the Campanian coast, showed up around four o'clock at a summer beach club on the Lido di Scauri, where the prefecture had hastily improvised an operations center. They showed their evacuation notices and were promptly given keys to three of the waterfront apartments available.

No sooner had they been accommodated than the authorities expressed concern. What would happen now, when the anticipated great migration of the next couple of days would wash over the whole region? By midday of October 12, the census-taking and requisitioning resumed, but this time less abruptly and violently than during the early hours of the crisis. The pig's foot, government spokesmen began to assure everyone, had been a mistake, an understandable excess of zeal on the part of conscientious officials entrusted with a difficult task and trying to cope as best they could with a major emergency. All would now proceed in order, with appropriate regard for the law and due process, as well as concern for the rights of property owners, most of whom, several commentators pointed out, were not rich people speculating in real estate, but only private middle-class citizens with family vacation homes for which they had saved and sacrificed over the years.

Even as local officials were preparing to resume requisitioning, however, and were now bracing themselves for the arrival of the thousands of Puteolani due in a matter of hours, telephones had been ringing all over Italy, and in parts of Europe and America as well, with the news. Mistrustful, as usual, of their own government, alarmed by the public statements being made—especially in Latina by Signor Barbato—and outraged by media accounts of the pig's foot, the embattled bourgeoisie was already either on the scene or rushing to it in defense of its property.

IN POZZUOLI, almost nothing was going according to plan. During the forty-eight hours the minister had allotted for the evacuation, a vast confusion reigned. Some people did manage to leave, but mostly in their own cars and camions and usually to move in with friends or relatives living in the vicinity. The army trucks commandeered for the operation were parked here and there around the city, but no one had given the drivers specific orders as to how to proceed or where and they simply sat it out. Squads of soldiers and police did from time to time sweep through Zone A, urging the inhabitants to leave, but many refused and were not forced to do so. Those who tried to soon found themselves milling about for hours in a great mass of people surging back and forth around the offices of the municipality and the Ministry of Civil Protection, which occupied temporary headquarters in a two-story school building a couple of miles to the south of the tottering *centro storico*.

There the Puteolani spent their time swapping rumors, squabbling over precedence in line, asking questions and receiving contradictory answers from the harassed officials inside, who were themselves evidently being kept in the dark by the authorities in Rome and were unable to inform the would-be refugees exactly where they were to go and how. An approximate count made by a reporter on the scene estimated that, of the thirty thousand people scheduled for evacuation, about ten thousand had already made their own living arrangements and about twelve thousand were precariously installed in temporary quarters, leaving roughly eight thousand people still living in Zone A, where they had achieved, as one of them put it, only "the right to be afraid."

By this time, the social life of the city had reached a state of almost complete paralysis, with many shops and businesses closed. Here and there people managed to improvise solutions, like the doctor forced to evacuate his palazzo, who left a sign on his door informing his patients that his office had been transferred to "the tent in front." During the day inside Zone A, the streets and alleys were full of people hurrying about on various errands and moving their belongings out of their threatened homes. This constant coming and going caused traffic jams everywhere, with only one young man, a private citizen who had spontaneously taken on the task himself, making any effort to untangle the worst knots.

At night, the quarter became a ghost town, the suddenly empty streets threading their way between the skeletal frameworks supporting the darkened palazzi that seemed to creak and rumble in the silence. Along the waterfront on the evening of October 12, a crowd gathered to watch two teenage boys scrambling over a row of abandoned houses with cracked and lopsided walls to fasten long ropes to the worst-looking cornices and window sills. Back on the ground, the boys tugged and jerked on the ropes, bringing down bits and pieces of the buildings in thumping clouds of dust. When an observer asked why the firemen did not intervene, he was told, "They're not here, they've got other things to do." And what if the boys got hurt? "They're killing time," another voice answered. "What else are they supposed to do?"

Killing time is one of the occupations the Puteolani are famous for. Another is the ancient Italian art of *arrangiarsi,* a term that means literally "to arrange oneself," but is better translated as "fixing oneself up"—an invaluable talent in times of adversity. Pozzuoli is one of the poorest towns in Italy, with a constant unemployment rate of about 25 percent, an unfortunate distinction it shares with Naples. Once a flourishing spa, with an important fishing industry and several large factories, it was recently described by Raffaele Giamminelli, an official of the Italian ecological society Italia Nostra, as "a glaring example of urbanistic pillage and of social and human degradation." The fishing port, thanks to the rising ground, had been closed to all but the shallowest boats, and the factories, including a rubber works and an Olivetti plant, have either shut down or greatly cut back, idling hundreds of workers.

Thrown upon their own resources, the Puteolani have had to survive for years as best they can, mostly by hand-to-mouth manual labor and improvised jobs of the kind Naples has become famous for, such as guarding illegally parked cars, "painting" days-old fish to make them seem fresh, guiding tourists to restaurants and hotels from which they receive kickbacks, and so on. Not surprisingly, the Camorra, the Neapolitan Mafia, flourishes here, and petty thievery, smuggling, and small protection rackets of one sort or another are endemic. Furthermore, according to a Neapolitan historian named Alfredo d'Ambrosio, "The previous ills have grown out of all proportion in these last years because of the inactivity of the public administrations, whatever their political color, and the passivity of a population more accustomed to charity than good government."

The reality in Pozzuoli, as in Naples, is that all public initiatives seem somehow to end up squandering vast sums of money without accomplishing their objectives, while enriching those entrusted with carrying them out and their friends. *Clientelismo* (roughly, patronage) is the most important fact of life here, because a friend or relative in the right government office can literally mean the difference between living well and starving. In 1970, when the administration in Rome passed a bill allocating several billion lire to rebuild and repair the older sections of the city most threatened by the slow quake, the money dribbled away without anything actually being done. Soon after, however, there was a sudden rash of construction, with private builders throwing up hotels, luxury villas, and high-rent apartment houses everywhere but in the poorer parts of town. Last September, the mayor was arrested for having apparently passed out illegal building licenses during this period and was eventually forced out of office, but only after it was also revealed that he himself had put up a couple of apartment houses without the proper permits and sold them at a sizeable profit.

In such an atmosphere, it's no wonder that the Puteolani have traditionally displayed a good deal of cynicism and impatience with all official efforts, however well intentioned, to take care of them. "The people trust everyone and no one," a reporter commented on October 13 in Rome's *La Repubblica.* "They read the mayor's posters. They shake their heads. They glance in alarm at the little circulars, distributed door to door in certain streets, informing them where to gather in case of another big quake. They make the sign of the horns (against bad luck and the Evil Eye). They pack more bags in preparation for the long agony. . . ."

Luckily, during these first two days of the evacuation, the seismographs of the research center registered only minor shocks, none of them felt above ground. Between five and ten A.M. on the morning of the fourteenth, however, the city was suddenly subjected to what the volcanologists called "a seismic swarm," a total of 169 tremors, as the earth began again to surge upward. Several of them were strong

129

enough to jolt everyone in the area awake. "There is a progressive increase in energy," was the way one of the experts later explained it. "The seismic crisis continues with small shakes that have provoked an enormous number of underground lesions. The situation, therefore, still remains difficult. The phenomenon is in a phase of prolonged evolution."

The Puteolani did not have to be told by the scientists exactly what was happening. At dawn they rushed out of their threatened palazzi, abandoned their tents and trailers, and gathered along the waterfront, where at 6:52 A.M. the strongest of the shocks, measured at between three and four on the Richter scale, caused panic and some people to believe that an actual volcanic eruption was imminent. By midmorning, thousands of citizens had gathered in front of the emergency headquarters demanding to be evacuated and calling out for the officials inside to take action.

No one, however, seemed to know exactly what to do. Mayor Gennaro Postiglione failed to appear and Signor Pastorelli, whose own personal headquarters had for some reason been set up fifteen miles away in Caserta, was also nowhere to be found. At eleven-thirty, a group of exasperated citizens shoved their way past police into the building to find many of the offices empty and only one minor official present, with whom a pushing and shouting match immediately broke out that finally ended with the forced eviction of the protestors. At noon, when Signor Pastorelli finally showed up, the building was empty. His arrival triggered another outburst from the angry crowd in the street and he, too, soon vanished. Frustrated, the citizens were thus reduced to arguing with each other, in what became a purely speculative hours-long debate over their own prospects and fate, a scene one eyewitness described as a Pirandellian tragicomedy.

Meanwhile, the army trucks remained immobile, their drivers as confused as the Puteolani themselves. "What do I know?" one of them told a reporter, who asked where the refugees were to be taken. "Orders come from everywhere, with the result that we're stuck here hour after hour. And the people run away on their own legs." Few of the latter seemed to know where they were headed. In cars, on trucks, on bicycles, on foot, and pushing carts heaped high with their personal belongings, whole families spent the day on the move out of Zone A.

"Where are we going?" a father of five driving an open camion answered one inquiry. "How do I know?"

Others, however, began to take matters into their own hands. Equipped with eviction notices and other documents establishing them as bona fide residents of Zone A, thus making them eligible for requisitioned living quarters, these Puteolani set about fixing themselves up. An Olivetti factor worker named Franco Maddaluno, at the head of a caravan that included his wife, his sister-in-law, his son and daughter, their spouses, three grandchildren, and a mountain of baggage, headed up the coast to look for a place to live. They were turned away everywhere and told by various officials to go back to Pozzuoli until their number came up and they could be legally assigned a house somewhere. Maddaluno ignored this advice and kept going until he finally spotted a small empty villa at Pineta Coppola, the largest of the summer housing developments, a few miles north of Pozzuoli. The men broke the lock on the gate, forced the front door open, and took possession of the house. "We couldn't wait any longer," Maddaluno explained, after describing to an observer how he had had to abandon their damaged home that morning.

Such scenes became commonplace in the area during the next couple of days, when dozens of families—some with documents, others without—found themselves on the move. Most, like Maddaluno, did not wait to be told where to go, but simply sought out empty quarters anywhere they could find them. Once inside, who could have the heart or, more important, even the legal right to evict them? Certainly not the authorities, who had by now proved themselves unable to provide adequate shelter. A few of the fleeing Puteolani did insist on some sort of quasilegal justification for their actions. An old man named Alessandro Di Spizio, who presented himself at the emergency center at Pineta Coppola late on the afternoon of the fourteenth, insisted on speaking to the functionary in charge. He described in detail how he had had to abandon not only his house on the outskirts of town, but also his two pigs, fifteen rabbits, and thirty chickens, as well as several barrels of good new wine, now destined to become vinegar. *"Signore,* I have found an unrented house, all the shades are drawn," he concluded his account. "Will you give me permission to break in the door?"

THE PART of Italy designated as the best place to house the majority of the refugees consists of a roughly fifty-mile-long coastal strip stretching from the outskirts of Minturno to Sabaudia. The whole area, known popularly as the South Pontine, includes the important fishing, agricultural, and commercial centers of Terracina, Fondi, and Formia, respectively, but it is mainly a tourist and resort area. Latina, the provincial capital, is a large and spectacularly ugly community founded in 1932, after the draining of the malarial Pontine marshes south of Rome. It has since flourished as an agricultural boomtown, but it is about twenty-five miles north of Terracina, in the middle of flat farmland, and has little in common with the zone of which it is the administrative capital.

When it was announced that requisitioning would resume and the prefect of Latina made it plain that he expected wholehearted cooperation from the municipal administrations under his jurisdiction, it was generally felt that he simply had no idea what exactly was involved. Signor Barbato was demanding accommodations for twenty-five thousand people and he evidently expected to be provided immediately with several hundred places and thousands more literally within a matter of a day or two. On October 12, he assigned three hundred men to find another couple of hundred rooms in the area between Scauri and Formia and delivered what amounted to an ultimatum to the rest of the South Pontine. "All right," he declared, after having been informed that so far only a total of about 130 lodgings had been volunteered in the whole district, "if good manners aren't enough, then we'll have to start up again with bad ones."

The trouble was that, by this time, opposition to the whole scheme had solidified. Most of the houses along the coast were no longer empty, but occupied, instead, either by their owners or the owners' friends and relatives, who had come swarming down from the north, suitcases in hand, to defend their vacation spots. People unable to get away sent surrogates—cousins, nieces and nephews, aged aunts, in-laws, grandparents, children, trusted friends—all prepared to resist any attempt to take over their possessions. They laid in supplies and prepared to sit it out. Many of the hotels and *pensioni* normally shut-tered during the winter months had been reopened, some with their registers showing every room to be occupied, even though very few guests were actually to be seen anywhere. At night, the shoreline between Terracina and Minturno, ordinarily dark at this time of year, twinkled like a Broadway marquee. "It looks like half the pensioners in central Italy have decided to winter on the coast," a municipal cop in Formia observed to a visiting journalist.

Everywhere meetings were called and committees formed to protest Minister Scotti's plan. A shower of resolutions, petitions, and demands fell upon the local authorities, most of whom clearly sympathized with the protesters and passed these communications on to Rome, as well as the government officials on the scene. "We sympathize with the inhabitants of Pozzuoli," read a typical letter handed to Antonio La Rocca, the mayor of Sperlonga, and signed by ten citizens, "but we feel the need to point out that these calamities are too often caused by the improvidence of the authorities."

Even in Formia, a relatively wealthy town where the local administration had cooperated to the extent of compiling a list of two hundred places ("all belonging to people who have between three and ten houses"), there were a number of serious objections. Why, for instance, had certain areas been exempted, such as San Felice Circeo, an exclusive little resort a few miles northeast of Terracina, where a number of Roman politicians happened to have luxurious villas? Such questions, mostly unanswered by anyone in charge and continually fed by the skepticism that characterizes the way most Italians regard all forms of authority, continued to agitate the whole area during the next few days. Furthermore, not content with meetings, protests, and passive resistance, some of the landlords in Gaeta, a large but very poor town near Formia that survives mainly on summer tourism, persuaded the municipality to file a legal appeal with the regional administrative court in Latina against the possible seizure of their property.

Of all the communities on Prefect Barbato's list, none was more vulnerable to requisitioning than Sperlonga, the small resort town with its year-round population of only about thirty-eight hundred. During the summer months, it teems with visitors, known to the native Sperlongani as "the Sunday Romans," many of whom rent vacation quarters in Sperlonga Mare's many small hotels and *pensioni*. The outsiders who have bought houses and apartments in the *centro storico* occupy them the rest of the year only on weekends, so it should have been no problem to come up with the roughly two hundred lodgings reportedly allotted as the town's quota.

Before a definitive count could even be made, however, the Sunday Romans had mobilized against it. They held meetings and drafted petitions. The more agile managed immediately to install leaseholding winter tenants in their empty apartments or established themselves as legal residents of Sperlonga, maneuvers that automatically exempted the property concerned from being taken. The municipal administration put a stop almost at once to such tactics for the duration of the emergency, so most of the returnees simply remained inside their houses to wait it out. As the days passed, they had to content themselves with hearsay alone, since no one connected with government was making any more official statements at this point.

The central meeting places became the tiny main piazza in the *centro* and the square outside the city hall, where every arrival and departure by anyone in authority was noted and widely commented on. Most of the information that leaked out into the town came from Sperlongani who had relatives on the public payroll, but no one could vouch for the authenticity of any of it. It was said, for instance, that requisitioning would affect only those people with more than two vacation homes; the large summer campground directly below the village; the so-called *case abusive,* houses built illegally, without proper permits; certain hotels and *pensioni;* the four very grand-looking beachfront villas belonging to an absentee contractor, who used them only as summer rentals. Mayor La Rocca, who spent much of his time secluded in his office, refused to declare himself, but made it known that, like his colleagues in the rest of the South Pontine, he was in daily negotiations with the prefect's staff in Latina. His supporters hinted that he was engaged in a delaying action, a time-honored way in Italy of riding out all sorts of public crises. "They are making lists," a middle-aged Sperlongana I'll call Pasqualina declared in the piazza on the morning of October 14. "There is a first list and a second list and a third list. When they begin making lists, nothing will happen." Pasqualina had a nephew who worked in the city registrar's office and her pronouncements were regarded as oracular.

Neither the news programs nor the daily papers carried much specific local information during this period, which left everyone free to make his own assessment of what was going on, not only in Sperlonga, but all over the South Pontine. Still, apart from the inconvenience and the tensions caused by what amounted to an almost complete news blackout, the Sunday Romans also managed to enjoy themselves during the wait. The weather remained sunny and mild, which enabled the hardier to spend part of the day at least on the beach, and at night people entertained each other at home, where they could swap the latest stories and continue to speculate on the eventual outcome of the crisis. "We should start this rumor every year, because it gets everybody back in October," a Roman novelist observed over a coffee in the piazza one morning. "We are like the eighteenth-century French aristocracy wining and dining and telling each other outrageous lies, while the mob gathers at the palace gates." Others compared the event to the mid-fourteenth century in Florence as described by Boccaccio, when the nobles fled the plague raging in the city to sit it out for ten days in their country villas, where they entertained each other in the evenings with the tales immortalized in *The Decameron.*

The main topic of conversation, of course, was speculation over exactly whose houses would be taken and when the first refugees, always referred to as "they," would arrive. A close watch was kept on the Via Flacca, the coastal road linking Sperlonga to the south, and every truck and bus heading north was rumored to be carrying fugitive Puteolani. Estimates as to the exact number of families to be settled in Sperlonga ranged from a high of two hundred and fifty to a low of twelve. On the night of October 13, the word was that *they* had reached Serape, a residential suburb of Gaeta, but that the Gaetani were erecting roadblocks and agitating in the streets against their presence. "It is like wartime," commented a retired businessman living in a villa behind Sperlonga, "when we did not know where the Allies were or if the Germans might come back."

After several days of continued silence from the authorities, some of the stories circulating became outlandish. One had a total of five hundred apartments about to be seized; another that the Camorra had dispatched spies to the village to make a list of the best places, which would then be auctioned off for occupation to the highest bidders. My own personal favorite had to do with the silence at city hall. There would be no official announcements from the mayor's office, it was said, until all the *bustarelle* had been collected. (A *bustarella* means literally a "little envelope," but indicates a bribe, traditionally stuffed into a sealed envelope and passed under the table.) It became hard, after a while, to take any of this information seriously or to remember that this comedy had started out as a genuine emergency and possible tragedy in Pozzuoli only a few days before. By Saturday evening, October 16, not one house had been requisitioned and not a single refugee had yet appeared in Sperlonga or, as far as anyone knew, anywhere north of Formia and Gaeta. According to Pasqualina, about forty families would eventually be settled in Sperlonga Mare, but they were now not expected to arrive before the following week. "Italy," an American journalist once informed me, "is a small country entirely blanketed by rumors."

DURING THE early days of the siege in the South Pontine, matters continued to deteriorate in Pozzuoli. Most of the would-be fugitives were unable to find any place to go on their own and were forced to return. The beach resorts immediately north of the city had quickly filled up and few people were brave enough to venture even as far as Minturno on their own, with no assurance of finding a place to stay. Discouraged by the reports filtering back into the city and accounts of the hostility being displayed by landowners everywhere, the majority of the several thousand Puteolani still in Zone A settled down to make the best of their precarious situation. Whenever their buildings began to shake, they fled into the streets, but returned as soon as it seemed safe enough. They ignored all orders to leave, because by this time it had become clear to them that little in the way of real help was to be expected from the government's badly snarled rescue efforts. These survivors clearly preferred to sit tight rather than live in trailers or allow themselves to be resettled miles away from their homes. Some of the families that had been successfully moved earlier had, in fact, already begun to drift back. They complained that they had been assigned unfurnished and unheated rooms, even garages, to live in and that they had been taken fifty or sixty miles away. Where would their children go to school? And how would they be able to support themselves?

Faced with such questions, the authorities seemed to have no definitive answer. Signor Pastorelli blamed Rome for his troubles. His administrative staff consisted, he said, of fifty-four harassed and badly overworked people, who were doing what they could in impossible circumstances. "We need new financing," he insisted, "technical resources, specialized personnel." How else could he be expected to cope in a few days with the urgent needs of thirty thousand people? As for Riccardo Boccia, the prefect of Naples, he seemed to believe that the Puteolani were residents of the Third World. "The psychology of the people is what it is," he told reporters. "To go away, they have to see their palazzo fall down. Otherwise they won't leave." And Mayor Postiglione complained that the scientists had first failed to predict accurately what would happen, then, after the big tremors in early October, had been so pessimistic that they had literally compelled the government to impose an emergency evacuation for which no one was prepared.

The scientists denied this. "It is not exact to speak of evacuation," declared a leading volcanologist named Franco Barberi. "We notified Scotti that new earthquakes were possible. From a scientific point of view, they won't be violent, but shocks like the one of October fourth are in the range of probability." It was an old problem, another expert named Giovanni Ricciardi pointed out, in a zone that had had to be evacuated three times since 1970 and contained "buildings that tremble when a truck passes in the street." The scientists had acted responsibly, according to Enzo Boschi, the president of the National Institute of Geophysics, because it was their duty as scientists to foresee the worst, "for which the severity in inspecting the stability of the houses [in Pozzuoli] is more than opportune."

Nothing the scientists said sounded reassuring. The slow quake had attracted a number of the world's leading volcanologists to the area, including Haroun Tazieff, a lively, articulate sixty-nine-year-old naturalized Frenchman from Warsaw, whose idea of a good time is to be lowered directly into an active crater so he can examine the activity inside firsthand. After having spent several days in Pozzuoli, he gave a lecture in Rome on October 16 at which he predicted a possible catastrophe. "Ah, Pozzuoli is a great question mark, a mystery," he said. "A mystery that began thirty-five thousand years ago with a tremendous explosion that caused eighty billion cubic meters of magma to blow up. An apocalypse, an enormous devastation."

Nothing like that would happen again, he assured his listeners, but he added that the continuous pressure could provoke an eruption. "That bubble down there is pushing up and has to find an outlet," he explained. "I don't mean earthquakes or Vesuvius, but a volcano is being born there." His findings confirmed those of Professor Narcisio, who had also predicted a couple of days earlier that the situation could get worse. "You can't exclude the possibility," he said, "that one day the molten rock pulsating under Pozzuoli, and sometimes causing the ground to shake more than a hundred times a day, may one day come breaking through to the surface in an explosion." He repeated his earlier estimate that such an event was probably not imminent, but admitted that it was impossible to tell exactly when it might occur.

Salvatore Sorrentino, the bishop of Pozzuoli, evidently regarded the affliction as a possible supernatural phenomenon. "Because of our sins," he wrote, in a pastoral letter he instructed his priests to read aloud at services throughout the diocese, "perhaps we have provoked the judgment of Our Lord." Luckily, he continued, His mercy would undoubtedly temper nature's rage. This letter aroused considerable controversy, since a number of people pointed out that the bishop himself should be among the last to accuse anyone of wrongdoing. He had been implicated in at least two building scandals during his twenty years in office and had the reputation of being such an able real-estate speculator, on his own behalf as well as the Church's, that he was known locally as "the bishop of cement." At least one of his younger priests refused to read this missive aloud to his parishioners. "It seemed inopportune to me, to say the least," he informed a reporter for *Panorama,* "also because the bishop has never seen fit to make even one visit to a tent city, to bring a word of comfort to whomever has lost his home."

Just on the chance, however, that a higher power could indeed be persuaded to intervene for Pozzuoli, a group of devout citizens and clergy had called on San Gennaro earlier in the week. San Gennà, as he is more affectionately referred to locally, is considered the patron saint of the whole Naples area and is, of course, best known for the periodic liquefaction of his dried blood. Apart from this purely symbolic marvel, the saint has also been credited over the centuries with having worked some really useful miracles in Naples, especially whenever his statue, which is kept in the Church of San Gennaro on the outskirts of Pozzuoli, is brought to the scene of whatever calamity requires his intervention. This time, the wonder-working icon, which consists of a youthful-looking carved figure wearing a bishop's miter and seated before a seven-pronged candelabrum, was carried in a procession through the streets of the city and finally to the entrance of the Solfatara.

Unfortunately, this visitation had disastrous consequences; the next few days were marked by greatly increased seismic activity, with hundreds of tremors every night. Nevertheless, the saint could hardly be blamed, most people seemed to feel, even though one participant in the procession felt that he was probably angry. Pozzuoli, after all, was where San Gennaro had been martyred, supposedly in 305, by decapitation. "He is unhappy," this critic said. "He does not wish to be reminded of Pozzuoli."

A T T H E end of the week, Signor Scotti himself returned to Pozzuoli. After again touring the city and taking note of the continuing muddle everywhere, he summoned his engineers and officials to a meeting behind closed doors in the prefect's office. "We have to emerge from this tunnel of chaos," he declared. With that in mind, he assigned four of his experts, including his deputy Pastorelli, to analyze and explain exactly what was happening. "The requisitions continue," he also announced. "There is a basic problem: We have to transfer the people in tents to hotels, to houses, because winter is at the gates and we have to bear in mind that the phenomenon is unfortunately destined to drag on for a long time."

Unhappily, nothing the minister said seemed calculated to overcome the resistance of the property owners to the north. Over the weekend, the prefect of Latina issued another of his dramatic ultimatums to the mayors, informing them that within forty-eight hours they were expected to provide enough rooms to put up at least five thousand refugees. This set off more public protests, especially in Gaeta, where an angry crowd staged a demonstration in front of the town hall and marched through the streets. Several roadblocks were set up along the Via Flacca, between Formia and Gaeta, but they were quickly dismantled by the police. The unions representing public services and the fishing and tourist industries called a number of brief work stoppages, and the schools shut down for a day. Although the anticipated innundation of Puteolani again failed to appear, the feeling throughout the South Pontine continued to be one of exasperation, especially with the distant authorities, who seemed to have no understanding of local needs and problems. "They're asking us to find furnished lodgings, and with all the services of light, water, and heat," the mayor of Gaeta explained, after pointing out again that most of the places available were summer homes, sparsely furnished and often without any heating facilities at all.

In Pozzuoli itself, however, as the second week of the emergency began, an unexpected calm settled over the city. Apart from the now much smaller crowd that showed up every morning outside the evacuation headquarters south of town, presumably still hoping for a solution to its problems, life elsewhere resumed a routine familiarity. Traffic in the streets seemed normal, many of the shops reopened— even in Piazza della Repubblica and other parts of the *centro storico*— and, along the waterfront, the fishermen hawked their catch to passersby, as they had for hundreds of years. If it hadn't been for the rows of tents, the army trucks, and the scaffoldings propping up the damaged palazzi in Zone A, no visitor could have imagined what the town had been through the past few months. Furthermore, since the last big shock early on the morning of October 14, the slow quake had become gradually less virulent, so that by the middle of the week only the delicate instruments at the research center were still registering any subterranean activity.

The scientists continued to warn that this could mean only a pause, while pressure built up for another upward surge, but by this time most of the Puteolani had pretty much stopped paying attention to them, just as they had ceased putting any faith in the utterances of the politicians. The citizens went about the business of reorganizing their lives despite the slow quake and the inadequacies of their public institutions. "A living city that wants to live," an observer on the scene reported. The phenomenon of brandyseism had become like a longterm illness afflicting a patient determined to ignore it.

The Puteolani were also doing their utmost to fix themselves up. It was revealed, for instance, that about twenty thousand applications for the monthly housing subsidy of 350,000 lire had been submitted to the municipality, which, allowing for an average of four persons to a family unit, meant that assistance was being requested for about eighty thousand people. This was not only far more than the total of thirty thousand presumably qualified to receive it, but also more than the whole population of the town. It had become almost impossible to verify all such claims anyway, because it turned out that the records in the city registrar's office had somehow mysteriously disappeared, probably in transit.

Other peculiarities began to come to light. The municipality, which should have had no more than 150 people on its payroll, apparently employed about fifteen hundred. Some of the more high-ranking civil servants, it was said, had been given first crack at the best of the empty apartments in Pineta Coppola. Mayor Postiglione denied that irregularities of any sort had been committed or knowing anything about such illegal favoritism; he simply explained that everyone wanted to be resettled as close as possible to his place of work.

The greatest mystery of all concerned the estimated forty-five hundred people supposedly precariously sheltered in the tented encampments along the shoreline. On October 18, when the weather suddenly turned cold and it began to rain, the authorities ordered the dismantling of the so-called *tendopoli*. A total of about five hundred lodgings was now available to house these refugees, who obviously could not be allowed to remain where they were any longer. That evening, however, when police and carabinieri went to make a check of the tent cities, they found only about three hundred and fifty persons living in them. Where had everyone gone? No one knew exactly, but over the next couple of days it became clear that most of the people assigned tents were only using them during the day; at night they went elsewhere, either to bunk in with friends and relatives, to already assigned temporary lodgings outside the city, or, in many cases, back into their condemned palazzi in Zone A.

The pattern of life in Pozzuoli had become like the tides. During the day people flowed into and about the city to work and carry on their usual household chores; at night they departed to sleep wherever they had managed to set themselves up. The citizens still living full-time in Zone A obviously felt they had no other choice, at least not one that made any sense to them. When the mayor was asked by reporters how people could be allowed to come and go as they pleased in the most dangerous part of town, he replied, "That zone will not be completely closed. . . . We will try, with the help of the technicians, to discipline the presence of citizens in the zone. We will try to restructure the center after the phenomenon is over. But we reject partitioning. Heaven help us if life stops!"

Two days after the check of the *tendopoli,* the administrative court in Latina issued an injunction putting a stop to all requisitioning throughout the province. The order did not rule on the legality of the government's overall emergency powers, but simply suspended this one action until the court could arrive at a final verdict. This promised to drag on for many months, however, so that the effect of the ruling was to lift the state of siege in the South Pontine. Demonstrations and strikes ceased in Gaeta and elsewhere, while the Sunday Romans began to go home. Within twenty-four hours, the whole vacation coastline had reacquired its somnolent off-season aspect.

The court's ruling caused no reaction in Pozzuoli, whose inhabitants had by this time lost all interest in moving to the South Pontine anyway. By October 20, only about 130 families, no more than five hundred people, had been settled there, most of them in Minturno-Scauri and Formia. In Sperlonga, not a single house had been requisitioned and not one Puteolano had showed up.

Confronted by this disquieting reality and blocked from putting any further pressure on the municipal administrations in the South Pontine, Signor Scotti and his staff placed their hopes on the swift construction of the new city at Monte Ruscello, which, the minister now assured everyone, would be ready in ten to twelve months. The project would be carried out under the supervision of the architectural faculty at the University of Naples. It would be necessary to work double shifts, a minimum of twelve to fourteen hours a day. "There mustn't be dead times, we must use to the utmost the technical and professional energies we have," Signor Scotti said. "I'm launching a challenge. We are pushing for a definitive settlement of the refugees, skipping over completely the phase of provisional arrangements." In the meantime, he continued, additional temporary space for the people still in tents or unsafe buildings would be found to the south, in Naples itself or along the coast toward Sorrento.

This announcement helped to set off a wave of unrest in Naples, with rallies and processions through the streets and piazzas against what the protesters felt was the favoritism being shown to Pozzuoli. It was a confrontation, in essence, between the earthquake victims of the two cities that one observer immediately likened to a "war of the poor." The problem was that in Naples, nearly three years after the earthquake of 1980 that had caused mass evacuations from the tottering palazzi of the *centro storico* there, about seventy thousand people were still living in temporary quarters, twenty-seven thousand of them in prefabricated shedlike containers. Thirty months after funds had been appropriated to build twenty thousand homes for these people, not one had been completed and assigned to a family. In such a climate of frustration, it was not surprising that the Neapolitans should have reacted angrily to Minister Scotti's rosy pronouncements; the wonder was that they hadn't taken to the streets earlier. "It is not that we are opposing the people of Pozzuoli," one woman told a reporter, "but we have our own unsolved drama."

As the second week of the crisis dragged to an end, with the light at the end of the tunnel of chaos as distant as ever, nature at least proved kind. It stopped raining and the weather again turned mild. Best of all, the slow quake seemed now to have stopped altogether. The seismographs continued to register a dozen or so minor rumbles a day, but none strong enough to be felt above ground. The scientists, too, had changed their tune. There was probably nothing to worry about, they had begun to say—the pressure below had found enough of an outlet to make an actual eruption or another major jolt unlikely.

And so, just as they have for centuries, the people of both Pozzuoli and Naples settled back into their lives, while awaiting the solution to their needs promised by the authorities, but mostly without any real hope that it would be forthcoming. A Neapolitan named Mario Cacciapuoti, who had been living for nearly three years in a tiny rectangular space inside an aluminum container, probably spoke best for all of the embattled poor of the region. "It's like dying slowly," he said.

ENTREPRENEURS

CHAPTER
TEN

THE QUEEN
OF THE BOGS

WELCOME TO THE Great Gray Queen of the Bogs!" began the note I found in my message box from a friend of mine, when I checked into my hotel in Milan during a recent visit. It seemed an appropriate greeting, as I had arrived in the city late at night by train to find it, as is often the case, shrouded in fog and bone-chillingly damp. Early the next morning I woke up to rain beating against my window shutters, while outside the narrow streets in the older part of town where I was staying were crowded with figures hunched under umbrellas, threading their way through parked cars on their way to work.

This sight, as well as my friend's salutation, cheered me up. I had not spent much time in Milan since the early 1970s and my first impression was that nothing had changed. I once lived here off and on for over a year and I can't remember ever having seen the sun from November to April, while the strongest memory I've retained from that period is of a constant, hurried coming and going by people impervious to climate and fiercely intent on the day's affairs. Milan is the industrial and commercial capital of the nation, "the most citylike city in Italy," according to the noted Sicilian author Giovanni Verga, who made that observation nearly a century ago. Its inhabitants pride themselves on their energy and business acumen, on their ability to "get things done" while making money, and most of the country's great industrial empires were created here. A typical Milanese tale is always one in which the protagonist rises to the top through imagination, determination, and sheer hard work. "The average Milanese businessman performs labors that would have daunted Sisyphus," Indro Montanelli, the editor of *Il Giornale,* once said. "And because he is a prodigious toiler, he always achieves the summit of whatever he sets out to do. Elsewhere in Italy this is considered luck." Lee Iacocca's autobiography was a clamorous bestseller here, just the kind of self-congratulatory managerial success story the Milanese can identify with.

During most of the seventies, while the country suffered through a prolonged recession, with high inflation, unemployment, and frequent strikes, as well as the terrorist "years of lead," Milan survived better than most other Italian cities. It remained, in Montanelli's words, "a happy island" in a sea of corruption, violence, and misery, where people continued despite everything to work hard and the city government, headed by its popular Socialist mayor, Carlo Tognoli, provided, beginning in 1975, a decade of stability and incorruptible efficiency. "There was once a Milan," a recent story in the weekly *Panorama* observed, with a beloved mayor, efficient public services, and "an enviable autonomy" from the political intrigues being played out in the corridors of Rome's ministerial palazzi. In Milan, Rome, the nation's capital, with its Byzantine bureaucracy and squabbling political factions, has always been considered the quintessential example of everything wrong with the society. The feeling here has always been that only Milan, with its energy and entrepreneurial spirit, could triumph over the inertia to the south and continue to keep Italy, at least the northern half of the peninsula, in the vanguard of the world's industrialized economies. "South of Rome is Africa," is the way I once heard it put, a definition most of my Milanese acquaintances would heartily endorse.

The spirit still dominates Milan and, after only a few hours spent here, it can become contagious; visitors quickly adopt a brisk Milanese pace. One soon discovers, too, that the Milanese are even prouder of their more recent achievements than their earlier ones. The central city bristles with modern skyscrapers, some of them stunningly beautiful. The Milanese design the best modern furniture, and the local fashion industry ranks with Paris as a trendsetter. Ask any Milanese what he likes best about his hometown and he is likely to mention one or all of the above, as well as point out other contemporary features—the many thousands of businesses, large and small; the hundreds of banks and hotels; the best public transportation system in Italy.

No dynamic American executive could fail to appreciate this place. Milan's stock exchange, which now handles about 90 percent of the nation's securities transactions, has recently been modernized. (While the work was under way, a temporary annex was built next door, swallowing up the entire piazza facing the exchange, thus depriving the citizens of badly needed open space. It is typical of Milan that almost no one protested—something that could not happen in Rome or Florence.) The shops seem to be always crowded, the hotels and restaurants full, the economic and scientific sections of the newspapers teeming with news of conventions, trade fairs, technological breakthroughs, international business developments, and announcements of endless opportunities for investment in all sorts of enterprises. Most significant, the want ads indicate a voracious demand for skilled personnel at every level, and there is far less visible misery in Milan than in most American cities. "We have our poor, of course," a friend of mine admitted at lunch one day. "But we take care of them. This is not Naples or New York."

Milan is not merely a commercial center, but, like every other Italian city, has its share of great sights. The Milanese spend a lot of time in and around them. They have a rooted idea that somehow the day has been mismanaged that hasn't put them within walking distance of the historic center, with its great Gothic cathedral, the Galleria and its sidewalk cafés, La Scala, the opera capital of the world, and the majestic Castello Sforzesco, the seat of ducal power in the late Middle Ages. Milan is built like a giant spiderweb with this heart at its center and the Milanese feel irresistibly drawn to it.

The Duomo itself is a fantastic sight. It looks like an enormous white wedding cake, all spires, curlicues, leering gargoyles, and saintly figures. Citizens used to picnic on its rooftop and they still take shelter inside, sitting and gossiping in the pews during the hot, humid summer months. They flock to La Scala during the opera season and are the toughest, most demanding audience in the world. At the cafés under the soaring glass arches of the nearby Galleria, the local buffs will spend hours debating the merits of various singers.

Traditionally, this city has always been receptive to art and kind to artists. In addition to such great public museums as the Brera and the Poldi-Pezzoli, with their dozens of Mantegnas and Bellinis and Tiepolos, Milan has the finest private galleries in Italy, where most of the country's modern art is sold. The town is full of painters and sculptors who feel supported and comfortable here. The tradition is an old one. Henri Beyle, the Frenchman who wrote under the name of Stendhal and haunted La Scala, wanted to be buried here, his tomb to bear the simple epitaph, *"Henri Beyle, Milanese."* And when Giuseppe Verdi lay dying in his hotel room on the Via Manzoni, the citizens laid straw over the cobblestones outside his windows so the maestro would not be disturbed by the rumble of carriage wheels.

And the Milanese also like to celebrate. Milan has by far the most active nightlife in Italy, with elegant late-night spots full of pretty people having a good time. Periodically, this nightlife has come under fire, with revelations that the Mafia owns some of the clubs and that drugs are readily available. "When will Milan decide to open its eyes?" the columnist Giorgio Bocca recently asked in the weekly *L'Espresso.* "When it's like Chicago in the thirties?"

Like every other industrial metropolis, Milan has always had a high crime rate, but in recent years there have been some huge scandals, mostly involving real-estate speculation and drugs. "A distracted, understanding city, Milan," Bocca observed. "Here there are people who buy everything at above-market prices, who keep huge fortunes immobilized in houses, lands, warehouses, but never anyone who asks where this sea of money comes from." He suggested that Milan's coat of arms ought to be redesigned to portray two hands separated by a check, with the left hand obviously ignorant of what the right hand was doing. As for what another commentator has called the "river of heroin" flowing undisturbed past the seemingly indifferent gaze of the police, the traffic has served to shed a disquieting light on an underground society of drug dealers, playboys, girls on the loose, and con men. "Milan is the capital of the fast-buck artist," an American businessman told me. "Everything is for sale here."

IN ITS headlong rush to prosperity, Milan has paid little attention to ecological or environmental considerations. The city's traditional colors are various shades of brown, gray, and burnt orange, but some buildings, including many of the elegant eighteenth- and nineteenth-century palazzi that line the avenues in the heart of the historic center, are beginning to turn black in the polluted air and some seem to be visibly crumbling before one's eyes. Only recently have the citizens begun to organize in defense of their patrimony. One of the oddest sights I came across was the Columns of San Lorenzo, a grouping of sixteen ancient Roman pillars originally brought here to form a majestic portico for the adjacent Church of San Lorenzo, which can trace its own origins back to 350 A.D. The marble shafts had been tightly wrapped in canvas and plastic to protect them from further erosion until they could be restored and the whole monument, one of Milan's most famous sights, resembled a huge package abandoned in the middle of the Corso di Porta Ticinese, one of the main avenues leading south, as if dropped there by a careless shopper. "We're going to ship them to you in America," I was told facetiously by a young Milanese ecologist, when I inquired about the monument's future. "You can set them up in Arizona, next to the London Bridge."

Sarcasm, irony, and a sort of doomsday wit are the shields behind which the people who care most about this city operate. "We are few but nice," I was informed by Luisa Toeschi, a journalist who devotes much of her spare time to working for the local chapter of Italia Nostra, the country's leading ecological organization. She and a colleague named Alberto Ferruzzi, an architect, told me that they keep running into the same people over and over at every meeting and conference having to do with cultural matters or the environment. Italia Nostra was founded in 1958 "to preserve and conserve the historical, artistic and natural patrimony of the nation without hope of gain," as one of the organization's recent bulletins put it. It has sixteen thousand members nationwide, two thousand of them in Milan. "Always the same faces, the same speeches," Signor Ferruzzi said. "It is like talking to oneself."

Nevertheless, over the years, Italia Nostra, aided by a handful of smaller but equally vocal environmental groups that have sprung up during the past decade, has managed to achieve some local victories, mainly by helping to create pedestrian islands inside the *centro storico* and over seventy small parks and gardens within the metropolitan area. WHY DOES MILAN HAVE TO BE UGLY? was the headline over an article published in a newsletter. The piece pointed out that people return-ing from summer vacations were invariably struck by their home-town's squalor and that there was no reason for such pervasive ugli-ness.

The traditional answer here to such arguments is that Milan has never been considered a beautiful city, even during its heyday, when it was traversed by its famous *navigli,* or canals, and it can't really com-pete as a tourist attraction with the rest of Italy, despite its famous sights, elegant palazzi, and splendid private gardens. "You don't go to Milan for beauty," a Roman relative of mine once observed. "You go there to work and that's all."

As the people at Italia Nostra never tire of explaining, however, the quality of life in Milan is no longer merely an aesthetic question but one of survival. There are few controls over the industrial emissions spewing daily from the city's thousands of factories and nearly a mil-lion automobiles, nor is there any emergency system in place to warn people of dangerously high pollution levels in the air or to compel fac-tories to shut down and drivers to park their cars. Milan sits in the heart of the Po Valley, Italy's breadbasket, tucked up under the protec-tive rim of the Swiss Alps. It does not benefit from the onshore breezes that protect Naples and Rome or the winds that periodically blow off the peninsula's central mountain ranges. The atmospheric inversion layers that cause the most rapid build-ups of pollutants often last ten days or more here and the area is also subject to thick ground fogs that trap harmful chemicals and prevent them from being dispersed. Al-most every day the local newspapers report on the poor quality of the air and often issue warnings of potential disaster, but the authorities seem not to be listening. "It will take a major calamity, with people dropping in the streets, to get our politicians to do anything," a re-porter on the daily *Il Giorno* said to me. "And it will happen."

Milan is also one of the few major cities in Western Europe still without adequate sewage-disposal facilities. Every day millions of gal-lons of untreated waste flow into the ancient system of canals and un-derground rivulets on which the city rests, are carried into the Po and its tributary network of rivers, then out to the Adriatic. Although sew-age is only one of the ills afflicting the Lombard streams, which have been dying for years and have become conduits for all sorts of pesti-cides and other potentially lethal chemicals, it is certainly not the least of the system's problems. For years the municipal administration acknowledged the need to build some sort of disposal facility, but has only recently set about constructing one. This, despite the fact that recent national surveys reveal that most people believe "respect of the environment" to be the country's most important priority, even if it means loss of jobs and a lowering of material living standards. Eventually, it is hoped, the politicians will begin paying more attention to what their constituents want and have been trying to tell them for years.

Despite its ecological problems, most of which are common to every large industrialized city, Milan seems likely to remain what some local wag once called it, "an international capital in search of a country." It is less than two hours from Paris and London by air, three hours by train from Venice, and less than half an hour by car from the romantic lake country Italy shares with Switzerland. And the city's ferocious concentration on materialism also has its compensations. The Milanese, only about 1.5 million strong, account for less than 7 percent of Italy's population, but 28 percent of the country's national income. With one of the highest per capita earnings in Italy, they own more telephones, computers, household appliances, video games, and cars than other Italians. They drink in the country's best bars and eat in its finest restaurants. They publish most of Italy's books and magazines, put on the biggest trade fairs, sell the most art, and set the fashions for the rest of the nation. If that means the quality of life must suffer a little, many Milanese seem quite ready to pay the price. "In Milan these days everyone's interested only in success and material well-being," the manager of my hotel informed me over a glass of wine one afternoon. "Who cares how you got it or what you did before? The important thing is to have it."

That point of view is also reflected in the activities of the young, few of whom belong to social or political movements and take no interest in politics in general. They are much more likely to join gangs, and all over town there are sizeable contingents of skinheads, punks, "rockabillies," and other groups identifying themselves mainly with pop-music trends. By far the largest and hottest new wave, however, consists of the *paninari,* a term that can only be roughly translated as "sandwichers." They are mainly teenagers, but the fad has now begun to include children of elementary school age and has become an authentic rage.

The movement, if it can be called one, was born sometime in the early eighties at the Panino, a sandwich bar in Piazza Liberty, a small square just off the Corso Vittorio Emanuele, in the heart of the *centro*. Milan, in addition to having some of the best restaurants in the world, has also become the fast-food capital of Italy, with many more Wendys, Burghys, and other junk-food emporiums than any other city. These places are heavily patronized by teenagers, and during the past few years have quite naturally become meeting places and unofficial private hangouts for gangs of kids following a trend or bound together by their own way of looking at the world.

Unlike any other teenage group, the *paninari* are united exclusively by the clothes they wear. Their wardrobes must consist entirely of jackets, shirts, pants, socks, and shoes that not only look American but have been made by one of perhaps a dozen approved designers and companies. They are expensive, with shirts and sweaters priced from a hundred dollars up and shoes as high as two hundred dollars. Each complete outfit costs a minimum of about eight hundred dollars and money-saving imitations of the genuine article will not pass; immediate ostracism is the fate of any would-be *paninaro* who tries to sneak a counterfeit article past the watchful eyes of his contemporaries. "To dress well means to dress with things that cost," a sixteen-year-old named Maurizio Gelati recently told a reporter. When asked if wealth was so important to him, the boy answered, "It's almost everything."

Appearance, however, is more important than reality. The offspring of an unemployed laborer will be accepted into any contingent of *paninari*, provided that he has been able somehow to put together an authentic ensemble that will enable him to blend indistinguishably into the group. Stories in the media of escapades and excesses committed by and for the *paninari* frequently feature episodes in which families of modest means practically bankrupt themselves to keep their children attired in the latest "in" fashion. Few Milanese parents see anything amiss in this attitude. "Let's tell the truth, we adults buy ourselves a Rolex, sports cars, designer clothes," one of them told an interviewer. "Why shouldn't they also have the desire to own the best?"

From Milan the *paninaro* craze has spread to most other major Italian cities, and there are now several magazines and comic books catering to them in which the characters express themselves in a jargon as distinctive, mysterious, and almost untranslatable as the "Valley talk" of Southern California. The phenomenon has alarmed a number of social commentators, who have accused the movement of being right-wing, if not Fascistic. They have pointed out that the *paninari* often greet each other with the Roman salute and that Benito Mussolini is a romantic figure to some of them. The kids themselves deny the political implications. "I have no political ideas," young Gelati declared. "And even my friends who say they are right-wing understand nothing of politics." Another *paninaro* explained that having a photograph of Mussolini in one's room probably meant only that the owner had failed to find a poster of Rambo.

Nevertheless, there is a growing dismay, especially among the young adults who lived through the difficult years between 1968 and 1980, concerning the *paninaro* phenomenon and what they perceive to be the attitude of the young in general. "To think that we educated our children to refute consumerism," one of them observed not long ago. "What surprises us most of all about their gangs, their groups, is the absolute absence of any kind of subversive, contesting messages. All that counts for them is riches, success, power." When I quoted this observation to a Milanese friend of mine, he said, "These kids are not setting any standards; they are merely reflecting the society they live in."

CHAPTER
ELEVEN

LA FORTUNA

A FEW MINUTES after six o'clock on the morning of February 18, 1983, the editor Angelo Rizzoli was awakened by a commotion outside his bedroom door in Milan. Except for the servants, he was alone in the house; his wife, the actress Eleonora Giorgi, was in Rome with their little boy, Andrea. Before he could get up to find out what was going on, a maid stuck her head into the room and said, "There are some people here who have come to take you away." The editor opened the door and walked out into the hall, where he was confronted by a captain and two other officers of the Guardia di Finanza, the special police force under the jurisdiction of the Ministry of the Treasury. "Doctor Rizzoli, we're sorry, but we have to carry out a warrant for your arrest," the captain said, showing it to him. "If I had been told even two years ago that I would wind up in jail," the editor later told an interviewer, "I wouldn't have believed it."

Rizzoli was driven immediately to a prison in Como. The building had been a monastery in the seventeenth century and the inmates were housed in the monks' cells—tiny, damp stone rooms with vaulted ceilings and primitive sanitary arrangements. At first he was alone, then he shared a cell for a while with a young heroin addict, who was also in jail for the first time. "I was kept pretty much in isolation for reasons of personal safety," the editor explained, "because, you know, prison is a fairly violent place." He also recalled, however, that the guards and other officials were humane and that the contacts he did have with the other inmates were "cordial enough." "And there were smugglers, pushers, robbers, kidnappers, murderers," he pointed out. "In short, it's not a foregone conclusion that all the worst people are in jail."

The basic charge against Angelo Rizzoli was that he had misappropriated his company's funds, creating a so-called hole in the accounts of over 28 billion lire (then worth about 23 million dollars). The company was Rizzoli Editore, the largest, most powerful and supposedly richest of Italy's publishing houses, owners of the country's most prestigious daily newspaper, the *Corriere della Sera;* its most popular sporting sheet, the *Gazzetta dello Sport;* book and magazine divisions rivalled in numbers and volume of sales only by Rizzoli's chief competitor, Arnoldo Mondadori Editore; and overseas interests, including Rizzoli International, with its handsome bookstore and art gallery in midtown Manhattan. It had been generally known for some time, however, that Rizzoli Editore had been losing money in large amounts. The previous October the company had sought protection from creditors under Italy's bankruptcy laws, which called for the implementation of a court-supervised procedure of "controlled administration." The hole had come to light during a perusal of the accounts by the judicial commission appointed to look into the firm's affairs.

The statistics uncovered by the investigation were astonishing. During the previous three years, Rizzoli Editore's losses had amounted to some 300 billion lire. It owed various banks 275 billion lire, 55 percent of that amount to a single Milanese institution, the Banco Ambrosiano. The missing 28 billion lire had disappeared sometime between 1976 and 1980, with very little documentation to account for where they might have gone. Eleven billion three hundred million lire were vaguely accounted for as a personal loan to Angelo Rizzoli, but no one seemed to have any idea what might have happened to the other 17 billion. To find out, the magistrates had issued their arrest warrants.

Also taken into custody that morning were Angelo's younger brother Alberto and the company's managing director, Bruno Tassan Din, who had recently been forced to step down by the judicial commission from his post as general director, the company's chief operating officer. The three men were brought back to Milan on Saturday, February 19, and quizzed at length in the solicitor general's office.

Alberto Rizzoli defended himself vigorously during his five hours of testimony. He declared, first of all, that he had never taken part in any of the firm's administrative or financial maneuvers; his own role had been strictly that of a technician, in charge mainly of the company paper mill in Marzabotto, where he spent much of his time. "I occupied myself with operational matters," he said. He had differed profoundly, however, with the policies being pursued by his brother and Tassan Din, ever since the firm's acquisition of the *Corriere* in 1974, and had resigned in May, 1979. "I had absolutely no idea," he testified, "where the money (about 5.5 billion lire in property and Treasury certificates) came from to buy me out, when I left the business."

Angelo Rizzoli and Bruno Tassan Din were questioned for twelve hours that first Saturday, until about 10:30 P.M. They denied having stolen or mishandled funds in any way and portrayed themselves essentially as well-intentioned businessmen, who had fallen on hard times through no fault of their own. According to one of their lawyers, Gaetano Pecorella, the missing money consisted of so-called *fondi neri,* or black funds, payments made in cash under the table, mainly to evade taxation, to authors and contributors to various Rizzoli publications. The list of recipients supposedly included some of the most illustrious names in Italian letters and journalism. Pecorella also hinted that some of these black funds had found their way to representatives of various political parties, but he refused to be specific. Three days later, in fact, he denied having made any such insinuations concerning the *fondi neri* and insisted that the investigators would eventually find all of the financial operations properly accounted for; all that needed to be cleared up were the reasons for them.

It was only a matter of a few more days, however, before Angelo Rizzoli himself began to talk about the black funds. When asked by one of the examining magistrates to explain what was meant by the phrase "payments that pass through the president," he replied that it was a euphemism for "payments in black." "They pass through the president, that is, through my hands," he explained, "because they are payments destined for persons of a certain prestige, authors with

159

whom we have a relationship of trust that has to be administered at the highest company level."

"But why did Rizzoli pay in black?" the judge asked.

"You see, Your Honor, it was a necessity," the editor answered. "You either pay certain authors under the table, as they wish, or they back off and even go over to our competitors. It's a rule of the market-place."

"It's a general custom?"

"No, Your Honor, we're talking only of the top, the authors of a certain fame. Writers like Giorgio Bassani or Oriana Fallaci, they want the black. And that's the way certain big names who contribute to our journalistic titles want to be paid."

By the time Angelo Rizzoli was provisionally released from jail, thirty-seven days after his arrest, he and Tassan Din had both done a lot of talking about the *fondi neri,* which presumably accounted for the now firmly established 29-billion-lire gap in the company accounts. The list of recipients had by then greatly lengthened to include not only authors and journalists, but politicians, bureaucrats, state functiona-ries, business colleagues, financiers, and various free-lance go-betweens and influence peddlers, all of whom pocketed stacks of lire notes for promised favors. From the time Angelo Rizzoli began to show up regularly in Rome in 1975, when it had already become clear to him that his company was sinking ever deeper into debt and desper-ately needed additional financial as well as political help, he found himself paying off in all directions.

The sums ranged from relatively modest amounts, such as 50 million lire disbursed to an ex-magistrate and state official named Ugo Niutta for his presumed political connections inside the Christian Democratic Party and the 20 million lire handed to a woman named Maria Angiolillo for entré into her elegant Roman political salon, to re-ally sizeable sums of money for the flashier wheeler-dealers. Mauro Leone, the son of Italy's current president, reportedly pocketed several hundred million lire for his valuable contacts, which included such powerful international and financial guns as David Rockefeller and West Germany's Franz Josef Strauss. It also turned out that the Chris-tian Democratic, Socialist, and Social Democratic parties benefitted, at least indirectly, from Rizzoli's largesse. Outright donations in the hundreds of millions flowed out to individuals and organizations, including newspapers and publications, associated with various politicians and political groupings. Unfortunately, none of these payoffs brought relief of any kind. By 1980, the company was floundering, over 150 billion lire in debt and unable even to keep up with the interest on its existing loans. In looking back on that period, Angelo Rizzoli described his situation as that of a man held hostage by greedy bankers and politicians, who intended to cut his property up between them.

One person had no doubts as to who was to blame for the catastrophe. From his villa at Cap Ferrat, on the French Riviera, where he had been living since his retirement from the presidency of the company in 1978, Andrea Rizzoli, Angelo and Alberto's father, blamed Tassan Din. In a series of interviews with Italian journalists, he portrayed the managing director as a Borgian plotter, who had manipulated his older son into a series of disastrous business deals and whose only goal from the beginning had been to acquire control of the firm. "It is he who wrecked everything, bringing my son Angelo to ruin and to prison," he declared. He compared his policies to that of a man trying to get to Mars with a stepladder and said that he might as well have printed his own money to carry out the "lunar projects" the company had embarked on in recent years. As for Angelo, Andrea Rizzoli described him as a befuddled innocent, who had been blinded by Tassan Din's grandiloquent visions and had become as self-deluded as he. He said that he would do all a father could do in such circumstances, which was to forget the past and all the mistakes made and to stand by his son.

Few people were moved by the elder Rizzoli's distress. It was pointed out, by Angelo himself as well as the reporters covering the story, that the origins of the company's difficulties could be traced directly back to the purchase of the *Corriere* in 1974, which had been insisted upon by Andrea Rizzoli. Furthermore, even after his retirement, he had continued to draw 100 million lire a month from company funds, well into 1979, partly to support a gambling habit in the Riviera casinos. Both he and his second, much younger wife, a dashing ex-jet-setter named Liuba Rosa, were known to have been heavy losers in bouts of roulette and chemin de fer that sometimes lasted for days. Andrea Rizzoli justified his addiction by telling the writer Camilla Cederna, who had known the family for many years, that he preferred "the sickness of the green table to that of the white powder," a clear implication that he believed his older son to have been a cocaine user.

What began to fascinate everyone who had been following the story, however, was not the banal account of simple mismanagement and embezzlement that had brought about the ruin of a successful business, but the names of the participants. It had been known for months, for instance, that Rizzoli Editore had been deeply enmeshed in the subterranean maneuvering of a number of shady characters, including the bankers Michele Sindona, a Sicilian-born financier then serving a long prison sentence in the United States for having looted and caused the failure of an American bank, and Robert Calvi, the head of the Banco Ambrosiano, whose corpse had been found hanging, a possible murder victim, under a London bridge the previous June. Also involved were Licio Gelli and Umberto Ortolani, two scheming entrepreneurs who were both fugitives from Italian justice for having founded a secret Masonic lodge called Propaganda Due (known as the P2, for short), through which they had plotted and finagled to acquire control of banks, businesses, and publications, with the possible long-range goal of actually overthrowing the state.

The names of both Angelo Rizzoli and Tassan Din had cropped up on the P2 membership roster, as had those of well-known politicians, civil servants, members of Parliament, military and police officers, jurists, bankers, industrialists, and other prominent citizens. It was reported that the Vatican was deeply involved, especially through its Istituto di Opere Religiose (IOR), the Holy See's investment arm, which was headed by Monsignor Paul Marcinkus, an American priest known to be close to Pope John Paul himself. To lend a touch of glamour to the unfolding drama, the names of celebrated TV personalities and movie stars were also mentioned, including, of course, Eleonora Giorgi.

The scandal spread like an oil spill, fed week after week by new revelations and the sort of dramatic happenings only a popular novelist could have dreamed up. It confirmed what so many Italians have suspected for years—that the interests of many politicians and private speculators are one, essentially aimed at corrupting and subverting democratic institutions and bringing into power a right-wing totalitarian form of government. The involvement of Rizzoli Editore in the vast plot also struck many Milanese as tragic, not because it was an attempt by special interests to take over the country's leading publishing house and newspaper, but because it represented the bankruptcy of a whole system and, even more important, the betrayal of an old Milanese dream. Within that context, the saga of the rise and fall of the Rizzoli dynasty over a span of only three generations achieved for many the status of a folk epic.

THE MILANESE believe that their city's primacy and commercial success is due largely to their own character, which could have been invented by Horatio Alger. The Milanese traditionally see themselves as dedicated toilers, who are in love with their work and are smarter and more innovative than everyone else. It has little to do with blood or history, but is simply the result of something magical in the air, as if Milan itself were the catalyst. It has often been pointed out that many of the city's great fortunes were made either by humble immigrants or local poor people, who worked their way up from scratch. Milan, in fact, regards itself as the only place in Italy for a man to build himself a better mousetrap; it will inevitably reward his enterprise with fame and money.

No one fitted more snugly into this complacent vision than the first Angelo Rizzoli, the founder of Rizzoli Editore. He was born in Milan on October 31, 1889, and spent ten years of his childhood, until 1905, in an orphanage, where he learned to become a typographer. From the age of sixteen, he worked at various factory jobs, then caught on as an apprentice and delivery boy at a local printing plant. In 1909, he made a down payment of 500 lire, almost all the money he had been able to save, to a German salesman for a secondhand press, promising to pay the balance of 6,000 lire over a period of five years. He borrowed a pushcart and went himself to the railroad station to bring his machine, a Victoria Dresden, home. "I was twenty years old and I owned something," he later recalled. "My working capital was 100 lire and two healthy arms. I spent 200 lire renting some space in Via Monte di Pietà, near Piazza della Scala. My private office was a somewhat modified water closet. I was the firm's boss, the worker, and the messenger boy. In this way, in 1909, my lucky career as an industrialist began."

The reference to luck was typical of him. "To make a fortune, you need good fortune," he liked to say. Another of his favorite aphorisms was, "You have to know how to be forgiven by luck," and he was celebrated for his legendary *"la fortuna."* Actually, *la fortuna,* pure and simple, had little to do with his success. It was once analyzed by Indro Montanelli, in an article on the editor in the *Corriere della Sera.* "The luck of Rizzoli is his common sense and his absolute faith in whatever he is doing," Montanelli wrote. "Owing to his faith, he was able to launch enterprises that would have discouraged a Hercules. . . . And owing to his common sense, he established these enterprises without ever losing his shirt. This is the famous luck of Rizzoli, to which he often refers with humility." He began as a commercial printer, but by 1970, the year of his death, the Rizzoli publishing empire was worth over 100 million dollars. The original Victoria Dresden press still stands today, in the lobby of the Rizzoli headquarters in Milan, where the old man installed it as a monument to himself.

Like many self-made men, Angelo Rizzoli used to boast of his lowly beginnings and limited schooling, but he clearly also had a great editor's nose for hiring the best journalists and writers for his publications. He was not at all reluctant either to explain to anyone who asked him how he had obtained his success and especially how he went about financing his ventures. "I've always been my own banker," he once told Camilla Cederna. "And I've continued to expand without ever selling any of my private property, without ever making debts, without ever having to bend my back to anybody." A short, stout man with a large bald head, heavy black eyebrows, and an animated forceful manner, he liked to dress in white, sucked often on a plastic mentholated cigarette holder, and kept his accounts on various current projects scribbled on bits of paper and matchbook covers in his pockets. He was a genial and fascinating eccentric, who was nicknamed by his employees the "Cumenda," short in Milanese dialect for "Commendatore," an honorary title of respect.

He was also understandably an intimidating figure to his only son, Andrea, as well as to his own grandsons, all of whom worked at the firm while old Angelo was still on the scene. (Andrea's sister Pinuccia and daughter Anna never took an active part in the management of the company, which from the beginning was run as a typically Italian patriarchy.) He kept Andrea on a tight leash and frequently denigrated his abilities in public, while also disapproving of his second marriage and gambling habit. Angelo, too, was a frequenter of the casinos, but he was a smart, tough player who often won and knew when to quit, whereas Andrea almost always lost and never seemed able to walk away from the table during his worst losing streaks. Toward the end of his life, when Angelo was frequently asked whether he ever intended to retire and step aside to allow his only son a chance to show what he could do, the old man liked to say, "He's too young to take command and too old to inherit it."

Angelo Rizzoli died at the age of eighty-one on September 24, 1970. Andrea was fifty-six at the time and had already had two heart attacks. He was spending too many of his days on the Riviera, where he and Liuba Rosa continued to gamble heavily and lose. The previous Christmas, the family had gathered as usual at the Cumenda's house in Milan for the traditional festivities. The old man had begun to feel his years and had for some time expressed a fear of death. ("Ahi, ahi," he was reported to have exclaimed, when he was told of one of Andrea's heart attacks, "it's a warning bell for me.") At Christmas dinner, with the family gathered around the table, Angelo delivered his usual little closing speech. "This is perhaps the last time we are together at Christmas and I am here to toast with you," he reportedly said. "The only thing I regret is that I built up this business like a jewel and in five years you will bring it to ruin."

THE GREAT unrealized dream of the elder Rizzoli's long career was his desire to own and publish a major daily newspaper. He had discussed it frequently all during the sixties and had put out feelers toward the *Corriere della Sera,* which was then owned by the Crespi family of Milan. Rebuffed, Rizzoli then planned to bring out his own newspaper, under the title of *Oggi* (Today). He bought printing presses in the United States, hired several top journalists and even made a few trial runs. Unfortunately, he couldn't make his figures add up. One of the little slips of paper he carried around in his pockets contained detailed notations on all costs, which the old man frequently consulted and periodically brought up to date. Many of his colleagues and outside observers believed he would take the plunge, if only to cap his glorious career. Most newspapers in Italy lose money and are propped up either by political parties or rich private interests, largely out of vanity. Few people believed that Angelo Rizzoli, at this stage of his long career, could be intimidated by the prospect of losing money. "The Cumenda is the only one who has the courage to do it," one of his employees told a reporter. "He isn't afraid of the political and financial gamble."

The people who knew the old tycoon best, however, doubted that he would go through with it. One of his oldest friends, Raffaele Mattioli, who also owned a publishing venture and was the chairman of the board of the Banca Commerciale Italiana, Italy's largest private bank, predicted he would back off. "He achieved everything he set out to do, but he knows he can't achieve this thing," he said, "and he's too smart to risk a failure." When the figures refused persistently to promise him a profit, Angelo Rizzoli did, indeed, abandon his dream. He converted *Oggi* into a picture weekly full of gossip and pop reportage that quickly began to sell in the hundreds of thousands of copies (a circulation of half a million was considered excellent in Italy) and made the company a great deal of money.

After Angelo, Sr., died, the company continued to flourish for a while under Andrea and his two sons, both of whom, along with Nicola Carraro, their first cousin, took an active hand in the business. "We have to let the young people do things now," Andrea Rizzoli, who by then was only intermittently in his office, told a colleague. One of the new ventures was the launching in the early seventies of the Italian edition of *Playboy,* under a contract with the American publisher in Chicago that turned out to be unexpectedly costly to Rizzoli Editore. It should have been a portent of things to come, but the losses of this venture initially amounted to only several million dollars and no one paid much attention to such a minor fiasco.

The beginning of the firm's real troubles can be dated July 17, 1974, when it finally acquired the *Corriere della Sera,* by buying the roughly two-thirds of the stock then owned by the Crespis and a group of investors headed by a financier named Angelo Moratti, for about 44 billion lire. The overall price for complete ownership was about 65 billion lire, but the rest of the stock was in the hands of the Agnellis, the enormously wealthy Turinese proprietors of the Gruppo Fiat, which includes the famous automobile company. The Agnellis seemed to be in no hurry to sell, but Andrea Rizzoli insisted on arranging to buy them out as well. Pinuccia Carraro objected strongly to what seemed to her an unnecessary outlay of funds and she, too, asked to be bought out, which Andrea did, thus effectively removing the Carraro branch from the company. Everyone involved recalls that it was Andrea who was absolutely obsessed on going through with the deal at any cost. "It was his revenge against the patriarch who had frequently humiliated him," a reporter named Alberto Mazzuca later wrote, in the Milanese daily *Il Giornale Nuovo*. "The foundations for our ruin had been set," Angelo Rizzoli, who was then only thirty, commented twelve years later.

The internal finances of the *Corriere* were far more precarious than the Rizzolis had anticipated. Not only was the newspaper itself losing a 1.5 billion lire a month, but the parent company that controlled it, along with several other losing editorial ventures, was in disastrous shape. "No sooner had we set foot in there than we found ourselves confronted by a gap of 40 billion lire," Angelo Rizzoli later recalled, bringing the actual purchase price to over 100 billion lire. They had also expected to lose about 4.5 billion lire that first year, but discovered that they were actually being drained of money at four times that rate. The Rizzolis were forced to turn to outside financing. "We ignored one of the principles our grandfather had preached, the one of never getting into debt," Angelo Rizzoli commented.

His father had counted on financial help from a well-known but highly controversial industrialist named Eugenio Cefis, who was then president of Montedison, a huge private conglomerate with investments in nearly every sector of the national economy, and who had impressive political connections inside the ruling Christian Democratic Party. Cefis had strongly urged Rizzoli to buy the *Corriere* and promised to assume half the interest costs, estimated at about 20 billion lire a year, on the *Corriere*'s annual deficit. Montedison itself, however, was losing a great deal of money. By 1976, Cefis had been forced out and the promised aid never materialized. Angelo Rizzoli eventually came to believe that Cefis had never had any intention of sharing costs, but that his whole purpose was to weaken Rizzoli Editore and put the firm at the mercy of the conservative political interests he favored. The Rizzolis were, therefore, forced to turn to the banks, which, as inflation mounted, had begun by then to charge usurious rates of interest.

And as the situation continued to deteriorate over the ensuing months, the Rizzolis also decided that they needed political allies, who would be able to intercede for them with the financial institutions that had begun to squeeze them. It was a fatal mistake, most observers pointed out, because the only stake the country's politicians could possibly have in any editorial operation was to take it over or to make it a sounding board for the political lines they favored.

It was during this precarious period that the name of Bruno Tassan Din began to emerge as a powerful figure inside the company. He had been hired originally by young Angelo Rizzoli, with his father's approval, in September, 1973 as general and financial manager. He had worked at Montedison and had excellent references, especially as a prodigious worker. A tall, thin, silver-haired man of about forty with a long, vulpine face, he toiled fourteen to sixteen hours a day, always at full speed. He made an immediate impression inside Rizzoli Editore, which had until then been a fairly calm, well-organized place to work, with a number of managers, department heads, and editors who had been there for many years. Most of the company officers had been against the purchase of the *Corriere* and complained openly and constantly about it. "But they didn't propose anything constructive," Angelo Rizzoli recently recalled. "They limited themselves to tearing out their hair. They were annihilated, dismayed. The company had fallen into a sort of paralysis. The only one who gave an impression of activity, of not giving up, of hanging tough, of knowing how to react was this very Tassan Din."

He always seemed to be confidently in charge, bristling with ideas and projects, and his support reassured Angelo Rizzoli, who prided himself on his editorial abilities but admittedly knew little about financial matters and had had no experience in politics. The two men became inseparable and began to move together through the Byzantine corridors of power in Roman political and financial circles, where they were sometimes referred to as Cric and Croc, two cartoon figures (one tall and thin, the other short and fat) similar to our own Mutt and Jeff.

Basically, Tassan Din's tactic was to become friends with "the people who count," which to him meant also buying their friendship and support, just as they had set about buying the loyalty of their authors and contributors by paying them in *fondi neri*. Unfortunately, they found Rome to be a far more difficult and costly operation than they had anticipated. And as the pressure for additional sources of financing mounted month to month, they discovered increasing resistance from the financial institutions they approached, which, they began to feel, had been orchestrated by the politicians in power. In fact, Rizzoli later accused Emilio Colombo, the minister of the treasury, among others, of blocking every attempt to arrange reasonable financing for their beleaguered operation.

As it proved more difficult to obtain credit on almost any terms and it became increasingly clear to both men that there were political forces arrayed against them, they began to spend most of their time in Rome in an effort to find out exactly what was expected of them. "It was a traumatic, chilling experience," Angelo Rizzoli remembered. "I didn't know the Roman political world. Traditionally, Rizzoli had always kept its distance from it, and I was used to working in an environment of industrialists, where yes was yes, no was no, white was white. And instead we found ourselves talking with these Medusas, who when they said yes it was no, when they said white it was anything but white." He did not find himself alone in this situation. Rome was full of frustrated Milanese businessmen fluttering about the confines of ministerial reception rooms in an effort to get a hearing from some influential power broker. It was an old story to the older hands at the game, who have always blamed Rome for whatever goes wrong in Milan. "Politics is a Roman industry, and the only one they have," a Milanese journalist once said. "We make the money, and they steal it."

On December 22, 1975, with an additional payment of over 20 billion lire looming to complete the deal for the Agnelli interests in the *Corriere,* Angelo Rizzoli and Tassan Din went to a meeting in the Roman office of a promoter named Umberto Ortolani. Ortolani had begun his career as a stationmaster in Viterbo, but had made a small name for himself in the 1950s as a wheeler-dealer and investor with useful contacts inside the Christian Democratic Party. He had spent most of the sixties in Argentina and other parts of South America, where he had acquired interests in a number of banks, then resurfaced in Italy during the early seventies. He also had highly placed friends inside the Vatican, was a Knight of Malta, and seemed to know everyone. In fact, he claimed to be an old friend of Andrea Rizzoli's and had been entrusted a few years earlier with selling some resort hotels the Rizzoli family had built on the island of Ischia.

Also present at that meeting was Licio Gelli, whom Angelo Rizzoli had never even heard of and who looked, a portly man dressed all in gray, like the ex-mattress salesman and small-town clothing manufacturer he had once been. Gelli had also spent much time in Argentina, apparently done very well there, and enjoyed dual citizenship. He told Angelo Rizzoli that he knew of the company's business interests in Argentina and said, "If you have any problems, you must know that in Argentina I can do a lot." Ortolani assured Cric and Croc that Gelli's influence and power were not limited to Argentina. "Gelli can make useful, important contacts for you." It was he, in fact, who subsequently introduced the two men to Roberto Calvi.

One of the many strange aspects of this connection is that it should have originated at a meeting held in Rome. The home branch of Calvi's Banco Ambrosiano was in Milan, only a few blocks from Angelo Rizzoli's house. The editor had, in fact, already tried several times to contact the banker, but had always been rebuffed. "He shut the door in my face," is the way Rizzoli recalled it. The only way to get to Calvi was apparently through Ortolani and Gelli, who received a fee of 7 billion lire from Rizzoli Editore for their trouble.

The Banco Ambrosiano, which was known to have close ties to the Vatican, now began to extend the necessary credit. The publishing house's new allies began to move in all directions. Through a series of convoluted, barely legal stock manipulations and loans, Rizzoli Editore acquired the necessary capital to maintain an illusion at least of solvency. Instead of trying to pay off its obligations, however, the company immediately embarked on a frenetic program of investments with these borrowed funds in various dubious ventures in Italy and abroad. It purchased shares in strange little banks and holding companies in countries such as Luxembourg and Panama, where capital seemed to flow in and out without being subjected to annoying government controls. Rizzoli Editore also acquired other publications, even set about launching a brand-new tabloid called *L'Occhio* (The Eye). "No one does anything for nothing," Tassan Din later told a reporter, and he was also heard to declare at the time, "With money, I've discovered, one succeeds in obtaining everything."

As far as Rizzoli Editore itself was concerned, however, the money flung so recklessly in all directions might as well have been interred in an Etruscan tomb. Billions of lire, for instance, were lavished through Gelli in Argentina, with no apparent return. Every investment tended to disappear in clouds of promissory notes and stock options. Gelli, one of whose favorite assurances to his colleagues was, "I know everything, I can do everything," seemed intent on draining the firm of its last lira. Tassan Din, however, remained unperturbed and acted, as usual, on the theory he claimed to have mastered during his years at Montedison, namely that the ultimate winner in the game was always the investor who made the most debts, "because the inflation will pay him off."

Recently, when Angelo Rizzoli was asked by an interviewer how he and Tassan Din could have put so much faith in a trio of such equivocal characters, the editor pointed out that at the time no one even suspected them of being anything but respectable citizens and highly reputable businessmen. "Gelli and Ortolani were received by everybody," the editor explained. "They spoke with everyone, they were revered by everyone—industrialists, managers, and politicians at the highest level." And the names bandied about were impressive, including most of the leading financial and political figures of the day. As for Calvi, he was regarded by many as a brilliant investment banker, a man who would by himself one day revolutionize the Italian banking industry. Gianni Agnelli, the epitome of the suave international entrepreneur, asked to be introduced to him, though, as a true *magnifico,* he was put off by the softspoken banker's diffident personal manner and his habit of talking while staring intently at the points of his shoes. Even after Calvi was exposed as a common swindler, who had looted his own financial institutions for his personal gain (much in the manner of Michele Sindona, whose protégé he had once been), a number of leading political figures continued to defend him. When he was arrested, Flaminio Piccoli, then the leader of the Christian Democratic Party, was scandalized that a Catholic banker could be treated in such a disrespectful way.

IN EARLY July, 1977, Rizzoli Editore finally completed its transaction for the purchase of the *Corriere* by paying the Agnellis a total

of 22.4 billion lire for their third. A week later, it was announced that
the company had received an additional capitalization of 25.5 billion
lire, apparently in the form of a loan extended by the Banco
Ambrosiano, acting in concert with several other financial institutions. The appearance was that of a perfectly legitimate financial operation, in the form of a loan guaranteed by the family-owned stock of
the publishing house. What actually happened was that the Rizzolis
had effectively lost control of their company. To secure the needed capitalization to keep going, they had actually sold the 80 percent of the
stock they owned in Italy, retaining only the right at some future time
to buy it back—with interest, of course. The remaining 20 percent of
the stock seems to have been shifted about between various foreign
and Italian banks, in a series of suspect transactions that would later
lead to a charge against Angelo Rizzoli of having illegally exported
capital abroad.

The appearance offered to the world was that of a publishing
house in serious disarray, certainly, but which had succeeded in acquiring additional financing and was backed by several well-known, reputable institutions. The reality was quite different. The Banco
Ambrosiano itself, it turned out, had actually only played a part in an
elaborate charade. It was Calvi himself, acting in concert with Gelli
and Ortolani, who had become the real owners of Rizzoli Editore.
(Ortolani, in fact, had become a member of the board of directors.)
And behind Calvi and his friends loomed the Istituto di Opere Religiose, which, it would eventually become clear, had financed the entire
operation. In other words, the largest publishing house in Italy and its
most important, supposedly independent newspaper had fallen into
the hands of a group of swindlers with totalitarian political ambitions,
who were being backed in their maneuvers by the main investment
arm of the Roman Catholic Church.

Nevertheless, Angelo Rizzoli apparently continued to believe for
some months that he would somehow one day be able to recapture
control of his inheritance. He had counted heavily on Tassan Din, only
to discover, however, that his chief officer now appeared to be playing
a complicated game of his own. "It was then I realized that Tassan Din
no longer answered to me," he said, "but to them." Whenever Tassan
Din needed Rizzoli's consent or signature for any reason, the editor recalled, he would make a great show of complicity, as if he and the

Rizzolis were united on a policy of action, whereas the orders were actually coming from Calvi and his people. When the editor tried to contact the banker directly, he was never able to do so, but was always informed that he would have to operate through Tassan Din. Alarmed at last, and with the support of his father and the board members still loyal to the Rizzolis, the editor made a serious attempt late in the year to fire his general director, only to be indirectly informed by Calvi a few hours before the scheduled board meeting that any attempt to get rid of Tassan Din would mean cancellation of the existing financial arrangement. As this would have meant the immediate collapse of the company, Angelo Rizzoli was forced into what he accurately called "a shameful retreat."

The details of all these maneuvers, and the extent of the incredibly convoluted plot in which the Rizzolis now found themselves enmeshed, began to come to light in 1979, after the temporary disappearance of Michele Sindona. The banker was a fugitive from both American and Italian justice, but it began to be hinted that he had powerful political allies working behind the scenes in Italy to save him. After he had resurfaced (he claimed to have been a terrorist kidnap victim), been arrested, and brought to trial in the United States for the looting in the early seventies of the Franklin National Bank, on Long Island, the Italian police, aided by the FBI, were eventually able to reconstruct his movements. They discovered that one of Sindona's main contacts in Palermo had frequently travelled to the Tuscan town of Arezzo, where he had been the guest of Licio Gelli at the Villa Vanda, the clothing manufacturer's country estate. When the authorities, armed with search warrants, raided the villa and Gelli's private office during the winter of 1981, they found a filing cabinet containing a list of the names of everyone belonging to Propaganda Due, as well as many other documents concerning public and private financial speculations, supposedly secret government investigations, dossiers on criminal cases, and other evidence implicating all sorts of prominent people in what appeared to be a scheme to take over the government. The ensuing uproar did, in fact, cause the administration headed by Prime Minister Arnaldo Forlani, a Christian Democrat, to fall. It also precipitated the investigations that are still going on and will probably continue for years, since no scandal involving well-known, highly visible public personalities is ever quite satisfactorily laid to rest in Italy. It will finally perish behind a great cloud of conflicting documents and an uproar of endless testimony.

Shortly after the P2 list became public knowledge, Gelli and Ortolani fled the country, probably to South America. Gelli was actually caught and incarcerated for a time in Switzerland, but he managed somehow to escape, on August 11, 1983, before he could be extradited to Italy. Most Italian observers feel this coup could not have been engineered without the connivance of the Swiss authorities, who had no interest in having their own secret international banking operations publicly aired in a court of law, especially abroad.

Roberto Calvi was arrested on May 20, 1981, along with six of his associates, for having allegedly smuggled huge sums of money out of the country and looted his own financial institutions to the tune of over 200 billion lire, in much the same way as Sindona. Basically, it was charged that he had used investors' funds for his own financial speculations and transactions, many of them in violation of Italy's banking and currency laws. He was brought to trial in Milan on June 10, convicted on July 20, and sentenced to four years' imprisonment and a fine of 16 billion lire. Almost immediately, pending an appeal, he was set free on bail, though forced to relinquish his passport. Incredibly, he also quickly reassumed his position at the Ambrosiano, as if nothing had happened and with the full support of his board of directors. He continued to operate until June 10, 1982, when he disappeared from his Roman apartment. His body was found ten days later, hanging from a scaffolding under Blackfriars Bridge in London. Although the English authorities at first declared the banker to have been a suicide, hardly anyone in Italy, including his wife, believed that he had killed himself, and the English expressed serious doubts of their own. His death has remained unsolved, another in the many loose threads the scandal has left dangling.

ON JUNE 1, 1983, Andrea Rizzoli died of congestive heart failure in Nice. He was sixty-nine years old and, as one commentator pointed out in his obituary of him, he had "lived fifty-six years of his existence crushed by the unrestrained and dominant personality of his father." He was blamed by observers for having opened the door to disaster in insisting on the purchase of the *Corriere della Sera*. He had been rich, but unhappy and mostly unlucky—in both his professional and personal life. His gambling had brought him psychic relief, but at a cost that is still under investigation. Not long ago, it was revealed that in 1978 he had reportedly lost about 30 billion lire in a single emporium, the Casino Ruhl of Nice. The casino was apparently closely linked to the Ambrosiano Overseas of Nassau, another of Calvi's foreign agencies. The suspicion is that somebody close to Calvi engineered Andrea Rizzoli's horrendous losing streak, in order to force him to knuckle under to Calvi's demands.

Less than a month later, on June 29, 1983, Angelo Rizzoli was again arrested, under a warrant issued by the same magistrates investigating the Calvi case and all its ramifications. Once again the police showed up very early in the morning at the editor's house and this time took him to the San Vittore Prison in Milan, where almost at once his interrogation began. The main charge against him this time was that he had illegally exported funds, in the form of 26 million dollars' worth of Rizzoli shares paid for by the Banco Ambrosiano and routed illegally out of the country through Switzerland. He was also accused of having helped to orchestrate a fraudulent bankruptcy, designed to keep creditors at bay while spiriting assets of Rizzoli Editore abroad.

This time the editor and Bruno Tassan Din did not present a united front in defense of their actions. A few days after his arrest, Rizzoli was taken to the prison in Piacenza, where his ex-administrator was being held, and the two men were set face to face for about seven hours and asked to testify to the various charges against them. Each accused the other of wrongdoing and the editor denied having benefitted in any way from the transaction. By the time it took place, he pointed out, he had effectively lost control of his firm and had become a victim of the interests Tassan Din now represented. He accused his ex-colleague of having himself exported capital abroad and of having enriched himself in the process, the very maneuvers of which he stood charged, mainly on the statements given to the magistrates earlier by Tassan Din himself. After several days of such conflicting testimony, Angelo Rizzoli was transferred again, this time to Lodi, a small town south of Milan with a prison popularly referred to as a "jail for gentlemen."

About four months later, on October 27, Angelo Rizzoli was released a second time. The bail of 200 million lire was put up largely by his mother, who was forced to pledge her entire personal art collection to raise it. The charges against him remained and the investigation was still going on, but he was deemed not to be "a social danger" by his judges and allowed to go home.

Since that time the editor has spoken freely about his business affairs and personal troubles. His wife has left him and also given out interviews, which have shed further light on Rizzoli's troubled past. He portrays himself, essentially, as a man brought to penury by the calumnies and schemings of others, especially Bruno Tassan Din. About the only aspect of their joint past the two men still agree on is that various Christian Democratic and Socialist politicians, working behind the scenes with Gelli, Ortolani, Calvi, and the Vatican, had a great deal to do with the ruin and collapse of Rizzoli Editore. The firm remained for months in public receivership until it was eventually acquired by private investors and set back on its financial feet.

For Angelo Rizzoli himself the game is over, but he predicted quite accurately how some of the players in it would fare. Gelli, Ortolani, Paul Marcinkus, and a number of others involved in the caper managed to escape pretty much unscathed from the rubble of his company's collapse. He reminded one interviewer, too, that his nemesis Tassan Din, according to the magistrates who questioned both of them, had somehow managed to secrete about 70 billion lire in various foreign bank accounts, a sum, the editor sarcastically observed, he could certainly not have saved out of his salary. "I'm finished," Angelo Rizzoli said. "After a few years in prison, he will escape abroad to enjoy the money he has accumulated."

A frequently recurring theme in Milanese life is that of crime rewarded. The city has always had the highest rate of violent lawlessness in the nation and has sometimes been referred to in the media as "the Chicago of Italy." Most of the political scandals, of course, originate out of Rome and the south in general, but Milan is also the city of the great business swindles, not the least of which have been the Calvi and Rizzoli affairs. Criminals have traditionally been regarded here as fascinating and often romantic figures, as in the work of Carlo Bertolazzi and Piero Chiara, two well-known local writers, who have immortalized the doings of the so-called Milanese *mala,* or underworld.

One of Chiara's favorite characters, whom he names Prezioso Bonalumi and whom he affectionately recalls from the early 1930s as a good friend and great man in general, liked to sum up his view of life for him. "The world," he used to say, "is half for sale and half to buy, but all of it to steal."

CHAPTER
TWELVE

THE MODEL
AND THE PLAYBOY

WHEN AN AMERICAN fashion model named Terry Broome shot and killed an Italian playboy in his apartment early one morning in June of 1984, a lot of people in Milan, where the crime took place, were shocked but not surprised. Francesco D'Alessio, the victim, had a reputation in his circle for violence, and it was well known that he had been publicly rude and obnoxious to his murderer on a number of occasions. As for Terry herself, she had a history of violence in her own past as well as an ugly residue of broken dreams and smashed hopes to sustain it.

At the time of the killing, most people had no way of knowing anything about either Francesco or Terry, until they began to read about them in the press after the murder. The act itself, however, seemed to many the perfectly natural outcome of a way of life the city has fostered, gossiped about, and glamorized for years—a nightly fandango of fast cars, pretty girls, easy money, and cocaine. It's a wonder, some observers have noted, that it took so long for this ingrown fringe world, where scandal-mongering passes for casual conversation, to explode into the headlines.

In addition to being the industrial capital of Italy, Milan ranks with Paris and New York as a hub of world fashion. Its modeling agencies and photo studios attract young women from around the globe and especially from America, all seeking fame and money. "They arrive here used to eating hamburgers made out of ground bones, and they're catapulted into luxury restaurants," declared a popular hairdresser named Franco Battaglia, through whose midtown establishment dozens of these hopefuls passed every week. "From Coca-Cola they go to champagne, from the occasional sniff of cocaine they find themselves surrounded by trays full of the white powder. They arrive shy, naive, and afraid. After a month of this life, they've already learned how the world works, and they're completely changed. But it's not their fault. It's these rich characters who ruin them, delude them, promise them dazzling careers."

Many of these young women have never been abroad before. They arrive in the city with a few hundred dollars in their purses, a promise of work from some agency or other, an introduction or two to a well-known photographer or art director, and much hope. The agencies, especially those with offices in New York, sometimes pay for their plane tickets and loan them enough money to stay alive for a month or two while they're out making rounds.

If a girl gets lucky, the money is good, ranging from two hundred to a thousand dollars a day. Equally important, she can build up her portfolio, eventually move on to Paris or New York, where she can become an international cover girl, fashion star, and very rich. And what lies beyond? Why not Hollywood, true celebrity, millions? The dreams are real, at least.

The first few weeks in town are crucial. If a model can get herself hired for a fashion layout or an advertising campaign, she begins to earn a little money, out of which she has to repay the agency and keep herself alive. More than alive, she has to look all the time and everywhere just as beautiful and alluring as possible. And she has to go on making the rounds, get herself known, not only inside the studios, ad agencies, television-producing offices, and magazines but in the party circles, nightclubs, restaurants, luxury apartments, and country villas of the powerful, the well-connected, and the merely rich.

Some few women can and do succeed merely on their extraordinary good looks and talent, but most can't. They need help, they need connections, the kind that can get them the break they want—an introduction to a top photographer, a meeting with a powerful director, an audition for a TV commercial. And they also need support, money, a little flattery, a hand to hold in the dark. "They know we're alone like dogs here," a twenty-one-year-old model from Houston named Rochelle Redfield told a reporter shortly after the D'Alessio murder, "without roots, far away from our friends, and that their company is the only one offered us."

The available men are cast from a classic mold. They all have plenty of money but are usually not the ones who made it. Francesco D'Alessio's father, Carlo, is an industrialist and the proprietor of Italy's most successful thoroughbred racing stable. Francesco's closest friends were Guido Borghi, whose family makes refrigerators; Carlo Cabassi, the brother of a powerful financier; and Umberto Caproni, heir to an airplane business. These typical *figli di papa,* or "daddy's kids," consider any evening wasted in which they fail to show up at some fashionable gathering or watering hole without at least one long-legged beauty, preferably foreign, on their arm. "It's not by chance that Francesco was married to a model, courted only models, spent the last night of his life with a model, and was killed by a model," an acquaintance of his observed.

Meeting the new arrivals on the scene has never been much of a problem for these men. One way is to hang around a midtown residence hotel called the Principessa Clotilde—better known everywhere in the fashion world as the Princess Clitoris—most of whose 220 rooms are rented out either to the women themselves or permanently occupied by the hunters. The latter are hard to resist, even if their advances tend to be a little crude. "I was sitting on a sofa at somebody's party, talking to a girlfriend," one ex-model recalled, "when some little fat guy sat down next to me. He's looking me up and down, and then he pulls out his checkbook and shows me he's got millions in the bank. He sticks it back into his pocket and says, 'I'm tired of this. Want to go to my place?' Then he asks me if I've been there before. So many girls come and go that he can't even remember."

Usually, the wooing is a little less brutal and accompanied by masses of flowers and small gifts. Some of the girls move in with these men, a few even get married, but most soon find themselves being passed around until they discover they've become used goods and the phone stops ringing. Yet given the dreary alternatives, it's understandable they would let themselves be whisked into this corrupt life. "I never gave a damn about hanging around that world," a twenty-six-year-old model from Chicago told a reporter, "but I can understand my colleagues who are blinded by those siren calls."

She went on to describe a daily life made up of hours wasted on useless interviews and auditions, bad treatment at the hands of photographers, contempt from fashion editors. And all the time the obsession to be perfect, to stay thin, the fear of putting on that deadly extra ounce. "And then, when the day is over, the four walls of your hotel room. Not even the comfort of a movie, because you don't speak the language. No possibility of meeting people outside the fashion world. Loneliness, squalor, boredom." Obviously, it's much more fun to be wined, dined, and showered with presents, even if there may be a small carnal price to pay at the end of the evening.

What most of the women caught up in this self-indulgent game fail to realize is that the rules are largely dictated by the Mafia, which secretly owns not only many of the nightclubs and restaurants they frequent but some of the hotels they stay in. Milan, with its hordes of flashy entrepreneurs, has become celebrated as the crime capital of Italy. Several local commentators have compared it to Chicago in the 1920s and '30s, the only difference being that today's gangsters are making their fortunes mostly in the narcotics trade. Through the city's streets and piazzas flow what one columnist has called a "river of heroin," and drugs of all kinds are available practically on any corner.

One of D'Alessio's acquaintances from the club-and-disco scene was Joe Maserati, a hood reported to be the king of the cocaine traffickers. And the fact is that the story of Terry Broome and her victim is also a tale of cocaine addiction. "I have nothing against the sad little girl who fired the shots," Cheryl Stevens, D'Alessio's widow, testified in court, "but with this miserable world that destroyed my marriage. . . . Cocaine drove [my husband] crazy. Once, when he'd taken too much, he tried to rape and strangle me, he who at the start of our relationship was so sweet and gentle."

By the time Terry Broome and Francesco D'Alessio met in the spring of 1984, they were both living on the edge of catastrophe, united in their little dance of death by their mutual desperation. Terry was twenty-six, with a long history of failure already behind her. For her, the Milan adventure was another in a series of misguided attempts to haul herself out of a pit and achieve success in a world for which she had few qualifications. One of five children, she was raised on various military bases all over the United States and grew up envying her younger sister Donna, who was prettier and more popular than she. Terry was terrified of her father, Bill, a career air force sergeant who raised his kids as if they were a combat platoon and used to knock them around. "He threw us from wall to wall and punched us like we were big men," she remembers. Terry was, in fact, his favorite victim.

At fifteen, she ran away, was hitchhiking in South Carolina when picked up by a couple of bikers and raped. Then the man she approached for help near a local bus station also attacked her, but this time, though nearly hysterical, she managed to fight him off. Her father's reaction was that she probably deserved whatever had happened to her.

She tried to escape again at eighteen by marrying a high-school beau, but the union quickly failed. Donna, meanwhile, had moved to New York and was already launched on a successful modeling career. Terry joined her there but couldn't find much work. She was a little too tall, a little too gangly, and her freckled, irregular features didn't photograph as well as her sister's. She drifted into a party circuit of drugs and alcohol. "I was drinking maybe a bottle of Scotch a day," she recalls.

In 1979, she followed Donna to Paris, where everything at first was "marvelous, fabulous, divine." After a few weeks, however, Terry found herself once again tagging around after her sister and finding no work. She thought she'd become known, but everybody knew her only as Donna's sister.

She fled back to New York and, in 1980, tried to kill herself. Finally, she returned to her family in Columbia, South Carolina. There, helped by her mother, she fought to break her habits, but her old acquaintances would telephone from New York and she would go up on visits and fall into booze and cocaine again. Nevertheless, despite a number of such setbacks, she did manage to pull herself together and save enough money to rejoin Donna, this time in Milan, for one more try at modeling.

Terry arrived in the city on April 20, 1984, with about a thousand dollars in cash in her purse, which was snatched by a pickpocket the very next day in the subway. Suddenly destitute, she became totally dependent on her sister and moved into her apartment. But Donna was deeply involved with a rich businessman named Giorgio Santambrogio and couldn't cope with Terry's disorderly intrusion into her life. "I used to spend days cleaning up her messes, putting things back in place," Donna explained in an interview. Eventually, she moved Terry into the Principessa Clotilde, where she was immediately snapped up by a thirty-eight-year-old playboy named Claudio Caccia and introduced to the city's extravagant nightlife.

Caccia took Terry to all the best places—the Caffè Roma, the Plastique, the Vogue, and the Nepentha, the last everybody's favorite late-night hangout in the shadow of the curlicued Gothic spires of Milan's great cathedral. In these hot spots, where the cocaine provided by the Mafia is passed around on little trays and everybody sniffs, Terry quickly became hooked again but didn't think she was in trouble. Whereas Donna and her boyfriend would show up in this milieu only occasionally and then merely to have a drink or two before moving on, Terry became a regular. Her days were spent hoping for jobs that never materialized, her nights being taken from one place to another, passed from one bed to the next and always high on coke. Still, she had convinced herself she'd made it. "If I don't get the success I expect, I'll content myself with a husband," she told a friend.

She even thought she had finally met just such a man in a jeweler named Giorgio Rotti. He had a shop on the fashionable Via Manzoni and a pied-à-terre at the Princess Clitoris. Chunky and hairy, with a big nose, he was not good looking, but at least he treated her well. He gave her a gold necklace, a ring, an expensive watch, and he drove her around in a Mercedes with a telephone in it. He also used drugs. "Sometimes, he'd drive holding the steering wheel between his knees while he sniffed cocaine," Terry later testified. Nevertheless, he seemed to be genuinely smitten by her and even introduced her to his parents, a sure sign in Italy that he was serious about her. In early June, Terry moved in with Rotti. "I can't believe this," she told Donna. "I'm so happy."

The happiness was not destined to last more than a couple of weeks, because by this time Terry had already met her nemesis, D'Alessio. Their first encounter was at a party Caccia had taken her to on the night of May 6 at Carlo Cabassi's villa in Casorezzo, a few miles out in the suburbs. A gray-haired, elegant-looking man, Cabassi had a reputation for giving parties that started out innocently enough but often degenerated into drug-and-sex orgies. On this occasion, after the servants had gone to bed, Terry remembers his preparing "lines of snow" with a razor blade for his guests to snort from a tabletop. Under questioning in court, Cabassi couldn't recall whether cocaine had been used that night, "but I can't exclude it, because I can't know what my guests have." He did admit that he himself sometimes used the drug but continued to deny Terry's version. "Nobody's going to make a demon out of me," he told his friends during the trial. "I'm vaccinated against this and other things."

Later that night, Cabassi persuaded Caccia to let him take part in a sexual threesome with Terry. Francesco had fallen asleep on the floor, but a few hours later, after hearing that he had missed out on the fun, he walked into Terry's bedroom and woke her up. He began to masturbate in front her and insisted that she make love to him immediately. Terry refused; she was afraid Donna would find out about the party, and she was sober enough by now not to want to give herself to anyone. To Francesco this must have seemed like a slap in the face; he was not used to being turned down. As Terry would testify, "I think he was very well known and very well liked by girls." In any event, from then on, Francesco never let up on her. Because they moved in the same circles, the two kept bumping into each other, and on every occasion he would proposition her or make disparaging remarks, then touch himself in the crotch. Terry told her friends about these incidents, but even those who witnessed them advised her to ignore them. It was just the way Francesco was, nothing to take seriously, nothing to worry about. But for Terry, his behavior became a daily nightmare. "He used to call me a whore, a bitch." She couldn't understand why he wouldn't let her alone; she didn't realize he was as desperate as she.

On the surface, Francesco D'Alessio appeared to have everything. He was forty, a ruggedly handsome man of six feet four who had been born rich, knew everybody, had a beautiful wife, two healthy children, and had succeeded at whatever he tried. He also liked to gamble. He knew more about racehorses than anyone except perhaps his father. In his teens, he sat up late at night studying bloodlines and breeding charts, and he could judge the racing potential of an animal in five minutes. "Women didn't matter to him," recalled a bookmaker who used to go to the races with Francesco. "They came after everything else, and everything else came after horses."

D'Alessio had always been rude and headstrong, probably as a result of his pampered childhood, but after he found drugs, he became something more than merely a big, undisciplined kid used to getting his own way. One acquaintance remembers Francesco's beating up an American girl in a nightclub because she wouldn't go to bed with him. And several years earlier, at the Nepentha, he kicked and slapped his wife around because he had found out that she wanted to leave him. He cracked up cars, fell asleep in his clothes in hotel lobbies, didn't wash, rarely shaved, created public scenes everywhere, from which only his money and connections extricated him.

As his life went to pieces and his personality disintegrated, he turned his self-hatred against all women. "He used them, that's all," a friend recalls. "Love? An invention of novels, according to him," says another. He developed sadistic psychological techniques for making women fall in love with him and then left them. He became obsessed by the idea they were all trying to put something over on him. An acquaintance remembers bumping into him at a private sporting club in the company of a beautiful blonde. Francesco pulled him aside. "What do you say, shall I drop her?" he asked. The friend didn't know how to answer, so he mumbled, 'Why rush it? Sooner or later, probably, it'll end anyway." To which Francesco replied, "So then better do it at once. Thanks for the advice." Then he turned back to the girl. "From this moment, you've had it," he announced and walked away.

His gambling became a metaphor for his urge to self-destruct. Although a superb handicapper who could read an odds board at a glance, he made impossible bets. He played to lose, and not only on the horses but at cards, tennis (a sport at which he had been a champion), even the most routine aspects of daily life. By the time he met Terry Broome, he had convinced himself that nothing counted except the pleasure of the moment and that existence was meaningless. "Life is a bet," he liked to say, "and I want to lose it."

On the night of June 25, Terry and Rotti joined Donna and her boyfriend at the Caffè Roma, where Terry spotted Francesco at the bar. Anticipating trouble, she persuaded her party to leave, and they moved on to the Nepentha. But at about two A.M., Francesco showed up and walked over to their table. "Hi, look who's here," he said to Rotti and smiled at Terry, who was already high on pills, alcohol, and coke. She fled to the ladies' room, but he waited for her to come out, then hung around the table dropping crude insinuations about Terry's penchant for group scenes and homosexual affairs. "How come when

the girls are with Rotti, they don't want to [have sex with] me anymore?" he asked at one point.

The jeweler did not rise to the bait, and the group soon left the
club. On the way home in the car, though, Rotti maintained a sullen silence, then suddenly asked for the return of his gifts. "What happened
at the Nepentha must have made Giorgio change his mind," Terry later
told one of her defense lawyers. Although she eventually found out
that Rotti had treated other so-called fiancées of his the same way, she
believed at the time that the incident had ruined her marriage plans.

Back in the apartment, Rotti went to bed, but Terry was too upset
and agitated to sleep. She moved restlessly about, then rummaged
through bureau drawers looking for electronic games, for which she
had a passion, and came across Rotti's gun, a Smith & Wesson
.38-caliber revolver. She put the weapon in a brown bag, dropped it
into her purse along with some plastic envelopes of cocaine, put a
jacket on over her blouse and jeans, and telephoned Francesco at his
apartment on the Corso Magenta, an elegant part of town. She made
an attempt to pass herself off as "Diana" and was invited to come over,
even though she had the clear impression that Francesco wasn't alone.

After a ten-minute cab ride across town and a couple of snorts of
coke, she showed up at D'Alessio's place at about five o'clock. As she
had suspected, he wasn't alone but in the company of a tall, pretty
blonde named Laura Marie Royko. Francesco grinned at Terry and invited her into the bedroom. "I knew you'd show up," he told her and
again made more of his ugly advances. When she refused him, he
asked if she wanted him to invite some of his friends over, since one
man clearly wasn't enough for her, and he also called her a bitch.

It was too much. Terry suddenly reached into her purse, took out
the gun, and fired. The first shot missed and Francesco moved toward
her. The second one struck him in the chest, but he managed to reach
her and grab her wrist. They fell to the floor, wrestling for the gun, and
Terry pulled the trigger three more times. The last bullet caught
Francesco in the temple, from a distance of about five inches. Terry got
up, put the gun back into her purse, and left, but not before assuring
the woman in the next room that she had nothing to fear from her.

The horrified Royko, who had been dimly aware only of an argument going on in the bedroom prior to the shots, ran out of the apartment to inform Carlo Cabassi, who kept a penthouse flat upstairs. "I

shouted, 'Carlo, Carlo, wake up!' " Royko recalled, " 'Francesco's dying!' " He got up, got dressed very slowly and went downstairs. While an ambulance and the police were being summoned, Cabassi set about eliminating any evidence of drugs, then calmly telephoned various friends to tell them what had happened. Francesco was apparently still breathing, but he had not much longer to live.

At home, after Terry had told Rotti what had happened, the jeweler reloaded the gun and put it back in the drawer. Terry called Donna, then hung up on her when her sister began to shout that she had been nothing but trouble ever since she arrived. While Terry packed a suitcase, Rotti cleaned the blood off her sneakers. Then he drove her to the airport. "I had a round-trip New York–Milan ticket," Terry later explained to a magistrate, "but I didn't want to go back to the United States." At Rotti's suggestion, she flew to Zurich on a ticket he bought for her and holed up there in a cheap rooming house that happened to be opposite a police station. When the Swiss, alerted by the Italian authorities, began to look for her, all the cops had to do to arrest her was cross the street.

Extradited to Milan, Terry was stunned by the crush of reporters and the popping of photographers' flashbulbs that greeted her return. "What is this?" she asked, confused and apparently unaware of the sensation the crime was causing. "I didn't want to kill Francesco," she kept repeating to anyone who would listen. "I didn't mean to kill him."

Terry spent the next two years in jail awaiting trial. She was held first in an old and overcrowded prison in Milan and then Pavia, where she was mixed in with hardened criminals, drug addicts, and lunatics and became addicted to methadone, a chemical substitute for heroin mistakenly prescribed for her by someone on the medical staff. Twice she tried to kill herself by slashing her wrists. Finally, she was moved to a more modern facility near the ancient hilltop town of Bergamo, east of Milan. And there she started at last to rebuild her life.

She was immediately befriended by a former terrorist named Vincenza Fioroni, who helped Terry with her rudimentary Italian and eased her into the prison routine. The two young women shared a cell, and Terry began to find security and peace in this new relationship. Her mother continued to stand by her; so, too, did Donna (she was still a top model, and her career, in fact, benefited from the attendant publicity).

When the case finally came to trial there was no doubt where the sympathies of the public lay. Terry was regarded as the victim, not the protagonist, of the crime. Her codefendants—Rotti, Caccia, and Cabassi, who were up on various related charges but had spent almost no time in jail—were referred to in the press as "the three little pigs" and pilloried as the architects of her ruin. In his summation, one of her defense lawyers told the judges, "You see before you a living being, but in effect she is deader than the one whose life she inadvertently took. Only your sentence can bring this girl back to life." The spectators burst into applause and many people, including Terry's interpreter, were crying, but the presiding magistrate sternly reminded the courtroom that "a hall of justice is not a theater." All Terry had to say in her own defense was that she had not meant to kill Francesco and could do nothing to indemnify his death. "I can only guarantee that I will try to change my life."

After eight hours of deliberation, she was found guilty of voluntary homicide (second-degree murder) with attenuating circumstances and sentenced to fourteen years in prison. Her lawyers appealed the sentence, but Terry seemed resigned, even content, to be where she was. She got up every morning at seven and spent her day in jail making pottery, studying Italian, writing, reading, working in the prison vegetable garden and laundry, for which she was paid about a hundred dollars a month, enough for her immediate needs. Free at last of her dependency on pills and coke, she looked tanned and fit. She also seemed to have acquired a pretty clear understanding of her own involvement in a scene she no longer missed and had no regrets about the world she had left behind, most certainly not the men in it. In jail, she assured everyone, she had met a far better class of people.

As for the three little pigs, they were all found guilty of a number of offenses, ranging from possession of drugs to giving false testimony, but were handed suspended sentences and sent home. Of these men and the scene in general, a well-known columnist named Giorgio Bocca observed that "they had no desire or capacity to love" and had to resort to drugs and the lures of the flesh to make it through the night. The women, he continued, were incapable of having valid desires or of living real lives, but allowed themselves to be exploited and used simply in order to be thought desirable, to be valued solely for their looks and immediately availability. We had been asked to witness a drama of impotence, he wrote, without heroes or heroines, played out against a background of trivial pursuits and easy money.

Produced and directed, he might have added, by the real villains of the piece—the quasi-respectable Mafia hoods who kept the rivers of drugs flowing through the great cities of the world. None of them were on trial in Milan.

CHAPTER
THIRTEEN

THE IMAGE
OF THE PRINCE

THE ONLY MAN in Italy better known than the Pope, according to a national poll, is Gianni Agnelli, the head of Gruppo Fiat, the giant automobile company that has its headquarters in Turin. Every year Agnelli's likeness appears on national and international magazine covers and on the front pages of newspapers, not always in the most flattering light. Some years ago, he was caught from the rear in the act of changing his pants while on board his yacht by a paparazzo using a telescopic lens. This photograph, too, was published in several picture magazines and was reportedly a great favorite with the assembly-line employees of the Mirafiore plant in Turin, the citadel of Agnelli's industrial empire. A woman reporter who wrote about the incident in *Grazia,* an Italian fashion magazine, commented that the photograph revealed a middle-aged man in excellent physical shape and that he remained an attractive figure to women, despite the stupidity and vulgarity of this particular act of intrusion, which had caught him unawares. His looks, in fact, are frequently commented upon by interviewers. "What strikes you are his large eyes, circled by fine lines," one woman wrote about him. "They shine with a distant and intense light that reminds me of certain Byzantine mosaics. So does his nose, lightly hooked like that of an aristocratic sire, and the mobile cut of his mouth, breaking into an affable smile."

Agnelli is of medium height and weight, but his rugged good looks have become as exportable as his famous company's products. It's not unusual for the rich and successful to be singled out by the press, especially if they happen to be physically attractive, but to become a supercelebrity, a Kennedy or a Pavarotti, the added requirement is an intangible. Federico Fellini, the movie director and himself a member in good standing of this exclusive group, once had this to say about Agnelli: "He's pleasing, the way an actor is pleasing, and because fortune has singled him out. He's a victor. Stick a helmet on his head, put him on horseback. He has the face of a king."

Real kings have gone out of fashion almost everywhere, although in Italy the longing for a royal line persists in some sections of society. Shortly after the end of the Second World War, in 1945, Italians voted in a national referendum to abolish the monarchy, which had thoroughly compromised and discredited itself, first by King Vittorio Emanuele's failure to take a stand against Mussolini's more onerous domestic policies, and later by its open collaboration with the Fascist regime at home and abroad. When Prince Umberto, the heir to the throne, was banished with his family and took up residence in Spain, the assumption in most quarters was that the monarchy had become a dead issue in Italy. Nevertheless, although no one today seriously advocates a return to power of the House of Savoy, the nation's hereditary dynasty, there is still a nostalgia for the sort of stability in public life that a monarchy represents. "Italy has been waiting for a real political leader for nearly thirty years," an Italian journalist has observed, "and it's no accident that Henry Kissinger used to spend more time talking to Gianni Agnelli about the country's problems than to the political mediocrities who have succeeded each other in power for decades here."

Many Italians feel that Agnelli himself should run for office, because, as a charismatic figure, he would be able to influence the course of events in a way no ordinary politician can. The only problem with this scenario is Agnelli himself. On the subject of politics in general he has always shown himself to be well informed, but his views have consistently been those of an outsider. "If you are in Italy and you have the responsibility of the Fiat," he has declared, "that's already a big chunk of responsibility. To believe that there could be another greater one or that it might be up to you or that it could be destined for you is a presumption and would be highly unlikely to occur. That's a practical argument, let's say. And then there's also another one—a diffidence, in a sense. One could end by acquiring an infinity of commitments one could never afterward bring to fruition." He went on to express a fear that he might find himself involved in what amounted to a swindle. "Symbolically, you see that you could unite, let's say, the more or less conservative world, the whole middle-class world, perhaps even some of the younger people, who might see in you a symbol, an emblem, a promise that would then not correspond to the reality of the power you could exercise."

Agnelli is convinced that most of Italy's ruling politicians have been in power too long. "We grew up together in a sense, I know them all," he says. "It's a relationship that weighs on me. When I see our country's problems, the political class that deals with them, and then I see the problems of other nations and the kind of political class that deals with them, I have to say that usually the country where one was born gets the class that resembles it the most. And when I see how we cope with our problems, it makes a certain effect on me . . . . Here we improvise and solve our problems as they come up. It's very hard to find anyone who can look ahead."

Any chance that Agnelli could have been persuaded to enter politics was probably squashed when his younger brother Umberto, then also a top Fiat executive, suddenly became a candidate some years ago for the Chamber of Deputies as a Christian Democrat and was elected. The move startled some members of the Agnelli clan but turned out to be without consequence, since Umberto was quickly relegated to the back ranks of his party and failed to alter the comfortable status quo in which the party functionaries have basked for decades. His lack of success helped to persuade his older brother that little was to be gained by attempting to take a direct hand in the nation's internal affairs. In any case, every Italian government has to deal with Gianni Agnelli. If the Gruppo Fiat were ever to become insolvent, the crisis would be far more severe than the mere toppling of a political coalition. "Rulers now are made, not born, and sometimes not even elected," an Italian political commentator pointed out not long ago. "Italy today, for better or for worse, is the Italy of Gianni Agnelli, not the politicians."

THE BASIC source of Agnelli's power is the Fiat, which makes the cars that four out of every five Italians buy, but which also manufactures metal products, tractors, airplane engines, industrial vehicles, buses, and railroad and production systems. The company also has engineering investments in a number of Third World nations and owns several of the country's most influential daily newspapers and magazines, including Milan's *Corriere della Sera* (which it acquired after the collapse of Rizzoli), and Turin's *La Stampa*. Furthermore, the Fiat is itself a subsidiary of a privately owned company in which the shareholders are Gianni, Umberto, his four sisters and four first cousins.

The Agnellis have invested heavily in a number of unrelated activities, ranging from a national soccer team (Turin's Juventus) to publishing houses, building concerns, international resorts, a mass retail chain, manufacturing, banks, and real estate. No one, probably not even Gianni himself, knows the full extent of his investments or his net worth. The only certainty is that his interests are so diversified that he and his family could easily survive the collapse of his automobile empire, though such an unlikely eventuality would undoubtedly cause a crisis of such magnitude in Italy that the nation's fragile democratic political institutions might not survive it. The Fiat employs about three hundred thousand Italians, which makes it, next to the state itself, the largest single provider of work in the peninsula. In addition, its products feed and are nourished by a host of complementary businesses that employ another quarter of a million Italians.

During the boom years of the fifties and sixties, the ownership by ordinary citizens of a Fiat car became a symbol of the country's postwar affluence, in much the same way that possession of a Model T epitomized the prosperity enjoyed by middle-class Americans immediately after the First World War. A serious financial crisis at Fiat would necessarily bring the organs of the state to its rescue, in a far more drastic way than our own government chose to act on behalf of Chrysler, because the collapse of the Italian firm would be comparable in the United States to a simultaneous shutting down of all of our major automobile manufacturers and steel companies. Hundreds of thousands of workers would be forced into the streets, with the probability that such an eventuality would cause first a financial panic and then rioting and political violence. This possible scenario is the negative factor on which the Agnelli family's power rests and so pervasive is its company's influence in national affairs that one expert on its operations commented a few years ago, "The French government owns Renault, nobody knows who owns Volkswagen, but Fiat owns Italy."

The Fabbrica Italiana Automobili Torino (Fiat) was founded in Turin in July, 1899, by nine men, who raised 800,000 lire for the "construction and sale" of new cars and hired fifty workers to produce the first model. This was the Tipo A, a two-seater with carbide headlights and wheels not much larger than those of a bicycle. It could attain a speed of about twenty-two miles per hour and cost 420,000 lire, which made it a luxury item to most people. Within two years, however, the Fiat had begun to export cars, and its early clientele included the King of Spain, Kaiser Wilhelm II, twenty-two members of the British aristocracy, five Austrian archdukes, seventeen Indian maharajahs, and a sprinkling of Vanderbilts and Whitneys. By then the company had already begun to diversify and was producing buses and other industrial vehicles. In 1912, it launched the Zero, the first model built as a series and aimed at the less affluent buyer. By then production had climbed to 3,400 units a year and the firm employed 4,000 workers. It had begun to transform Turin, a sizable but sleepy provincial capital, into a company town.

Although he did not become president of the company until 1920, the man who from the beginning had been the moving force in its affairs and rapid growth was Giovanni Agnelli, Gianni's grandfather. He came from a middle-class family in Villar Perosa, a Piedmontese mountain village, and had moved to Turin after some years of military service. He had become obsessed with machines in general, but especially with the possibility of designing and building automobiles. It was he who found the backers, created the company and ran its day-to-day operations. Count Carlo Biscaretti di Ruffia, the son of one of the company's founders, remembers him as by far the most powerful personality on the scene. "From the first day he lived as though he were fighting a battle against all opposition," he recalled many years later. "He was always right, and he won by reason of his indomitable spirit, courage and self-sacrifice . . . . Fiat has made some wonderful machines, but Agnelli made the company into a really great, sound, and powerful organization, by his tenacity, his power of persuasion, and his way of imposing his will on others, almost by suggestion."

Giovanni was a tall, athletic-looking man, with a mustache, thinning hair, an intimidating way of gazing fixedly at people and a parade-ground voice. His military background had made him used to giving orders and being instantly obeyed and in later years, whenever he faced opposition, especially from within the ranks, he was not shy about reminding everyone that he had built the Fiat with his own money. This fact alone, he felt, gave him the right to make any decision, however despotic, he wanted to. He was known to everyone, including his own family, as "the Senator," an honorary title conferred upon him by the Fascist government in 1923 that suited him to perfection. He was, in fact, the portrait of a late nineteenth-century captain of industry—obsessed, tyrannical, energetic, an empire builder on a grand scale. "I have a profound admiration for these men," wrote Antonio Gramsci, the cofounder of Italy's Communist Party and its most articulate spokesman. "They are the dominating figures of our time, kings much stronger and more useful than the rulers of other epochs, even those of our own. They are the ones who tear the ignorant, backward masses of the countryside from their tranquil, supine somnolence in order to hurl them into the heated crucible of our civilization. . . . And that is why I am not scandalized if they succeed in earning millions by an exploitation compared to which the thievishness of ordinary bandits—that is to say, the founders of every nation's civilization—is a laughing matter."

The Senator, like most of Italy's leading industrialists, took little interest in politics, except as they affected the successful operation of his business. After the First World War, even as the Fiat continued to expand and make money, the nation, betrayed at the Versailles peace conference, savaged by inflation and the failure of many businesses, was being shaken by labor agitations of one sort or another. On September 1, 1920, the workers occupied Turin's factories, including Fiat's, and stayed on the premises for a month. Agnelli reacted predictably. "As things now stand, relations between management and labor are impossible," he declared in Turin's *Gazzetta del Popolo*, after the strike had been settled. "The workers don't want to work anymore.

They are fascinated by political ideas and don't want to admit the gains they have made. It's impossible to conceive of constructing anything, when one has to rely on the cooperation of twenty thousand enemies." He threatened to resign and proposed forming a cooperative with his workers, an idea he knew would be rejected by labor and which was calculated to entrench him in power. In fact, on October 30, 1920, after his bluff had discredited the metallurgical union's leadership, he was elected president and managing director of the company.

The crisis in Turin and continued agitation in the nation's streets and piazzas, however, had served to focus attention on the newly formed Fascist Party of Benito Mussolini, whose squadrons of roughnecks staged their March on Rome in 1922 and seized power, with the tacit acceptance of the King. The Senator played no part in these events and, in fact, was regarded as aloof by the party functionaries in Turin, but, like most businessmen, he welcomed the calls for law and order and the antilabor stance of the Fascist oligarchs. When, shortly afterward, he was sent an unsolicited official party card and became a member, he is said to have explained in Piedmontese dialect, "This is only because they forced it into my pocket." But he never openly opposed any of the regime's repressive policies and, like every other leading industrialist and financier, he remained silent even when Giacomo Matteotti, the Socialist leader, was murdered in the streets of Rome by Fascist thugs on June 30, 1924. The business community was repaid by the banning in October of that year of the country's troublesome independent labor unions. This guaranteed the Fiat a period of continued rapid expansion without having to disperse too large a slice of the pie to its workers. And when the company felt itself threatened in the mid-twenties by French and American attempts, especially by Ford, to invade its home markets, the Fascist government raised import duties and granted the Fiat enough special tax advantages to make the firm practically immune to foreign competition.

By the end of the 1930s, with Europe divided into two camps and busily rearming itself for war, the Fiat dominated the Italian industrial scene. In 1939, it opened a new automobile assembly plant occupying a million square meters at Mirafiori, on the outskirts of Turin, and employing twenty-two thousand workers. Like most other Italian businessmen and many ordinary citizens, the Senator had become convinced that, despite Mussolini's displays of public affection for Hitler, the dictator would never actually commit his country to waging war. Agnelli continued to run his industrial empire as if the political confrontation abroad could not possibly affect its profitable operations.

T HE HEIR apparent to this burgeoning industrial empire was the Senator's only son, Edoardo, born in 1892. The boy's older sister Aniceta, better known as Tina, had married a young engineer named Carlo Nasi, who came from a well-to-do middle-class family of building contractors, but who was never fully accepted by his father-in-law and pursued an independent career as a construction engineer and architect. He and Tina had five children over a span of fifteen years, but soon after the birth of their last one, in 1928, Tina died. The focus of the Senator's personal life became Edoardo, who is remembered by his niece Clara Nasi as "a most intelligent person, somewhat charming, but quite different from his father." He was, in fact, a social butterfly as well as a gambler, who squandered a small fortune in the casinos.

He was also apparently something of a dandy. He never wore a hat and is remembered by several contemporaries as always being impeccably dressed, "very elegant, like an English gentleman." He was tall and slender, with blue eyes and fair, curly hair that he combed straight back off a prominent forehead. A good talker and highly social, he was also well regarded by the local Fascists, who cultivated him and thought of him as an ally. He was considered a lightweight by many, but, like most scions of wealthy Italian families, he became a sensible citizen from the day he married and began to raise a family.

His wife was Virginia Bourbon del Monte di Santa Maria, the daughter of a Roman prince and his American-born wife, Jane Campbell. Attractive and well connected, Virginia is remembered by her daughter Susanna as "beautiful, fragile, in love with gaiety, completely uneducated and madly generous." The marriage delighted the Senator, because it presaged the end of his son's playboy years and his deeper involvement in the internal affairs of the empire. It was a perfect example of the kind of marriage the children of self-made tycoons are expected to conclude; it put a dynastic stamp of nobility on a conquering warrior class. But their contemporaries also recall that the marriage was not an especially happy one, and their children suffered in childhood from a lack of affection and personal attention that only the parents themselves could have provided.

Virginia and Edoardo had seven children, four of them girls. Gianni, the second-oldest, was born in Turin on March 12, 1921. He was actually named after his grandfather, but from the first he was called Gianni, a contraction of Giovanni, in order to distinguish him from the Senator. He is remembered by two of his sisters, Clara and Susanna (who was usually called Suni) as a bright and lively child, quick to make friends, talkative, adventurous, but not a diligent student. With his teachers, he was, in fact, a *contestatore,* an argumentative, feisty sprite who liked to challenge authority and accepted very little on faith. He occasionally flunked courses and was always being disciplined for one small social infraction or another.

The family spent the school year in a large villa on the Corso Opporto, a tree-lined avenue in one of Turin's wealthier residential areas. The house was full of servants and the children's lives were dominated by a series of English nannies, who every day walked them to and from their various schools, regardless of the weather. In *We Always Wore Sailor Suits,* an autobiographical account of her childhood, Suni recalls every day as being dark, with fog swirling along the cobblestoned streets between the dark stone palazzi and gloomy arcades for which the city is famous. Life in the *centro storico* of this provincial capital was still unhurried, serene, uncrowded, seemingly impervious to the industrial growth around it. Suni recalls the bright lights of the shop windows under the covered walks as being the only relief from the prevailing gloom. Even in summer, which they usually spent at the fashionable beach resort of Forte dei Marmi, they were dressed in blue sailor suits and were expected to behave like miniature adults.

The dominant figure in the children's lives was their grandfather, whom they visited during holidays in Villar Perosa, a town of about four thousand inhabitants where there was little for them to do, and a number of Saturday nights the rest of the year for dinner. Their grandmother Clara remained a dim, complaining figure, almost always in bed with some ailment or other, where she nibbled on yogurt or bits of spinach while criticizing amusingly everyone around her. The Senator, however, was a good host, even though he paid very little attention to the children, and the succulent meals, prepared by a talented Neapolitan chef, were a relief from the austere formality of the less elaborate repasts, presided over by their various nannies, routinely provided at home.

Occasionally, the Senator would call on them, an event that made everyone in the house nervous because it was felt that he disapproved of their worldly way of life. He usually came alone and always arrived on time. He would climb the stairs rather than ride in the elevator to the second floor, where he was met by his son, who ceremoniously shook his hand and offered him a glass of sweet vermouth. Virginia would come running late into his presence from some other part of the house to be met by his disapproving eye, but she could usually manage to charm him at least into a semblance of cordiality. The children would be ushered briefly into his presence to greet him but were otherwise shut off from these formal dinner parties, which always ended with the men clustered in a corner to discuss politics and business and the women left to their own devices. "From his childhood Gianni derived a way of looking at life, a way of dealing with human relations that, though it tends toward self-control, also induces skepticism," a close friend of his once commented.

Gianni's childhood ended abruptly on Sunday afternoon, July 14, 1935, when his father was killed during the landing of his small, private seaplane near Genoa. Edoardo was forty-three, Gianni only fourteen at the time. Thousands of people came to the funeral in the Church of the Blessed Angels, on the corner near the family home, and walked in silence behind the horse-drawn hearse through the streets of Turin. The account in *La Stampa* of the funeral ceremony, held the next day in Villar Perosa, noted that the eyes of many in the crowd at the church were fixed on "that adolescent who now represents the family continuity of an enterprise around which the lives and hopes of a hundred thousand workers revolve."

After his father's death, Gianni's teenage years were agitated and complicated by his mother's social life and love affairs. Capricious and intemperate, the beautiful widow began to move in the sort of artistic, party-going circles that the Senator despised. She fell in love with Curzio Malaparte, an opportunistic, flamboyant writer and journalist, who had been fired as editor of *La Stampa* by the Senator himself. Gianni remembers this d'Annunzian figure as "affected, perfumed, dressed in blue jackets with gold buttons, glossy, and oiled," addicted to puns and word games the boy found boring. When Virginia refused to break off the affair and tried to run away with her family to Rome, the Senator had her train boarded in Genoa by police agents and took the children away from her.

Eventually, Mussolini himself was persuaded to intervene and the children were restored to her, after she agreed to renounce Malaparte. When she decided to move permanently to Rome, however, the Senator again took custody of the children. This time they rebelled and became all but unmanageable, until at last he relented and the family was reunited during the summer of 1937. After some months on the French Riviera, they moved to Rome. Virginia was happiest there, because the city was, after all, the artistic and social capital of the country as well as the political one, and she was surrounded by her friends, so unlike the Torinesi, "who only kiss you when someone dies."

BY THE time the Second World War began, Gianni was already being groomed to take over at the Fiat. He was studying toward a degree in business law and in 1939 he made the obligatory trip to Detroit, the Lourdes of the automobile industry. "Our people have always looked toward Detroit with enormous respect," he once said, "from the assembly lines of the thirties to all the systems of production and the evolution of automobile technology." But he was also disagreeably surprised by the chaos and filth of the American factories, where blacks and whites worked separately in settings "much more infernal than our own." When he returned, however, after having crossed the States by train and car with his cousin, Carlo Nasi, he was struck by how much smaller everything looked at home—buildings, roads, every aspect of the countryside.

When the war broke out, the family was scattered. Virginia remained in Rome, where she continued to give and to go to parties and dabbled riskily in salon politics. The Senator remained at his post in Turin, where his factories were now turning out equipment for the dictator's war machine. Despite his grandfather's opposition, Gianni enlisted and fought as an officer with an armored division in Russia and North Africa. By 1943, when he came home on leave, he knew that the Allies would win the war. Never a Fascist sympathizer, he had fought only as a patriot; it was not difficult for him, nor for many other Italians, to change sides, once Italy had declared an armistice and the Germans had subsequently occupied the country. He and his grown sisters spent the last few months of the German occupation shuttling back and forth across the Swiss border and scurrying about the countryside, trying to avoid being caught by the Germans or the Fascist patrols of Mussolini's hastily organized puppet government in the north.

Meanwhile, the Senator continued to go every day to his office, although there was little he could do now except sit in it and hope that his factories would survive the war. They did, although badly damaged by Allied bombs, but after the liberation of Italy on April 25, 1945, he was accused of having collaborated with the Fascists and was refused admittance to the premises by his workers. The Fiat was administered by a committee headed by Giancarlo Camerana, who had married a Nasi, on a sort of caretaker basis, until it could be decided who would take over the empire. There was talk of nationalizing it for the benefit of the workers, but at the time it had not even been decided what sort of government Italy would have after the war and everyone's energies were largely concentrated on staying alive and restoring essential services, such as power and public transport, all shattered by the campaign that had been fought for two years the whole length of the Italian boot.

The Senator, however, could not understand what had happened to him. Every morning he would summon his driver, Paolo Bogetto, and tell him to take him to his office. "But, Senator, they won't let you in," the driver would protest. "It's mine! What can they do about it?" the old man would shout at him. Bogetto would drive him to the Mirafiori plant and park some distance away, from where the old man would peer stonily through the window at his suddenly inaccessible creation.

It was a tragic year. Gianni was still recovering from an accident suffered when he and Suni were being driven south at night from Florence by a deserting German soldier. The car had overturned, shattering his ankle. Then, in November, Virginia was killed in a car crash near Pisa, while driving north to console the Senator. The latter died on December 16 of a heart attack, after having taken a bad fall in his bathtub. He was seventy-nine and it was the end of an era. "I thought only of my work," he had been fond of saying. "Perhaps that was a mistake." The old man's funeral cortege passed slowly by the gates of the Mirafiori, from which no one dared emerge to pay a last respect to his coffin. At Villar Perosa, however, the entire population defied the orders signed by the National Committee of Liberation not to take part in the ceremony and turned out to say good-bye to the man who had, in effect, been the town's feudal lord.

Gianni was twenty-seven when the Senator died. As the next in line to the throne, he was allowed to occupy a small office on the premises at Mirafiori, but he was given almost nothing to do. The company was in the process of being taken over by a managerial genius named Vittorio Valletta, the Senator's handpicked successor to Edoardo, and he was not the sort of regent to step gracefully aside for an heir apparent. Gianni was handed graceful speeches to read on ceremonial occasions and told, in effect, to run along and play. Traditionally, the Agnellis have always come late to power, in their middle years. And Gianni also remembered that the Senator had once told him: "Enjoy yourself for a few years, so you'll have gotten it out of your system when it's time to get down to work." Gianni now took the advice and the opportunity seriously and began to enjoy himself with a vengeance.

He was at the time the most attractive and desirable bachelor in Italy, with a personal income later estimated to be about 6 million dollars a year. He set up a pleasure court in exile in a splendid twenty-eight-room villa at Beaulieu, on the French Riviera, which became the headquarters for a rollicking troupe of international revelers, among them Errol Flynn, Ali Khan, Prince Ranier of Monaco, Porfirio Rubirosa, and Baby Pignatari, who had listed his favorite hobby in an edition of *Who's Who* as "girls." Gianni, too, cultivated this pastime. He reportedly dispatched private airplanes to run them in and out of his life by the dozens and displayed a decided preference for slender, elegant blondes of the sort that graced the covers of fashion magazines.

Like Shakespeare's Prince Hal, Gianni, too, had his Falstaff, in the person of Prince Raimondo Lanza di Trabia, an Italian playboy who had been a close friend of Galeazzo Ciano, Mussolini's son-in-law, and had paid court for years to Suni. This extravagant personality approached each day as a personal challenge. Absolutely fearless and indifferent to social consequences, he treated the great with a familiarity indistinguishable from contempt, summoned servants by firing a pistol in the air and coped with temptation by always yielding to it. "He was my great friend," Gianni later recalled. "The rascal, what times we had!" To such men, everything, from a dangerous ski run to the conquest of a beautiful woman, was a challenge that had to be met and overcome.

Adventurers of this sort rarely die tranquilly in bed, surrounded by loving friends and relatives. On a November morning in 1954, Raimondo hurled himself naked to his death from a third-floor hotel window. Errol Flynn was to die of a heart attack while paying court to a teenager. Rubirosa perished in his Ferrari against a tree in the Bois de Boulogne. Ali Khan killed himself in his car by crashing into a wall in Paris on his way home from a party. Gianni, too, had his brush with death. In 1952, he emerged from a high-speed collision with a truck on the French Riviera with a crushed and now permanently stiffened right leg. He spent three months in a hospital, where he began to realize that the party might be over.

The turning point, most of his friends agree, was his marriage in 1955 to Marella Caracciolo, the daughter of a distinguished Italian aristocrat and his American wife, Margaret Clark. Marella was the childhood friend of two of Gianni's younger sisters, Cristina and Maria Sole, and she had the sort of delicate beauty that immediately appealed to him. She had dark blond hair, brown eyes, and a slender, graceful figure. Her outstanding feature was the longest and most aristocratic-looking neck her friend Truman Capote had ever seen. She dressed elegantly and simply, usually in black or white, had worked for *Vogue* and had already been photographed by Avedon. She was twenty-six when she married Gianni in the fall of 1955 and he, at thirty-four was presumably ready to become a responsible citizen.

They apparently brought out the best qualities in each other. "Gianni gave me a taste for life, for having fun," Marella told an interviewer several years ago. "I was in love with the way he was then. I'd heard so much about him and the myth had been created. He's changed a lot and for the better. He never used to get involved, but now he's more open to the problems of others. Basically, he was just the same, but oriented toward things I considered second-rate." During the next ten years, the couple had two children, a boy and a girl, and Gianni began to take a much more active interest in the affairs of the Fiat, which by that time had established itself as the driving force behind the economic boom of the fifties and sixties that has permanently altered the social fabric of Italian life.

From the firm's point of view, Vitorio Valletta turned out to be the right man to preside over the two decades prior to Gianni's assumption of power. Trained as an accountant, he had been with the Fiat since 1921 and, through sheer diligence and efficiency, had made himself indispensable to the company. He remained at his post during the last months of the war, survived first the hostility of the Fascist fanatics, then the equally virulent opposition of organized Communist cells inside the factories, and devoted all of his energies in the immediate postwar years to maintaining the hegemony of the Agnellis over their property and preparing it for the economic boom that was to ensue. It was under his guidance that the Fiat began to produce during the 1950s the small, inexpensive cars—the 500, the 600, the 850 models—that motorized Italian families and helped to transform Italy from a nation of artisans, shopkeepers, and farmers into an industrial power now among the top five in the world. He was able to accomplish this, of course, because Italy, after the referendum banishing the House of Savoy and the subsequent adoption of a new democratic constitution, had clearly opted for an economy based on American concepts of free-enterprise capitalism. It is significant in this context that, during the first decade after the end of the war, most of Italy's major industries were rebuilt or created with large infusions of American aid in the form of low-interest loans, as well as outright grants through the Marshall Plan.

Valletta was always called the Professor. He was a small man with a toothy smile who had tenaciously worked his way up in life from a modest middle-class background (his father had been a career army officer) to make himself indispensable. He was an early riser who neither drank nor smoked, at meals nibbled mostly on vegetables and fruit, and was the complete company man. "The Fiat, the Fiat, then the family," he liked to say. He resolutely avoided the limelight and loathed publicity of any sort. "I can't stand everything that is merely appearance," he once said. "There's no need for it." His only other passion was for horseback riding, which he indulged in for two hours in the early morning, before heading for the plant, where he spent most of the rest of his time, including holidays and weekends.

His attitude to the company and its workers was proprietary and rigidly paternalistic, blindly consecrated to a nineteenth-century concept of profits at any cost, and indifferent to the ecological and social realities that would later cause havoc throughout the nation. The economic boom that began in the mid-fifties and lasted uninterrupted for a full decade destroyed the centuries-old economic fabric of Italy and created problems that remain largely unsolved. The burgeoning factories of Turin and Milan lured many thousands of young men away from the impoverished rural areas of the southern provinces and the Veneto, where unemployment and low wages had been endemic for generations, to work on the assembly lines. These badly educated, mostly untrained workers poured into the northern cities every day by train to join the growing labor pool and settled into a life ultimately far more destructive of human values than that of the sleepy villages they had left behind.

The national and local authorities had made no plans to accommodate them and they settled mainly in outlying areas of the cities, either into newly constructed blocks of grim-looking apartment buildings, thrown up by private builders with no concern for zoning laws or basic public facilities, or into so-called ant-heap *pensioni* and shanty towns, where dozens of people shared a few rooms and sometimes slept in shifts. Although everyone in power was aware of the chaotic, unsanitary conditions in which most of these industrial workers lived, no one imagined that the situation might one day become intolerable to many of those trapped in it or lead to the fearsome social conditions that bred and nurtured the terrorism of the seventies. Valletta's attitude was typical of the managerial class then in power and whose views were reflected by the series of governments, all dominated by the Christian Democratic Party, that succeeded each other in office for decades. "The secret is only one," Valletta said at the time. "To make a bigger pie so that when it comes time to cut it, there will be enough slices for everyone." His view of his employees was quintessentially condescending in its simplemindedness. "The worker has a right to have every day his cup of broth and his slice of boiled beef," he once told the editor of *La Stampa*.

According to Gianni, Valletta was convinced that what was good for the Fiat would ultimately be good for everyone, and in this he was no different from most businessmen everywhere. He saw no need for the sort of social planning that smacked to him of government meddling in private affairs. The complete autocrat, he surrounded himself with technicians who would not interfere with his policies and he brooked no intrusion into administrative matters. "He believed in the mass," Umberto Agnelli said not long ago. "He paid very little attention to the individual."

He was eighty-two years old when he finally stepped down. He had been asked sometime earlier what he would do when he retired and he had replied, "Die as quickly as possible." On April 30, 1966, at a meeting of 489 shareholders, he obliquely endorsed the succession to power of Gianni. "Doctor Agnelli is not merely his grandfather's grandson," he said. He died two years later, during the summer holidays, so that, according to one commentator, he would not cause the Fiat to lose so much as an hour's labor on the assembly lines.

O N T H E morning of April 18, 1969, a caretaker at the Agnelli villa in Villar Perosa named Guido Pascal happened to notice a blue canvas sack leaning against a side door of the house. It contained ten sticks of dynamite rigged to a detonator and timer and set to explode at six o'clock that evening, an hour when presumably most members of the Agnelli family, including Gianni himself, would be home. According to the experts who later examined the device, the explosion would have destroyed the entire rear of the villa and probably killed everyone on the first and second floors.

The attempt to blow up the Villar Perosa residence and its occupants was one of a series of such incidents in Turin in previous weeks. Less lethal bombs had gone off or been discovered in time at the American Consulate, various university buildings, the Mirafiori plant, the houses of local magistrates, the Church of St. Cristina, and the headquarters of the Industrial Union. The day before the attempt at Villar Perosa, two incendiary devices had been hurled against the driveway entrance of the new offices of *La Stampa*. None of these attacks were solved and no one was ever arrested in connection with them. They were attributed to no particular group, but simply lumped in together in police reports as examples of "anarchic terrorism." The well-organized, highly publicized attacks launched by such terrorist groups as the Red Brigades had not yet begun, but the incidents turned out to be prophetic.

In fact, from that moment on, the lives of Gianni Agnelli and his family were completely changed. During the 1970s, the so-called Years of Lead, they were escorted everywhere by armed bodyguards and their residences were protected by every means, ranging from electronic alarm systems to trained attack dogs. Even today, Agnelli's own movements are never allowed to become routine and are varied, usually at the last minute. No daily itinerary is ever publicized, and takeoffs and landings of his personal jet and helicopter are never openly scheduled in advance. Wherever he goes he is escorted by what he calls his "guardian angels," even to press conferences and other highly public functions. His wife and children do not go shopping or anywhere alone, at least inside their own country, and their every movement is under constant protective surveillance.

In retrospect, the attempt on the Agnelli villa figures as the opening incident in what became later that year the outbreak of violent confrontations in the nation's streets and piazzas now remembered as the "hot autumn" of 1969. By 1968, *il boom* had given way to what later became known as stagflation, a recession causing increasing unemployment along with an annual inflation rate that remained pegged at roughly 20 percent for over a decade. Italy's factory workers and public employees began to stage the series of strikes and other forms of protest that have plagued the country every since. The energy crisis of the early seventies exacerbated this situation and served only to underline the basic paradox afflicting Italy's status as a leading industrial power. "We are a nation like Japan, without natural resources to rely on," an Italian businessman recently explained to me. "Unfortunately, unlike the Japanese, we are not ready to make the sacrifices necessary to build a stable economy. Our industries and our industrialists have never been protective or caring of our workers."

It was entirely appropriate that the issue should have been joined most fiercely in Turin, where the nation's two central power blocks openly confronted each other in the form of the Fiat, which by 1967 had conquered 6 percent of the world automobile market, and the company's workers, who constituted the best-organized labor union in the country. The climate was one in which terrorism could take root and make converts. "The terrorists know what we all know," Diego

Novelli, the Communist mayor of Turin, declared in the late seventies, "and that is that this is a city of delicate balances, a tormented social scene, at the boiling point in suffering. Not only because of economic problems, but as much for the unrest and uncertainty caused by every strong contradictory change. Turin today is a city of displaced persons, in the actual physical sense, a city of provisionals—men without roots." He went on to point out that Turin had by then the third-largest population of southerners (about a third of the city's roughly 22 million inhabitants) after Naples and Palermo, but had not become a southern city; the newcomers had remained outsiders. "If you add up all these factors," Novelli continued, "you can understand what the terrorists set out to accomplish in Turin—the exploitation of the subtle malaise which derives from an identity crisis, the absence of a secure collective identity, from an uprooting. In a word, the exploitation of the effects of an incomplete integration. All this, they calculated, could guarantee a state of frustration and exasperation. . . ."

The Red Brigades and other organized terrorist bands became active during the early seventies, a period that coincided in Turin with the election of a Communist administration headed by Novelli. The young men and women who formed the terrorist groups turned out later to be mainly members of the middle class, who had become disenchanted with what they considered the Italian Communist Party's betrayal of the dogma of class struggle and revolution. These so-called *autonomi* were financed partly from abroad, trained in camps run by professional terrorists in Libya and the PLO-dominated areas of Lebanon, and linked to each other through an international terrorist network sponsored mainly by Soviet espionage organizations. More important, they were able to survive and to function as efficiently as they did because of the tacit support of many sectors of Italy's uprooted proletariat. Again according to Novelli, the violent transitions and alienations imposed on the new slum dwellers by the circumstances of their private lives and "the Dantesque bedlam that is the Mirafiori" created a climate in which terrorism flourished.

Ironically, this was the situation that Gianni Agnelli inherited when he became president of the Fiat in 1966, and ever since then he has been compelled to deal with it. He understood, when he assumed power, that Valetta's autocratic style had long outlived its usefulness and was in open conflict with the changing climate in the country.

Agnelli saw his main immediate task as the restructuring of the firm's internal hierarchy and the adoption of policies calculated to give his workers more of a direct stake as well as a say in its future successes. By his reforms inside the Fiat, he also intended to set an example that would prod Italy's industrial establishment to adopt more liberal policies toward its workers. His first thousand days in power were compared by several Italian journalists to those of John Kennedy's presidency and his social outlook to Franklin D. Roosevelt's at the time of the New Deal. When Agnelli was asked by a well-known journalist named Guido Gerosa some years ago whether he thought Italy as a whole could provide a version of the New Deal for its people, he answered, "Certainly, but where's our Roosevelt?" "Agnelli knew where the country's Roosevelt was to be found," Gerosa observed, "but he couldn't say it then, just as he can't say it today. The Roosevelt, if anyone, had to be him."

His first step was to unburden himself of Valetta's old guard, which he accomplished mainly by the simple expedient of making retirement mandatory at the age of sixty-five. He then reapportioned internal responsibilities within the company by decentralizing various power blocks and leaving much of the decision making to local departments. Like John Kennedy, whose style he had always admired, he installed his younger brother in a position of administrative power that left him free to deal with larger strategical concepts. Umberto, thirteen years his junior, was a less glamorous, less visible personality who, according to one commentator, happily played tortoise to Gianni's hare.

It was during this period of Gianni's regime that the Fiat became an international power even as its domestic markets were shrinking and its ability to compete was being undermined by strikes, terrorism, and violent confrontations in the streets. Gianni built Togliattigrad, the Fiat factory and workers' town inside the Soviet Union. (It was named after Palmiro Togliatti, the late Italian Communist Party boss and no friend of the Agnellis.) He launched a campaign to conquer European markets for his cars, quickly surpassed the Volkswagen in sales and took over ownership of France's Citroën, despite the open opposition of no less a personage than Charles De Gaulle. His view of the Fiat's position in the world transcended national politics and was perfectly expressed at the time, when he answered his critics by saying, "I do business with Franco *and* with

Tito." It was a cold-eyed practical outlook, typical of today's entrepreneurial businessmen, but startling to many at the time. He also told a friend not long ago that business per se had never given him pleasure; it was simply a question of estimating risks in terms of profit and loss.

It was during the 1970s that Agnelli became the glamorous international figure that he is today and largely because of the prominence achieved by his methods of operation abroad. "With the Vallettas and others we had moved for decades in a feudal atmosphere," Gerosa commented recently. "Our big businessmen had been managers, barons who had administered the lands of their lords. With Agnelli, suddenly we were restored to the image of the prince, the figure of the great leader by divine right, anointed by God, the *condottiere.*"

Nevertheless, even as Gianni Agnelli was becoming the symbol of this glamorous new world of international wheeling and dealing, the cornerstone of his empire was crumbling. By 1979, after a decade of rising energy costs and falling car sales, the annual losses of the Fiat had mounted to a net of 97 billion lire (then about 12 million dollars) and Umberto, in his role as general manager of the automobile company, had begun to threaten mass layoffs and to call for the devaluation of the lira. The latter step would have served to ease the burden of the high-interest loans the company had assumed during the years of expansion into foreign markets, but it alarmed the financial community as well as the nation's unionized workers, who viewed the step as an assault on the buying power of ordinary citizens.

When the Fiat actually fired sixty-one workers a few months later for "having constantly maintained attitudes not consonant with the principles of civilized behavior in working areas," the union called a three-hour protest strike inside the Fiat plants and demanded that they be rehired. The fired employees, management pointed out, had been little more than agents provocateurs inside the factories and were suspected of having collaborated with the Red Brigades and other terrorist groups. The incident was indicative of the chasm that still separated capital from labor in Italy, where each side still views the other as hostile. It came, therefore, as no surprise to many observers of Italy's economic scene when Umberto resigned as general manager on July 31, 1980, and turned over his job to someone not a member of the Agnelli family and so presumably not guilty by blood.

Some years ago, at the height of Agnelli's celebrity and when he was first being urged to involve himself actively in politics, a reporter for the Italian weekly *L'Europeo* interviewed a number of workers at the Mirafiori plant. It soon became clear that few, if any, of the Fiat assembly-line employees believed in the possibility that their employer would be able to solve any of the nation's problems. "Perhaps, in Milan or Rome, you still believe in the myth of Agnelli," a young woman in one of the body shops declared, "but here in Turin, no. Not only in the factory, where we're suffering with our skins for his choices, but in the city itself, where there are people who don't work at the Fiat. What sort of city has Agnelli created? What sort of a city has the Fiat created? Turin has the most serious social problems in Italy. It has no housing, only dormitory quarters or old buildings in which immigrants live sixteen to a room. The people have put Agnelli, the man you call the 'new prince,' to the test in these matters and they are paying the consequences."

IF GIANNI Agnelli remains a glamorous figure to so many people who are not employed at the Fiat, it is surely partly because he projects an image that conforms exactly to the one popularized in the so-called glitter novels of writers like Sidney Sheldon and Harold Robbins (both of whose books sell very well in Italy) and the movies and television shows inspired by them. With his good looks, money, and romantic past, Agnelli is the perfect projection of the modern pulp hero as international tycoon. And not the least of his attractions is his penchant for fast automobiles, which he drives himself at reckless speeds and with occasionally disastrous results. (Italian males in general tend to regard their cars as manifestations of their sexual grandeur.) Bernardino Aiassa, his personal driver from 1946 to 1973, declared after his retirement that his employer's driving technique was risky in the extreme. "I think I really must have a heart of steel to have survived some of the flights I took with him," he stated. "He always drove. I sat beside him, except when there was fog or ice, conditions he absolutely didn't care for." Aiassa recalled another accident in Turin, when Agnelli's automobile skidded on a patch of ice, sideswiped several parked cars, but continued on without stopping. Aiassa was later dispatched back to the scene to calm everyone down and assure the victims they would be adequately compensated for their trouble.

For some years after the 1952 accident, from which he emerged permanently crippled, Agnelli preferred not to drive. When he did resume, however, it was with the same blood-freezing panache as before. Not only does he himself enjoy driving fast, but he also likes to test the mettle of the people around him. Once, when Aiassa was driving David Rockefeller from Turin to Milan, Agnelli instructed the chauffeur to provide the eminent banker with a few thrills and telephoned him later to find out how it had gone and how long it had taken them to make the trip. Agnelli himself holds the unofficial record, having gone from a suburb of Milan to Turin in a Ferrari in forty-five minutes, at an average speed of about a hundred and fifty miles per hour.

Aiassa also recalls another incident between Milan and Turin, when he himself was at the wheel of a Maserati and pulled over because he thought there was some sort of problem developing with the steering mechanism. Agnelli, who had been sleeping, assured him that he must be mistaken and took over in the driver's seat. A few minutes later, he shouted that he had lost control of the machine and was going off the road. He barely managed to brake it to a halt in time to avoid a serious accident. When they got out, they found that one of the front wheels was about to come off. "Even today," Aiassa says, "he is every bit as daring a driver. He makes reckless maneuvers, especially in the city, and often scatters his police escort, which has a lot of trouble keeping up with him."

Such behavior, which in many other countries would have cost him his license, involved him in lawsuits, and perhaps even landed him in jail, is still tolerated in Italy, where the laws are often suspended or ignored in favor of the rich and well-connected. In any case, Agnelli's driving habits not only contribute to his romantic aura, but are also fairly characteristic of the way he conducts his life, always at full speed. "He is not methodical in his work," an associate has said. "He is rigorously punctual at his appointments, but he changes the times depending on what there is to do. He doesn't like to warm a seat, as they say, and so, if he has a free morning, he'd prefer to take his helicopter and go ski or go and take a sail rather than stay in his office, wasting time. He is very fast in his work and you have to be very quick to keep up with him."

Agnelli's working day begins at six A.M. with a quick perusal of the morning newspapers and an hour or so on the telephone with his contacts and minions all over the world. Whether in Rome or Turin, he is at his desk by eight-fifteen and remains there, if he is busy, until lunch. He naps until three-thirty, then goes back to work until eight. His day is equally divided between business appointments, correspondence and meetings, but none of them take up much time. "He's a man with whom you have to try to be clairvoyant and very quick in your dealings," a colleague points out. "By the time you've said half a sentence, he has usually grasped what you want to say. He's intolerant of details and of bureaucratic phraseology. The Fiat has made him famous for his impatience, intolerance and, above all, flightiness—in the sense that he willingly launches new projects, but then delegates their execution to others, because he doesn't want to follow them up in detail."

Agnelli plays every bit as hard as he works and he spends, by his own estimate, more time in the air in his two private jets than did his friend Henry Kissinger, even when the latter was engaged in shuttle diplomacy in the Middle East. He is liable to begin his day in Turin, fly to Rome for a business meeting, then up to London for an afternoon party, stop off at Monte Carlo for dinner and a little gambling, and get back home by midnight. He likes the feeling that his day is full and that he's always on the run. "They say the rich don't know how poor the poor are," he reportedly once commented, "but the poor don't know how hard the rich work."

He still spends some time in Villar Perosa, where the family mansion is staffed by twenty servants, including a gourmet chef who earns far more than the average Italian journalist, but he is more likely to be found these days in Turin or Rome. In the northern city, he lives in a hilltop villa surrounded by a magnificent formal garden and stocked with expensive art. His taste is eclectic and he buys only what he likes—Sèvres porcelains, sculptures by Moore and Giacometti, German expressionist paintings, Vlamincks, works by contemporary American and French artists, Italian moderns. "He's been formally very well educated in art," a friend of Suni's has remarked, "but his taste is instinctive and fearless. He can tell a phony from the real thing as easily as he can size up a potential friend or enemy."

The Agnellis also maintain an apartment in Manhattan, but,

when not in Turin, Agnelli himself is most often to be found in Rome, where he lives in a penthouse overlooking the Quirinal Palace and a portion of the ancient city. The rooms are spacious, featuring a great profusion of plants and flowers, as well as valuable art—a large Manzù horseman, a Modigliani, a Picasso. The general impression is of a place lived in by a very rich man with excellent taste.

That taste is also evident in what he wears, even at his most informal. He prefers custom-made light blue shirts to match the color of his eyes, white cashmere pullovers, tailored gray flannels, broadly knotted silk ties and the blue jeans that several years ago became the height of *alta moda* all over Europe. No one has ever caught him carrying a suitcase, even an overnight bag, and each of his houses is fully equipped to receive and outfit him whenever he chooses to show up. "He has a natural inclination to live well," Umberto says, "and an aversion to vulgarity."

He knows a great many journalists and writers and he likes talking to them on a casual basis. In fact, he has often said that he would have enjoyed being a newspaperman or an editor, if he had had his choice of another profession. He is not an intellectual, but, in addition to newspapers and periodicals, he claims to have read the major literary works of his time. Some years ago, he took a course in speed reading and he reportedly can zip through even the densest tome or a technical report at the rate of twelve hundred words a minute. He only sleeps five or six hours a night, but even so he clearly doesn't have much time for reading. He prefers books on military history and current topics in the news, but, if pressed, can rarely remember the title of anything he has read and will quickly change the subject.

Agnelli's closest friends are not from the literary world or the arts and have only two things in common: They are successful men of his generation and they have never bored him. David Samset, an Englishman, owns an art gallery in London; Ascanio Branca works in the movie business out of Paris; Galvano Lanza was in his regiment during the Second World War. With them and a relative handful of others, he allows himself to relax and converse on a casual basis. Abstract theories and philosophical speculation are not to his taste; like most businessmen, he prefers to deal in facts, practical possibilities, the here and now. The one constant in all he says and does, according to a number of people who know him well, is a thirst for the best of everything that the world has to offer. He has, in the words of one admirer, "a genius for enjoying himself."

His life also has deep roots in Italy's most traditional source of power—the family. Not the least of his appeal to many Italians is his devotion to his blood relations. If Agnelli were merely a modern-day *condottiere*, he would be considered, however romantic the aura surrounding him, simply another dashing figure in today's pantheon of pop-culture deities. The fact that he presides like a true paterfamilias over a regiment of more than 150 relations unquestionably establishes him as a serious person in a nation where the family, despite all the recent upheavals, is still considered the only reliable bulwark against disaster. "No Italian who has a family is ever alone," Luigi Barzini noted in his book, *The Italians*. "He finds in it a refuge in which to lick his wounds after a defeat, or an arsenal and a staff for his victorious drives. Scholars have always recognized the Italian family as the only fundamental institution in the country, a spontaneous creation of the national genius, adapted through the centuries to changing conditions, the real foundation of whichever social order prevails. In fact, the law, the state and society function only if they do not directly interfere with the family's supreme interest."

Agnelli conforms to this precept. He sees himself as an involuntary but nevertheless absolute patriarch, who concerns himself with everyone in the family's problems. "I've always been very available to whoever comes to ask me something—about work, various problems," he has said, "and I think I at least have everyone's complete trust—first, second, and third generation, even the youngest." He especially likes spending time with the latter and keeps in touch with most of them, even though they are now scattered all over the world. "Let's put it this way," he says. "If I had not always had the consent, the absolute trust of my family, it would have been very difficult. So it is their consent and faith that is reflected in the unity and continuity here [at the Fiat], because this is a business that from the first day has always, more or less, had a continuity of responsibility at the top. This has provided a notable element of security within." He is also fond of pointing out that throughout history "everything is destined to fall apart." Only the family, he implies, remains a secure bastion to fall back on. "To sum up, if I've been able to act as a single point of reference, it's exactly because of the support I've had from the beginning from my sisters, my cousins. . . ."

He talks today like a man who has renounced any political ambition and sees in his family the basic source of his power, although he has also represented Italy at the Council of Europe and is a strongly vocal supporter of the Common Market and its unification. No one who knows him at all can doubt that he sees his country's destiny as indissolubly linked to the ultimate fate of the Western democracies. "We'll go up and down with Italy," he once told an American reporter.

Nearly five hundred years ago, Niccolò Machiavelli wrote his famous political treatise, *The Prince,* in which he defined all the qualities a great ruler should have. According to some observers, he could have been writing a character sketch of Gianni Agnelli. "What doors would be closed to him?" the Florentine courtier asked. "What people would deny him their obedience? What envy would oppose him? What Italian would deny him homage?" In a political sense, of course, the Prince is still in waiting. Meanwhile, comments Suni, "he's doing what he was born to do and what he's able to do, and I think he carries it off pretty well."

EMIGRANTS

CHAPTER
FOURTEEN

ITALIANS
IN THE GARDEN

"WE'VE BEEN SWISS for not quite two hundred years," the young man said, "but we've been Italian for a thousand." He was dark, bearded, curly-haired, intense, and obsessed with his Italian heritage. We were strolling under a light drizzle along the lakeshore promenade of Lugano, watching boats full of happy middle-aged tourists crisscross the lake in pursuit of the simple pleasures, and idly tossing bits of bread to the ducks paddling in the shallow water. I had been in the Ticino, the Italian part of Switzerland, for several days by this time, and I had been telling my companion, a promoter of local cultural events, that I had so far found the area to be rather typically Swiss; that is to say, neat, clean, orderly, efficient, not like Italy at all. I had offended him. "You do not understand," he continued. "Here we have two hundred and fifty separate communities, some with as few as ten or twelve people, all very independent. We speak thirty-seven different dialects. We have seven newspapers, each with its own politics." He groped vaguely in the air with one hand for the clincher. "Ah," he exclaimed, his face lighting up triumphantly, "when we were asked to vote about seat belts in our cars, only the Ticinese voted against the law, by nine to one. We drive like mad people."

This man had obviously never been to Naples or Rome. I had seen no one in the Ticino drive like a mad person. I had, in fact, seen only one illegally parked car and it had sported a Como license plate, pure Italian. I thought it best at this point, however, to keep quiet. I had, after all, come to the Ticino as a visitor, not as an expert. So I allowed him to ramble on with his facts and figures, as we strolled past a small Greek rotunda containing a bust of GIORGIO WASHINGTON, IL FAMOSO LIBERATORE, executed by an Italian sculptor named Angelo Brunere and put on display in Lugano in 1859. "I go to Italy on my vacation every year," the young man continued. "I feel always more and more Italian." He suddenly spotted a chewing-gum wrapper desecrating the ground at the base of the statue, pounced forward to retrieve it and stuffed it quickly into his pocket, as if offended by this act of minor vandalism. The promenade, like every public park I had been in, was as spotless as a private golf course. Typically Italian? No, very, very Swiss. "I wish to explain something else to you," the young man said, as we parted a few minutes later in front of my hotel. "This William Tell—we don't give a dried fig for him."

I didn't really begin to understand this need to be Italian until I had been in the Ticino a little longer. It takes some time to penetrate a bit beneath the surface, especially because that surface, like so much of Switzerland, is so spectacularly beautiful. The area is roughly the shape of an inverted triangle, with its northern base planted against the Alps and its apex thrust into the heart of the Po Valley, about twenty-five miles north of Milan. From the St. Gotthard Pass in the north to the Italian frontier town of Chiasso is only about sixty-five miles, as the hawk flies, but the variety of the scenery is astonishing. The snow-covered peaks of the Alps, some of them over ten thousand feet high, loom over deep gorges and narrow valleys carved over the centuries by ice and water and probing southward like extended fingers toward Lake Maggiore. To the southeast, from the town of Bellinzona to Lake Lugano, the land is gentler, with forested hillsides and broader vales merging gradually into the extended flat plain of the Po, Italy's breadbasket. Everywhere villages of simple stone houses, clustered usually about a single church steeple, perch defiantly on the hilltops, while along the lakeshores the larger communities seem to frame the deep blue waters, as if to protect them from contamination by the modern world.

The easiest way to see all this is to hop onto the funiculars and cog railways the Swiss have built everywhere, swoop up to the peaks of the mountains on chair lifts, or ride comfortably on the slow boats that chug cheerfully about the lakes, stopping at every little fishing hamlet. One can also drive up into the valleys to gawk at the waterfalls and tramp about the countryside. Everywhere on the well-tended trails one encounters cheerful, ruddy-faced hikers and campers, all aglow with the joy of the great outdoors, and after a while one begins to think of the Ticino as a sort of huge public park administered and patronized by jolly health fanatics. The overall effect is one of great natural but severely regulated beauty, a typically Teutonic attempt to manage the environment. It reminded me at first of nothing I had become accustomed to in Italy, a country whose own spectacular scenic resources are simply taken for granted and have been largely neglected over the past thirty years in favor of unbridled development.

The names in the graveyards, however, are mostly Italian. On some of the tombstones photographs of the deceased have been permanently implanted. Here are the faces of the Lombard and Piedmontese peasants, descendants of the original hardy stock that settled in the area over a thousand years ago. The women seem prematurely worn and old, cheerless in their rectitude; the men wear hats, sport beards and fierce mustaches, and stare out at the visitor with stern, unsmiling eyes. They all seem to have learned that the world is not an easy place and that hard work guarantees, at best, only survival.

At Morcote, a small resort town a few miles south of Lugano, the dead lie quietly isolated on a hilltop beside their ancient granite church. Its dark steeple, soaring high above the lake, seems to point like a cautionary finger, an admonishment of a sort to the bustling new development of brightly tinted, stuccoed palazzi rambling along the shoreline below. The contrast is striking, a stark reminder of the strange, dichotomous history of the Ticino and a past its people once fled from, but which many, like my friend the promoter, were now clearly eager to recapture and defend. "Our history, from 1000 on," a writer named Basilio Biucchi recently noted, "is the existential history of a borderland and outcast territory (also cast out) between north and south, between the Alps and the Lombard plain, which already breathes the great Mediterranean Sea."

Basically, the Ticino, so called after the river that links Lake Maggiore to the Po, has always been, in the words of a local historian, "a part of Lombardy that has followed the destiny of Switzerland." It was contested for centuries between the militant dioceses of Milan and

Como, then was fought over by the Guelphs and Ghibellines, the ducal families of the Rusca, the Visconti and the Sforza, and a series of mercenary armies that trampled the local populations underfoot during the seemingly endless armed confrontations of the quarrelsome Middle Ages. Exhausted by these Italian and French conflicts, the Ticinese turned to the Swiss for protection, becoming for roughly three hundred years a colony, without self-government, major industries, or cultural centers. The people, fiercely independent and hardworking, struggled to remain on their land, but many were forced to flee abroad, mainly to Italy. The more highly skilled, especially the artisans in stone, immediately found work in Tuscany, Rome, Naples, and Sicily. They also travelled all over Europe, contributing to the construction of palaces, churches, monuments, and entire cities. (Moscow was partly built by Ticinese stonemasons.) Most, however, labored at humble jobs as porters, sweepers, peddlers, kitchen help, and day workers. The rural economy of the Ticino was able to export only the consistently small surplus of its produce; it depended for survival upon being able to unload its excess population. Emigration became a constant throughout the history of the region.

The main problem was that the Ticino was almost completely cut off from the rest of Switzerland by the formidable natural obstacle of the Alps. The country as a whole was populated, as it is today, largely by citizens of German origin. A strong French-speaking minority lived in the western part between Geneva and Lausanne, but it, too, had little contact with the area. Almost the only access to the Ticino was over difficult mountain passes or by boat across the lakes. Geographically, the Ticino depended upon Italy, but it found itself trapped between the Alps and the customs barriers along its southern borders.

Another negative factor was its dependence on the so-called Swiss League. The Ticino was not immediately admitted as a full-fledged canton, with all the rights and privileges of the vote, but was treated as a protectorate. In 1501, the first German-speaking governor was selected and installed himself in Bellinzona, a fortified town that became the capital of an essentially colonial administration, which lasted for three hundred years. These Swiss *landfogti,* as they were known, were appointed for two-year terms and their main concern was the raising of money. The post was auctioned off to the highest bidder and during the first year of his rule the governor spent much of his time trying to recoup his investment. The second year was devoted to milking enough out of the local population to put together a little nest egg to go home with. Even when the *landfogti* turned out to be well-intentioned and honest, the system worked poorly. "Ignorant of the language and the institutions of the subject country," the Ticinese historians Giulio Rossi and Eligio Pometta observed about this usage, "when, after two years they had become a bit acclimatized and used to the practices of their office, they had to give way to another magistrate, who was also completely new to the country." The Ticinese found themselves in the position of having, in essence, to pay protection money to their own government in order to be allowed to live in peace.

At the end of the eighteenth century, under the pressure of the Napoleonic wars and with French armies occasionally trampling across its territory, the Ticino finally became integrated into the rest of Switzerland, and in 1803 became a full-fledged canton. Then, in 1872, the opening of a railroad tunnel under the St. Gotthard Pass linked the area to the rest of the country and brought the Ticino to the attention of the rich, German-speaking burghers of Schwyz, Luzern, and Zurich. The first visitors from the north began to arrive to occupy the newly built hotels sprawling along the lakefronts and the Ticinese began to make money from the tourist industry. It was the only economic avenue immediately open to them, because the area had been isolated for three centuries and been completely passed over by the industrial revolution. The economy in general, however, remained, in Signor Biucchi's words, "weak, poor in resources and capital, with an emigrant working population." The tourist influx benefited only such well-situated communities as Lugano, Locarno, and Ascona, all picturesquely positioned on lakes; in the valleys and on the hillsides, the centuries-old poverty persisted.

The Ticinese, few of whom spoke any German or French, continued to feel themselves closely linked by blood and culture to Italy. The canton actively supported the Italian struggle for independence and dispatched volunteers to fight under Garibaldi. It sheltered refugees and fugitives from the Austrian domination of the peninsula and became such a hotbed of Italian revolutionary activity that the federal authorities had to close the frontier to keep the Austrian armies from invading Swiss soil. Nevertheless, a constant traffic of arms and plotters continued to scuttle back and forth over the waters of the lakes and the Ticino as a whole emerged from the conflict as an important contributing factor to the eventual liberation of Italy and the unification of the country under the Piedmontese House of Savoy.

This triumphant outcome turned out to be a major disappointment for the Ticino, which had expected a relaxation of customs barriers between the two nations and an even easier access to the Italian job market. Italy, however, had tremendous economic problems of its own to deal with, including widespread unemployment, and the Ticinese found themselves no longer welcome in the nation they had helped to create. "This was the beginning of our real love–hate relationship with Italy," a young radio producer and commentator named Gianni Bernasconi informed me one day in Lugano. "We found ourselves shut out of Italy and forced to emigrate now to America and Australia. At the same time, we had to continually ask the Swiss for bread. And to them we were *cincali,* a name derived from a simple northern Italian game played by two people matching extended fingers."

For the Ticino as a whole the period between 1860 and 1960 was the century in which the character of the region was defined. A population explosion continued to stock the columns of emigrants fleeing unemployment and poverty, while at home the survivors gradually began to integrate into the rest of Switzerland. "We finally discovered that we were not Italian, after all, but Swiss–Italian, with the defects and virtues of both," Signor Bernasconi said. "Yes, we are 100 percent Swiss," a tourist official named Marco Solari told me, "but we continually look to Italy. There is always this desire to open our arms to Italy."

NOT ONLY the Ticino, but all of Switzerland quite literally opened its arms to Italy during the 1950s and '60s. The nation was undergoing what came to be known in the Ticino as *il grande boom,* a period immortalized by an Italian movie called *Bread and Chocolate,* which portrayed the often comical and sometimes touching misadventures of a young Italian waiter working in a Swiss restaurant. The Ticino, too, needed workers and Italy had a labor surplus; the Italians poured across the border from the impoverished southern villages of the Mezzogiorno and the slums of the industrialized northern cities to work, mostly in the restaurants, hotels, and shops catering to the tourists or on the rich farmland and hillside vineyards between Lugano and Bellinzona. Many also found jobs in the building industry, but all were regarded by the Ticinese as *terroni,* a term of mild contempt indicating an ignorant attachment to the land.

For many of these immigrants the adjustment to Swiss life, especially in the north, was painful. Their main contact with home was the local railroad station, which became a meeting place and a source of information. The bewildered peasants stepping off the trains, suitcase in hand, often found themselves besieged for news from home and were in turn swept up into the local Italian colony. Most remained only during the heavier tourist seasons, but many, especially in the Ticino, stayed on and successfully adapted to their new life, finding in this corner of a foreign country not only a means of making a living but an Italianate ambience in which they soon began to feel at home. They sent for their relatives and started to raise families.

Unfortunately, this changed abruptly during the early seventies, when the economy suffered a period of stagnation and then a real recession. The tourist industry was particularly hard hit, because Switzerland, the world's banker, had become too expensive for the average traveller. The Swiss slammed the door in Italy's face, in much the same way Italy had turned its back on the Ticino a century earlier. The Italian workers and their families were coldly uprooted and sent home. Some Ticinese, upset by the ruthlessness of the procedure, protested, but in vain. "If Switzerland has a fault," I was told by a librarian in Lugano, "it is the incivility of civilization." The years of bread and chocolate left a bitter aftertaste that has only recently begun to fade.

During the past few years, the economy of the Ticino has been diversified and largely integrated into the overall Swiss structure, which is based on banking, construction, and specialized manufacturing. The industries—metalworking, plastics, clothing, shoes, watches, pharmaceuticals—are mostly small, many of them employing fewer than forty people. "The smallness of our ventures is characteristic of our Italian heritage," a spokesman for the Chamber of Commerce recently explained. "Every Ticinese wants to set up in business for himself."

Seventy-three hundred of them, however, are employed in the banks. The Ticino still has no stock exchange of its own, but it is the fourth biggest canton in terms of banking volume and has the most teller windows in the nation. "A lot of people invest across the Italian border," is the way it was explained to me, which essentially means that the Italians don't trust their own weakened lira and have for years exported funds, often illegally, out of Italy and into the safety of the Swiss banks, with their reassuring guarantees of secrecy.

One way to do this was by smuggling currency as well as other negotiable contraband—cigarettes, liquor, drugs—across the lakes in fast speedboats, and there is a museum on the shore of Lake Lugano testifying to the ingenuity of the smugglers. The collection is housed in an old customs building on the border and consists of a documentation of illegal activity over the years, as well as a display of some of the merchandise seized, including a miniature submarine once used to sneak in cargos of bacon and pork sausages.

Another method was by laundering money through the gambling casino in Campione, a tiny Italian enclave on Lake Lugano that is entirely within the borders of Switzerland. So much illegal money, known as "black funds," moved through there that the Italian government shut down the casino a couple of years ago for some months. The mayor of Campione and several members of his administration were arrested for allegedly being involved in the process. The casino has since been reopened, but under much stricter surveillance. As for the Swiss themselves, they have traditionally never really cared where the money came from, as long as it was deposited in their banks. The illegal export of funds into Switzerland is known to have contributed to a number of Italian financial scandals, including in recent years the failure of the Banco Ambrosiano and the bankruptcy of the Rizzoli publishing empire. Several Ticinese were arrested a few years ago for having helped to launder money earned from the illegal narcotics trade through Swiss banks, a case popularly referred to here as "the Pizza Connection." Although the Swiss refused in a recent referendum, by a vote of more than four to one, to open their books to outside investigators, they have given positive indications that some attention will now be paid as to how the money was earned that is still coming into the country.

THE MOST important Italian resource still flowing in a constant stream across the Ticinese border is people. Thirty thousand so-called *frontalieri,* or "frontier people," cross over every day to work, mostly in the hotels and restaurants. In order to qualify for their jobs, they have to live within thirty kilometers of the border and must return home every night. During the past decade, the smaller Italian towns along the frontier have doubled and tripled in population, while in the larger centers, such as Chiasso and Verese, blocks of new apartment houses have been built to accommodate these workers. The *stagionali,* or seasonal types, can remain for up to nine months; they also mainly serve the tourist industry. A much smaller group, known as *annuali,* or "annuals," can stay for a whole year and then renew their residence permits. At the end of ten years, the latter can ask for a permanent residence and eventually put in for full citizenship. Furthermore, if another economic slump should afflict the region, even the *frontalieri* can now apply for Swiss benefits, such as an unemployment compensation that will pay them up to 80 percent of their wages for one year while they are presumably out looking for work. The total population of the Ticino is about three hundred thousand, a third of whom are foreigners, most of them Italian. "As pure Ticinese," a local acquaintance informed me, "it is clear that we are on the road to extinction."

Ironically, it is the renewed and continued influx of Italians into the Ticino that is most likely to preserve the character and cultural traditions of the area. Since 1980, when an automobile tunnel was finally blasted under the Alps, the German-speaking Swiss have discovered the Ticino *en masse* and treat it as their own personal Riviera; they now swoop down onto its lakes and green valleys even for short weekends. Many have snapped up houses and land and built themselves vacation homes, which, as Swiss citizens, they have a perfect right to do. (Foreigners are not allowed to own property in Switzerland.) The trouble is that the Ticinese, having been looked down on as impoverished rustics for so long by their fellow citizens, are not ready to accept them into their community. "Now that we have at last become masters of our own destiny," Signor Bernasconi informed me, "we are masters being pushed off our own land."

The prosperous invaders from the north have the money to pay the inflated prices being asked for the choicer sites and there is now hardly a place anywhere in the Ticino that doesn't list German names on its roster of inhabitants. In a tiny village called Boschetto, in the Val di Maggia north of Locarno, all but one of the handful of once abandoned stone cottages are now owned by outsiders and I was told by the last Ticinese property owner there, a cheerful middle-aged woman who grew up in the area, that prices have tripled in the past five years. She was the only native-born Ticinese to hang on, even though she herself lived in nearby Cevio, a larger little town of a few hundred people from which she periodically fled as from a crowded slum. "Now even Boschetto is being taken over," she said. "For eight hundred years they ignored us and now they wish to swallow us up."

The attitude is a common one among the Ticinese, who have always felt themselves shut off from the mainstream of Swiss life. The total population of Switzerland is roughly 6.5 million, about two thirds of them of German origin, and undeniably the Ticino has been until recently all but ignored. The canton is without a university of its own and its citizens have to go to the French- or German-speaking ones to complete their education, whereas Italian is not a required language outside of the region. (Some Ticinese speak only Italian and attend universities in northern Italy.) The situation tends to feed the sense of inferiority and paranoia that has long characterized the attitude of the Ticinese in relation to the rest of the country. *"Landfogti,* go home!" and *"Landfogti,* hands off the Ticino!" are phrases I saw scrawled on building walls and every slight, imagined or not, is blown up and fiercely commented upon by the locals. A couple of years ago, a newspaper in Zurich conducted a survey on the sexual preferences and habits of the Swiss, but neglected even to mention the Ticino. The incident was indignantly played up in every Ticinese daily and rankled for weeks.

To combat what many citizens here see as a German invasion, some communities have begun to adopt tough local zoning laws to limit construction and conversion of old buildings into holiday apartments. The measures are designed mainly to keep strangers out. The village of Busino Arsizzio, an ex-fishing hamlet on Lake Lugano, was among the first to try to restrict the snapping up of its old houses by outsiders, but during a recent stroll along its narrow streets I noted that about half the names on the doors were Teutonic. "It is clear that to survive," Signor Solari declared, "we are going to have to latch onto the Italian train."

The Italians who now live and work in the Ticino have contributed greatly to keeping the area distinctively Italian. "At first, even under the more liberal rules of the past few years, they all imagined they would go home," Signor Bernasconi confided. "But now, ten to fifteen years later, there are children who have been born here and they have grown up as Swiss. In the beginning, too, mixed marriages were rare, but now they are quite common. *Their* children are pure Ticinese. And even the *frontalieri* influence our lives greatly. They have kept alive, for instance, *il gusto della cucina,* the taste for good cooking." He also pointed out that the obligatory military service all Swiss citizens have to participate in has contributed to easing racial tensions. "Next to Schmidt or Muller you will now find a Cacciotta. Many of the Italians who first came here were from the poorest parts and spoke only their local dialects, but their children have grown up Ticinese."

It doesn't seem likely that under the present system the Ticino will ever lose its Italian flavor, no matter how many German-speaking fellow citizens continue to pour in from the north. "You don't wipe out a thousand years of history overnight," the cultural promoter said to me. Several weeks later, when I was back in Rome, I fell into conversation with a local butcher who had married a Swiss woman and lived in Basel for eight years before returning to his native city. When I told him I had recently spent some time in the Ticino, he smiled and said, "All of Switzerland is very beautiful, but without the Italians it would be a garden without flowers."

CHAPTER
FIFTEEN

GOLDEN THROATS

THE FIRST TIME I heard Beniamino Gigli sing I thought of liquid gold. I was twelve years old and I had just walked into my grandmother's bedroom in New York, probably to ask her something about my homework, and she immediately shooed me into silence. She was sitting upright on the edge of her bed, listening to the small radio on her nightstand, and as I entered an Italian tenor voice began to pour into the room. I stood there transfixed, not knowing exactly what I was listening to, but overwhelmed by the mellifluous beauty of that sound. The aria, my grandmother informed me later, was the famous "Che gelida manina," from the first act of Puccini's *La Bohème.* "How this one can sing!" my grandmother said in Italian, when the last soft note had faded away. "Certainly he is a Fascist, but art does not know politics."

I already knew I had a nice voice of my own, even though it hadn't yet changed. My mother, who played the guitar and had been a singer and actress in her native Italy and on Broadway, most notably in a 1930s musical called *Revenge with Music,* had taught me some Neapolitan songs and a couple of *stornelli,* the popular local ditties she had grown up hearing in the streets of Rome. I sang them along with her at home, then later at school in New York, at assemblies and on more informal occasions. I had a cool, clear alto that people liked to listen to and, though I'd had no formal training, I had been told that I was musical and had talent.

I had spent most of the first eight years of my life in Italy, mainly on Capri and in Rome, and being able to speak a couple of foreign languages (French, as well as Italian) had provided a useful cachet I could bask in among my schoolmates. Being able to sing supplied another one, though it never occurred to me, until years after I'd heard Gigli for the first time, that I might actually want to become a professional opera singer myself. That came later, when I was seventeen and in love with a New York society girl named Lorraine, whose family had a Monday-night box at the old Met. By then I had become a fanatical devotee of the operettas of Gilbert and Sullivan, but had no interest in grand opera. In fact, I had never even been to the Met. My grandmother had once taken me, shortly after the Gigli episode, to see an *Aida* put on by a touring company, but I had been bored practically out of my skull. No second attempt had been made, even though I had gone on singing here and there, mostly in school choirs and glee clubs, and had begun to think about a stage career, but in musical comedy and operetta. When Lorraine's parents invited me to the opera, I accepted only because I didn't want her to think badly of me. I was pretty stuck on Lorraine and even rented a tuxedo for the occasion.

The opera performed that night was Wagner's *Tannhäuser*, hardly the sort of piece calculated to enchant a restless teenager. (Rossini is reported to have remarked, after hearing it in Paris for the first time, "It has some beautiful moments, but some very long quarters of an hour.") Lorraine was dreading the experience and clutched my hand for support, as we took our seats in the second row of the box, behind her parents. From the moment the orchestra began to play, however, I forgot all about Lorraine, and when the curtain rose on the Venusberg scene I stood up so I could see better.

The title role that night was sung by Lauritz Melchior, then nearing the end of his long career as the Met's leading heroic tenor. He was a tall, fat man with jowls and a florid complexion, who looked preposterous in a short tunic that revealed spindly middle-aged legs. He was also holding a lyre of some sort that he made a feeble pretense at playing as he sang his opening number, a paean of praise to his mistress, the goddess Venus, who was a large woman reclining languorously on a couch that her weight threatened at any moment to cave in. From our position to the left of the stage, I could also see how threadbare the sets were and distinguish the ropes holding up the flats. None of this mattered; when Lorraine began to giggle, I paid no attention to her. I was transported by the music and totally caught up in the singing. Melchior had a huge, dark voice with metallic top notes that cut through the orchestra like trumpet blasts. I stayed on my feet for most of the opera and by the end of the evening had become a confirmed buff. Not only that, but I had decided that I would become an opera singer. I don't even remember now whether I ever saw Lorraine again and I have no idea what became of her. But I can recall every moment of Melchior on stage and I also fell in love with Wagner. An excerpted 78–r.p.m. set of *Tannhäuser* was among the first purchases I made, when I began not long after to assemble an operatic record collection.

I knew, of course, that I myself didn't have a heldentenor voice and my newfound enthusiasm for opera wasn't limited to the Wagnerian repertory. What that first *Tannhäuser* accomplished was to open my ears to operatic music in general and I began not only to buy records and scores, but to haunt the old Met. I mostly bought standing-room tickets, then once inside I'd tip an usher a dollar or two to find me an empty orchestra seat. I went as often as I could afford to on my allowance and immersed myself in song.

It was 1943 and we were in the middle of the Second World War. There were few Italian singers on the Met roster, but it didn't take me long to decide that I liked the way they sounded. I especially responded to the talents of Licia Albanese, a lyric soprano whom I still remember as the most poignant Mimi I ever heard, and basso Ezio Pinza, whose full, open-throated, rolling tones came to symbolize for me everything I liked about the way Italians sang. Nino Martini was the only leading Italian tenor on the roster that season and he was all right, too, but I made my real discovery of tenors when I began to listen to records. Gigli and Enrico Caruso became my gods, though my personal pantheon of tenorial deities included many others—Tito Schipa, Aureliano Pertile, Galliano Masini, Giacomo Lauri Volpi, Giuseppe Anselmi, Alessandro Bonci, Dino Borgioli, Francesco Merli, to name the most prominent. I tried to sound like them and determined to become a great Italian tenor on my own, even if I had to change my name. My main argument with the war was not that we were losing it, but that it made it impossible for Italy to export what I considered its most valuable product, the golden-throated opera singers who knew how to fill the house with glorious music.

In the summer of 1944, I went off into the U.S. Air Force to serve fourteen and a half inglorious months in various southern military camps. When the war in Europe ended, I was discharged and came home determined to pursue an operatic career. My father insisted that I go back to Harvard, where I attended very few classes and spent most of my time performing with various Gilbert and Sullivan groups in the Boston area. What I wanted to do most, however, was study voice, so I left Harvard in the spring of 1946 and came back to New York, where I enrolled at the Manhattan School of Music and took two voice lessons a week from a woman on staff who had no credentials herself as a singer and had no idea how to teach me to sing. I still had a nice voice, but I couldn't hit anything about F-sharp without cracking. No one had spoken to me about breathing and supporting the tone on a controlled column of air. I knew that I needed better instruction than I was getting, but I had no idea how to go about acquiring it. And it was expensive even then; the best private singing teachers in New York charged ten dollars a half-hour.

Everything came into focus for me on January 10, 1947, with the Met debut as Rodolfo in *La Bohème* of Ferruccio Tagliavini. "Italy's trade balance took a favorable turn last night, with the return of its principal export commodity—operatic tenors—to the prewar standard at the Metropolitan Opera House," critic Irving Kolodin wrote the next morning in *The New York Times,* going on to note that Tagliavini's voice "floats superbly and reaches the ear with ring and vibrance at all levels of force." "He can give great pleasure to anybody who likes singing," Virgil Thomson agreed in the *Herald Tribune.*

None of this was news to me. I already knew all about Tagliavini and had heard him on records. I managed somehow to scalp a ticket for opening night and I was there when this dark, chunky little man appeared on stage that memorable night and began to sing. Not since Gigli had I heard a tenor voice of such grace and purity and I was transported. I suddenly realized that nobody I knew in New York could sing like that, with an outpouring of open legato, ringing top notes and the sort of soft, silvery head tones that could melt steel. Obviously it couldn't be merely a question of genetics, I reasoned; I'd read a number of books on singing, Italian-style, and I knew that it took a lot of slow, painful work to build a legitimate voice. But by then I'd also become convinced that only in Italy itself, the birthplace and cradle of opera, could I really learn how to sing.

I began to make plans. I had some money saved up, I had the government's so-called G.I. Bill of Rights, which would provide me with tuition expenses and seventy-five dollars a month to live on for a while, and my mother gave me a thousand dollars. My grandmother had already gone back to Rome to live and I had other relatives in Italy—aunts, an uncle, dozens of cousins of all ages and degrees—who would be helpful.

In the spring of 1947, I sailed from New York harbor for Naples on the *Saturnia,* an old Italian liner that had been used as a hospital ship during the war and had not yet been completely reconverted to the passenger trade. I was one of seven tenors on board, including old Giovanni Martinelli, a lion from the golden age of the Met, and I was the only one who couldn't sing a high note without cracking. I didn't care. The trip took ten days and I had never been so excited in my life, with an operatic concert every night in the main passenger lounge and my daily progress in Italian. Already I could feel my throat opening up and my voice begin to soar.

I SPENT most of the next five years in Italy, mainly in Rome, learning how to sing. I studied for a while with Riccardo Stracciari, an aging great baritone with phenomenal top notes, who told me that it was he who had persuaded Ruggiero Leoncavallo, the composer of *I Pagliacci,* to allow him to interpolate a high A-flat into the prologue of that opera. He sat at the piano in a frayed bathrobe, belting high notes off the walls of his musty apartment, but unfortunately, like many famous singers, he had no idea how to impart his skills to others and I soon moved on. Eventually, I landed in the welcoming arms of an elderly couple named Calcagni, who ran a vocal studio out of their apartment in an old palazzo just off the Corso, in the heart of Rome. She had been a well-regarded lyric soprano and was an accomplished teacher; he had had no career at all and hadn't the faintest idea how to sing, but was so enthusiastic about his pupils (he taught the men) that he somehow managed to convince us that we were all going to be great artists. He beamed and waved his arms furiously about every time one of us attacked a difficult passage, as if he could personally waft us over the vocal rapids.

The one-hour lessons cost the equivalent of about fifty cents each and I went every weekday. When I wasn't singing myself, I would hang around the premises with the other students and talk voices and opera. Sure enough, just by vocalizing and singing every day and hanging around with other young singers, I began to improve. Within six months I could hit some decent top notes and I could sustain a long legato line as well as anyone. At my debut, in a student concert about a year and a half after my arrival, I cracked my very first high note, in an aria from Thomas's *Mignon,* but I improved as I got my nerves under control and by the time my last big number came along, the love duet from *Madama Butterfly,* I was confident and actually enjoying myself.

My partner in this exercise was the Calcagnis' star pupil, a very large, jolly young woman named Caterina Mancini, who had already been signed by the Rome Opera and was on the verge of what we all felt sure would be a glorious career. She had a bright, rich soprano that sounded in my ears, as we sang together, like a fire gong. To this day I'm not sure I actually hit the high C with her at the end of the duet. I think I did, because my mouth was open and I was straining every muscle in my diaphragm to support the note, but I'll never know. All I could hear was Caterina. She went on to a successful debut, then was soon singing all over Italy and making recordings for Cetra. She undertook too many big demanding roles, like Norma and Aida, too early in her career and flickered out like a shooting star in less than a decade.

Still, I envy Caterina, because I was destined never to have much of a career at all. I did learn how to sing and I even became a passable musician, able to read a vocal line and careful of my diction. Everyone said I had a nice voice, a true *tenore leggero,* and some compared me to John McCormack, the great Irish songbird who had also studied in Italy, and Tito Schipa, the most musicianly of tenors. I worked on the lighter repertory and told myself that, as I got older, my voice would become bigger. Anyway, it wasn't size that mattered; it was a question of projection, supporting the tone and allowing it to float cleanly and clearly above the orchestra so it would be heard in the very rear rows of even the largest opera house.

Tito Schipa was still very much around and I went to hear him that first summer during the season at Caracalla, where he appeared as

Nemorino in Donizetti's *L'Elisir d'Amore.* The opera was performed outdoors in the majestic ruins of the ancient Roman baths, to an audience of thousands and with nothing overhead to capture the voices of the singers and project them outward toward the public. Schipa, however, was a consummate stylist and an impeccable musician. Every note he sang sounded as clear as the call of an amorous thrush and every word could be understood back to the rear rows where I sat, enthralled. When he embarked in the last act on "Una furtiva lagrima," the plaintive lament that is the opera's most famous chestnut, the delicate melodic line seemed to float in the air around me. I was amazed not only by the tenor's artistry but by the audibility of the music he created. It wasn't until later that I realized he could only have achieved such an effect through sheer vocal power; his voice may have sounded light in timbre, but it was also large. How else could it have carried so easily in the open air over chorus and orchestra? The quality of a voice is what establishes its category, as much as its size. I didn't fully realize that at the time or I might have stopped singing altogether. "Yes, I hear a voice there," a celebrated old baritone named Giuseppe De Luca had said about my instrument back in New York, when I had gone to audition for him at the suggestion of a family friend. "Yes, there is definitely a voice there, but I wouldn't count too much on it."

Schipa was only one of many singers I heard during those early postwar years. Like many of my fellow students, I haunted the back of the Rome Opera House, going to as many performances as I could get into and spending endless hours discussing the merits and demerits of every major artist. I was enthusiastically present at Caterina's triumphant debut, in Rossini's *L'Assedio di Corinto,* and for a *Tristan und Isolde,* sung in Italian, that starred a badly miscast but extraordinarily dramatic young soprano named Maria Callas. I heard Maria Caniglia, then in the twilight of her illustrious career, bluff her way through the role of Tosca, substituting dramatic bravura for her missing top notes, and sat appalled through a *Luisa Miller,* in which Giacomo Lauri Volpi, an aging star from the twenties and thirties, musically manhandled the delicate vocal line Verdi had composed for the part of Rodolfo. When I rose from my seat to whistle at him in protest (the Italian form of booing), I was nearly attacked by a band of his fans, too besotted by their worship of the great man's past to be troubled by his demolition of the composer's intentions. Every night at the opera in those years was an adventure, even if I didn't realize at the time how lucky I was to be able to hear all these great, once-great, soon-to-be-great, or never-to-be-great performers.

Beniamino Gigli was also still singing. Nobody cared anymore that he had been a Fascist; singers, especially tenors, were not supposed to have brains and to understand about politics. He was in his late fifties and devoting most of his time to the concert stage, mainly because it was easier on him physically simply to stand in place and sing exactly what he wanted to sing rather than have to portray a character in costume and make some attempt to act a role. He was short and fat, about as unromantic a figure on stage as one could imagine, but it made no difference to his public, which was vast and adoring and uncritical. His voice was darker than it had been in his prime and had a slight wobble, especially in the early part of his programs, which he would use to warm up. He began mainly with classical Italian songs that made few technical or physical demands on him and in which he could ravish us with the open-throated beauty of tone that had always been his trademark.

The second half of the evening, however, he would devote to arias from various operas. By then he'd have warmed up and that glorious sound soared out of him as if an angel had kissed his throat. I remember a night outdoors, in the ruins of the ancient Basilica di Massenzio in Rome, when I simply sat in place after his rendition of Eléazar's great aria from *La Juive,* too stunned even to applaud. I knew I would never be able to sing like that, but I consoled myself with the knowledge that nobody else could either.

NEARLY EVERY city and town in Italy of any size then had an opera season and I was able to hear opera everywhere. To help support myself, I had gone to work as a stringer for the Rome bureau of a news magazine, a job that not only established me to live decently but dispatched me periodically on trips around the country. Everywhere I went I'd pop into the local opera house to hear whatever was being performed and so I began to acquire a precious cache of operatic memories. I heard Galliano Masini, a dramatic tenor with a dark, velvety voice and an inadequate technique, swooping and scooping through Giordano's *Fedora,* in an outdoor performance in the main piazza of San Gemignano, illuminated by torches stuck into the walls of the ancient Tuscan towers that soared into the night. At La Scala, in Milan, I sat amazed through a performance of *I Puritani,* in which an unknown American tenor named Eugene Conley hit more high B's, C's and C-sharps in one night than I'd been able to achieve in two years of study.

At the Teatro Bellini in Catania, I suffered through a first act of *Rigoletto* in which the incorrigible Lauri Volpi, as the Duke, sang *mezza voce* all the way through. When the audience whistled its disapproval, a representative of management appeared before the curtain at intermission to explain to us that *"il Commendatore"* (an honorary Fascist title) was battling a ferocious cold. He would only attempt to continue if the public would show some understanding of his plight and heroic self-sacrifice. We all applauded heartily, after which *"il Commendatore"* proceeded to belt the rest of his way through the role fortissimo, an accomplishment that caused an outbreak of rapture in the house and a raucous standing ovation at the end of the evening.

In Parma, a small industrial city in the Po Valley, I again heard Schipa in *L'Elisir d'Amore.* I had never witnessed such enthusiasm from an audience before, with ovations at the end of each act for the singer that bordered on frenzy. The town was an operatic hotbed, fiercely proud of having nurtured Verdi, born in nearby Busseto, and Arturo Toscanini. The local buffs tolerated no deviations from what they considered to be the highest artistic standards and many careers had been drowned by the waves of disapprobation that pounded out of the cheap seats in the upper balconies, where the more fanatical upholders of artistic standards reigned. Around the corner from the opera house, at a small *trattoria* where many of the choristers hung out and people would occasionally rise up out of their seats to burst into song, I heard tales of the many ingenious ways in which offending singers had been punished. One tenor had been encored several times for his rendition of "Una furtiva lagrima" and had been compelled smilingly to implore the audience to allow him to proceed. "No," thundered a voice from the gallery, "you will do it until you get it right!"

In addition to the regular seasons, there were dozens of little opera ensembles that would tour the smaller towns and would occasionally show up in the larger cities as well. They usually starred one or two celebrated but aging so-called sacred monsters in parts they had made famous and used young singers or established second-raters in the other roles, while the chorus and orchestra were mostly recruited locally. These tours, sponsored by independent impresarios, were not noted for artistic excellence and almost always ended in insolvency, often with the casts unpaid and creditors in outraged pursuit. They did provide, however, an opportunity for young artists to try out a role under performance conditions and most of us expected to make our debuts in this way, in some small town where we could acquire the experience of doing a part without having to risk the disapproval of the critics, the sort of function now allotted to opera workshops.

One of my closest friends during these years of study and dreams was a young Italian baritone I'll call Vittorio. As a concession to his family, he had agreed to attend medical school, but his real love was opera and he had every intention of pursuing a singing career. He had a dark, well-focused voice that sounded large in a room, but which, oddly enough, failed to carry very far in the theater. I hadn't realized this about him and I was convinced that, with his solid top notes and musicianship, he would undoubtedly succeed. Then, one day, I went to hear him in a concert at the Teatro Argentina in Rome and found myself wondering why his voice sounded suddenly so thin and reedy, barely able to carry over the orchestra in the lighter passages and all but obliterated by the heavier ones. I put it down to the bad cold he told me he had been suffering from and continued to marvel at the sound he could make in close quarters.

When Vittorio informed me one day that he had been engaged by a touring company to make his debut as the Count di Luna in *Il Trovatore,* I fully intended to be on hand for his opening night, scheduled in a couple of weeks for some small town south of Rome, perhaps Frosinone. The star of the enterprise was an elderly diva, who was also reportedly the capital behind the venture. Vittorio would be paid barely enough to cover his travelling expenses for a total of three performances in three different theatres, but the opportunity, he assured me, was not to be missed. He'd be singing with an established star and he'd have a major role under his belt with which later to confront the managers and impresarios of the larger houses.

Unfortunately, I had to go out of town to cover a story for the magazine and missed Vittorio's debut. I had worried about him, though, because di Luna is one of the most vocally demanding of the Verdi baritone parts, and I could easily imagine a fiasco for myself in a similar situation. When I returned, however, and looked up Vittorio, he informed me that the performance had gone splendidly. He had been very nervous at first and not at his best, but, lucky for him, the disapproval of the audience had instantly focused itself on the tenor singing Manrico. He was a middle-aged Roman third-rater, who had made a minor career out of *comprimario* parts and by stepping into larger roles only at the last minute, when a performance risked having to be cancelled due to the indisposition of the singer originally hired. Dramatic tenors are the rarest of operatic commodities and even bad ones can make a living, if they can hit all the notes and just get through a part. This one, Vittorio assured me, had a voice like a goat in heat. "Then in the 'Di quella pira,' in act 3, he cracked the high C," Vittorio said. "The public is furious and this man in the front rows, he rise up, shouting, 'Ah, *bestia,* you animal, how is it possible to sing like this,' and so on. And then the tenor, he rushed to the footlights, sword in hand, and he shout back at this man, 'Hey, shithead, you come up here and sing the high note!' It was impossible, of course, to continue." So Vittorio never got to sing in act 4 and the rest of the tour was also cancelled, but he felt that he, at least, had made a successful debut.

I never sang in any Italian opera house. By the time I felt I was ready to audition, in the spring of 1950, I had also realized I didn't have a big enough instrument to have a major career in opera. I was then living in Milan, where I had been sent by the magazine to be its northern Italy correspondent. I had agreed to go partly because Milan, with its great opera house, La Scala, was the musical capital of Italy. Most of the agents and impresarios, who all seemed to be fat old men in rumpled dark suits, were there; they would gather convivially at midday in a corner under the glass arches of the Galleria, next to Piazza della Scala, stand around, sip coffee and do a lot of their casting on the spot. Like many other young hopefuls, I would also hang around from time to time, feeding on the gossip from the opera world that I longed to be a part of. I even went and auditioned for a couple of these old men, who sat impassively in small offices while I sang arias from *The Barber of Seville* and *Don Giovanni* and *Mignon* for them. One of them offered me the part of Alfredo in *La Traviata* with a small company then being assembled to tour a southern province, but indicated that I would be expected to pay him up front about twice what I would earn from the engagement itself. Not only did I object in principle to such an arrangement, I couldn't afford to accept it, especially since it would mean having to give up my job.

I did eventually get the singing lead that fall in a big musical revue called *Black and White* that opened in late December at the new Teatro Manzoni, physically only a few blocks from La Scala but light years away from it spiritually. I was the boy singer in a show that featured variety acts, comedians, and a chorus line of half-naked English girls, *"les* Bluebell Follies." I had two solos, one a number in which, dressed as a beachcomber, I sang "Go Down, Moses" in Italian ("Vaggiù, Mose, nella terra dei Faraoni"), after which a hula dancer gyrated in a cane field and the Bluebells kicked up their heels. I sang in all of the ensembles and both finales and we did nine shows a week, with matinees on the weekends. The curtain rose at nine o'clock and came down well after one. I was paid 4,000 lire a day, the equivalent of about twenty dollars in purchasing power, and I had no understudy. Two weeks into the run, I came down with a cold and continued to sing until I lost my voice completely and was replaced. It was six months before I could sing again, by which time I had moved back to Rome. I had had to turn down an offer to join the permanent staff of the magazine in order to accept my first professional singing engagement and I was unemployed, but I knew, after Milan, that my future lay in writing, not on the operatic stage.

SOME YEARS ago, when I was back in Rome, I bumped into Vittorio again. My wife and I had gone to the opera to hear Joan Sutherland in Donizetti's *Lucrezia Borgia* and I spotted Vittorio in the front row of a box. I waved to him and we got together in the lobby during the intermission. He looked sleek and prosperous, in a custom-tailored dark gray suit, and informed us that he was doing very well in his medical practice. He was affiliated with a well-known private hospital and also had his own practice. My wife asked him what he specialized in and he answered, "Rich Americans."

After the performance, Vittorio drove us back to his penthouse apartment overlooking the Tiber, poured us each a full tumbler of very smooth, ancient French cognac and played opera for us on his state-of-the-art stereo. As the sound of singing filled the night, we toasted each other and began to reminisce about our adventures as voice students, then as struggling young singers trying to get a foothold in the difficult world of opera. After a while, as the cognac took hold, we stood up and began to bellow along with the recordings. "My God, Bill," Vittorio said, "what fun we had! Now look at us. You are just another journalist and I am just another doctor. Let's begin all over. Let's quit everything and go sing in the Rome opera chorus. Think how happy we would be!"

Vittorio may have been right. I have never been happier than when I'm inside a major opera house, listening to some great artist in top form or a fine ensemble performance of one of my favorite lyric dramas. In the late fall of 1972, I was in Milan, working on an article about the city, and I went to see the late Paolo Grassi, then the newly appointed general manager of the theater. He was a moon-faced, short, heavyset man in his early fifties, with a mustache, a receding hairline, and alert dark brown eyes, who clearly considered his job a sacred mission. "Italy has thirteen major opera houses and symphonic organizations that receive state aid in the form of a subsidy," he informed me, "but the state must always think of La Scala first. We cannot be treated like the San Carlo of Naples or the Reggio of Turin. We are on another level of performance entirely. I don't say we don't make mistakes—we make many—but La Scala is still La Scala. Like Garibaldi, our name is internationally known and in places that have never heard of Giovanni Leone (then the president of Italy) and don't know what an Alfa-Romeo is."

After I had finished interviewing him, I asked if I could sit in on a rehearsal or two and he arranged for me to attend the first run-through on stage the next morning of act 1 of Bellini's *Norma,* featuring my favorite soprano, Montserrat Caballé. I already had in my collection every recording the Spanish diva had made, including pirated ones of various performances of hers around the globe, but I had never heard her in person. "But you must not allow yourself to be seen," Grassi warned me. "It is a closed rehearsal with orchestra and Maestro Gavazzeni is very strict about no visitors."

I showed up at Grassi's office at the appointed time the next morning and was escorted by an assistant into a second-tier box to the left of the stage. As I waited for the rehearsal to begin, I looked out over the elegant, cylindrically shaped auditorium, all cream and gold, with its tightly banked rows of boxes and balconies ascending into a void. Although the theater seats only about thirteen hundred, it seems huge and, with 193 years of operatic history behind it, completely intimidating. How could I ever have imagined I would one day have been able to stand there on that stage, where every great artist in history had sung, and dared even to open my mouth?

Soon after the rehearsal began, Madame Caballé, in the title role, appeared on the set to sing her introductory phrases, after which she would have to embark on the "Casta Diva," one of the most melodically intricate and technically difficult arias ever written. My initial impression of her was visually disappointing. She was a short, plump woman dressed in a black skirt and sweater, with a double strand of pearls around her neck and a beehive hairdo. She looked exactly like the Barcelona housewife and mother I had been told she was, not Bellini's ravishing Druid priestess. The minute she opened her mouth, however, the housewife disappeared and the tragic heroine of the drama took her place. Her warm, smooth, rich voice, perfectly supported on a seemingly inexhaustible supply of air, soared up above the orchestra, not skipping or slurring a single note as it spun its melodic web in the air around me. By the middle of the second verse, I was alone in the theater, in the very heart of the drama, and moved to tears.

When Caballé had finished, seeming to have expended no effort whatsoever in the casual accomplishment of this small musical miracle, the orchestra stopped playing and applauded. The soprano smiled and nodded shyly in its direction, as Maestro Gavazzeni good-naturedly rapped on his podium with his baton. The rehearsal resumed and I wiped my eyes, then settled back to enjoy the rest of it. You don't actually have to be Italian to have a golden throat, but you do have to be able to sing like one.

CHAPTER
SIXTEEN

THE LAST ITALIAN

For years the old Italians have been dying
all over North Beach San Francisco
For years the old Italians in faded felt hats
have been sunning themselves and dying
You have seen them on the benches
in the park in Washington Square . . .

—Lawrence Ferlinghetti

ALTHOUGH THESE OPENING lines of Ferlinghetti's poem commemorating, in effect, the end of an era in San Francisco were first published in 1977, some of the elderly citizens whose passing he mourns are apparently unaware that they are on the brink of an abyss. Most of the forty or so residents of the Casa Costanzo, for instance, the Italian retirement home on the south side of the square, are not much in evidence in the park. During the day they are likely to be out shopping, running errands, visiting relatives, or socializing in the local espresso bars that abound in the area. Giuseppe Ciardullo, for one, spends no time in the park and as little as he can at the Casa. His days are active, full of small, routine tasks and neighborhood projects—shopping for friends and clients, meals to be cooked, conversations to be enjoyed, jokes to be told, with, in addition, frequent afternoon forays in pursuit of winning horses. "I do not linger here," he says about the Casa. "There is nothing to do in here but be old."

Giuseppe is a slightly stooped but vigorous-looking man of eighty, with a thick head of iron gray hair, dark brown eyes, a long nose, pink cheeks, and a foxy smile. Every day he rises early and heads, coffee pot in hand, for the communal kitchen down a long beige-colored, dark-paneled corridor that is, like the rest of the Casa, spotlessly clean but institutional-looking. Even in the social rooms, with their comfortable sofas, armchairs, and color TV sets, the walls are devoid of pictures or other decorative touches. Giuseppe, therefore, prefers to eat breakfast in his room. It consists of biscuits, fresh ricotta cheese, and strong Italian coffee "corrected" by a shot of whiskey, after which he embarks on his day. He is almost always out of the premises by 8:30 A.M.

Dressed usually in slacks, an open-necked sports shirt with a foulard, and a sports jacket, Giuseppe emerges into what used to be the center of the city's Italian community, which radiated out from North Beach and consisted well into the 1950s of about thirty thousand people. On the north side of Washington Square, which used to be referred to by residents as *il giardino* (the garden), rise the twin spires of the Church of Saints Peter and Paul, with an inscription from Dante's *Paradiso* chiseled into the façade over the main entrance. On the east side is the Dante Building, which looks like a Venetian-Moorish palazzo and houses the Rossi Drug Company, one of the seven Italian pharmacies that used to flourish in the area. Next to it is the San Francisco Athletic Club, which is patronized mainly by its aging male members and whose walls are lined by fading photographs of long-dispersed winning soccer and baseball teams, its dusty rooms full of cabinets bulging with lusterless silver-colored cups and other time-worn trophies of long-ago triumphs. By lunchtime the bar of La Felce, the family-style Tuscan restaurant on the corner of Union and Stockton, will have filled up with club members, grizzled debaters sounding off in that mixture of Italian, Italian dialects, and American slang that characterizes the watering holes of second and third generation Italian Americans. And all around the square, as elsewhere in North Beach, are the other Italian establishments that have become more familiar to Giuseppe than the streets and piazzas of Viterbo and Rome, where he spent most of his first fifty years.

THE LAST ITALIAN

Giuseppe usually begins his day with a stop at his favorite haunt, the Café Italia on Vallejo Street, for an espresso. "Ah," he says, bowing formally to whichever of his friends and acquaintances he may find inside, "I have the greatest esteem for you, Excellency." He grins, he winks, he banters with the bartender, he makes his time a long, running commentary spiced with Italian puns, jokes, turns of phrase. "We must enjoy ourselves," he comments. "Was it not Mussolini who said that it is better to live one day as a lion than a thousand years as a lamb? Out of the mouths of cretins come small wisdoms."

He has become a well-known figure in North Beach and is welcome everywhere. At the Caffè Roma on Columbus Avenue, the proprietor treats him as an honored guest and he also benefits from special small discounts many of the merchants make on his behalf. In return, Giuseppe will cook for them from time to time, a talent he acquired from his childhood in Viterbo, north of Rome, where his father owned a *trattoria*. He whips up simple but delicious meals in the tiny kitchens many of the shopkeepers maintain in the back rooms of their establishments. He has an especially delicate touch with pasta and chicken dishes, and his *involtini alla romana*—thin, pounded slices of beef wrapped around onions and prosciutto and sautéed in a tomato-flavored meat sauce—are much in demand with his clients. These include the proprietors of several establishments on Columbus Avenue and the adjacent side streets, but he is especially sought after at the Caffè Roma, Stella Pastry, Biordi Art Imports, and the Gloria Sausage Factory and Delicatessen, where his cooking has frequently helped to keep him well fed.

On a monthly income of about five hundred dollars, Giuseppe is glad to be able to eat well at someone else's expense. "I do it as a favor, naturally," he has said, "but, of course, one hand washes the other." He shops for his supplies mainly in the Italian stores where he's known, but his favorite butcher is a Chinese establishment with whose personnel he communicates "à la Marco Polo," with elaborate hand signals, and he also gets tips on horses. Like Giuseppe, the Chinese in there are all horse-players and they give him a good deal on meat. "They are nice to me," he says. "We talk the language of catastrophe."

On days when he has no one to cook for, Giuseppe takes a bus to one of the local racetracks, either Bay Meadows or Golden Gate Fields. "I do it not to make money—the races are all arranged beforehand—but merely to distract myself," he explains. "After all, one must make the time pass." In the evenings, he returns to his room, cooks something for himself, then drops in at the Café Italia, where he is known to some of the younger patrons as "Joe from Rome." The walls of the Café Italia are decorated by faded Italian travel posters and the small room is usually crowded, full of smoke and the hum of active conversation. Giuseppe can count on finding someone around the pool table or at the bar to talk to in his native language, as his English is very limited. "I came to it too late," he explains, with a shrug. "What can you do?" Sometimes he plays pinball, but mostly he sits at one of the small round tables with other elderly friends to talk horses or reminisce, until, at eleven o'clock or so, it's time to go home.

T HE WORLD that Giuseppe Ciardullo and other first-generation Italian immigrants inhabit today in North Beach is a shrinking one. In fact, they appear to be living in a geographical time capsule, flitting from one small ethnic oasis to another within an area that is rapidly becoming homogenized. It was this disappearance of the Italians, made inevitable by the end of large-scale immigration in the thirties, that Ferlinghetti took note of in his poem and which Giuseppe and his cronies, however unaware they themselves may be of the trend, symbolize as they live out their days in the quarter.

In 1979, an independent survey of District Three, which comprises four neighborhoods—Telegraph/North Beach, Chinatown, Polk Gulch, and Nob Hill—showed a total of 13,400 people living in Telegraph/North Beach, 61 percent of them of "foreign stock," meaning "foreign born and persons of foreign born and mixed parentage." Over half of these people, however, were Chinese and since then that figure has greatly increased, due primarily to continued Asian immigration into the district, real estate speculation by foreign capital (so-called "Hong Kong money"), and the dying off and drifting away of the Italian families who only a generation earlier comprised over 90 percent of the inhabitants of North Beach.

Although no exact population breakdown has become available as a result of the 1980 census, primarily because Italians are no longer considered an ethnic minority but are simply lumped in with other whites, the exodus of Italians and their descendants from North Beach has continued, until today probably no more than a few hundred families remain. What North Beach has become can be compared to the façade of a baroque church, an ornate and imposing front of architectural and decorative wonders masking a plainer reality. The area today exists largely in guidebooks and the public fancy as a picturesque Edwardian quarter full of Italian restaurants and shops nestled against each other along the gridiron of narrow streets framing Washington Square, with its landmark buildings and rosy-cheeked old men dozing in the sun.

The portrait is accurate, as far as it goes, but many of the old people sitting on the park benches have Asian features, as do two-thirds of the children in the playground of the Salesian school attached to the Church of Saints Peter and Paul. The Dante Building, like many others, is now owned by Chinese, and the Rossi Drug Company is being evicted, while along Upper Grant Street the last few Italian establishments are sandwiched between rows of Chinese shops. The area bills itself, in fact, as New Chinatown and until very recently all of North Beach, for purposes of city planning and federal grants, had been subsumed at City Hall into "Greater Chinatown," a discovery that touched off a furor among the Italian merchants, most of whom, however, no longer live in the area.

The rapidly changing nature of North Beach even came as a surprise to people living in the quarter. The Casa Costanzo, for instance, was originally supposed to be a five-story structure and to occupy half the block, between the church and the corner of Filbert and Stockton. "We'd been talking about a home for our old people for years," Salvatore Reina, a semiretired banker still living in North Beach, recalled recently. "It was to be called the Villa Carina and would have cost several million dollars."

When his group couldn't raise the money, it was decided to take over the lease of an old hotel across the way that had become little more than a flophouse. Cleaned up, remodeled, and renamed (after Father Joseph Costanzo, a well-loved pastor of Saints Peter and Paul), the home opened in 1980 with forty-five rooms, but has rarely been fully booked. "The idea was to keep the respected elderly in the area where they are," Reina explained, "but it turned out to be a good thing we started in a small way." In other words, there simply weren't enough old Italians left.

If something of North Beach's Italian heritage does survive, it will be because some of the people who no longer live there have taken steps to perpetuate it. A distinguished-looking, middle-aged insurance executive from Bari named Marco Vinella, who lived in North Beach for eighteen years after his arrival here as an immigrant in 1955, is trying to mobilize the city's Italian-American community to preserve the neighborhood's traditional Italian character. A public relations man named Alessandro Baccari has even created a small museum enshrining it, in a couple of small rooms packed with memorabilia and a changing photographic display, over the Eureka Savings and Loan on Stockton, and he likes to point out that no one can alter certain basic facts about the district. "We grew up here, we went to school here, we come here for all our traditional holidays," he said recently. "No one is going to change that, any more than they are going to change the words of Dante on the front of our church."

Giuseppe Ciardullo was fifty-one years old when he and his wife Vincenza left Rome with his youngest daughter to settle in Washington, D.C., in 1951. Two of their children, all girls, had married American military men they had met abroad and were then also living in Washington, so that the move, made mostly at Vincenza's insistence, served temporarily to reunite the family. Giuseppe found a job as a waiter in a local Italian restaurant. Although he had worked most of his adult life for the Italian state railway system and had risen to the rank of a Capo Personale Viaggiante, a supervisory position with 375 employees, mostly travelling personnel, under him, he spoke very few words of English and felt unqualified in America to do anything but wait on tables. "It was a place that served spaghetti invisible under lakes of tomato sauce," he has recalled, "but at that time there were no good Italian restaurants there."

Within a few years, the sons-in-law were transferred to other parts of the country and the youngest daughter met and married a computer technologist, who spirited her away to Oakland. After nine years in Washington, the Ciardullos also moved to Oakland and Giuseppe found work as a waiter at La Felce, where he was employed for eleven years. After his retirement and then his wife's death in 1977, Giuseppe moved to an apartment in North Beach. All he has to live on now are his Italian government pension, reduced by inflation and the depressed value of the lira to about $200 a month, and Social Security payments of $233 dollars a month, supplemented by drawings from his personal savings. Although his three daughters are all married and flourishing in different parts of the country, he has no intention of asking them for help. He has five grandchildren and two great grandchildren, and he visits his scattered family several times a year, always paying his own travel expenses.

About a year ago, Giuseppe moved into the Casa Costanzo, where he occupies a small room on the second floor. It is spotless and furnished with a single bed, a chest of drawers, a TV set, a couple of framed landscapes, a woven red rug, and a table on which he keeps a bottle of whiskey, a Neapolitan coffee pot, and a few well-worn pots and pans. His single window looks out on a back wall, but he only pays ninety dollars a month in rent and goes there, he maintains, only to sleep. "This is what a train conductor is reduced to at the end of his life," he recently told a visitor, as he flung his arms out as if to embrace the scene. "But what else do I need?" He is cheerful about his circumstances and fond of cracking jokes about it. "We are forty-five at the Casa," he once remarked, "but only two of us take showers. It is healthier to be outside."

Giuseppe is now well known in the quarter, not only as a part-time chef but for his roguish sense of humor. He has a vast fund of jokes about his countrymen and, though he loathed Mussolini, he likes to quote the dictator on the subject. "Someone once told Mussolini that it must be very difficult to govern the Italians," he says. " 'No, it is not difficult,' Mussolini answered, 'but it is useless.' " He has also mastered a number of comic routines in various dialects. One of his best is a monologue spoken by a country bumpkin from a mountain village in the Abruzzi describing, as if it were a visit to Mars, his first and only trip to Rome. Giuseppe does not claim to be an original, but admits that he has adapted most of his routines from the acts of professional comedians he remembers from his years in Rome, when he and his wife went frequently to the neighborhood variety theaters. When he first moved to the Bay Area, he was occasionally invited to perform on local Italian television and radio shows, but these, like other manifestations of Italian culture in San Francisco, have been phasing themselves out over the past few years.

The Italian one hears in the streets these days is spoken mostly by the young, many of them native Italians, some of them here on student visas, who work on a temporary basis in the local restaurants and cafés, and the very old. The latter stay on in the quarter because it is all that remains of the Italy they left behind. They follow their familiar daily routines largely oblivious of the fact that most of the locales they frequent are now isolated between the storefronts of the Chinese and that they thread their way to them along sidewalks crowded by Asian shoppers.

Many have discovered that they can't go home again either. In the summer of 1977, Giuseppe Ciardullo went back to Rome, after an absence of twenty-six years. The city he had spent his first half-century in seemed foreign to him. His childhood neighborhoods had disappeared under blocks of new apartment houses and even Rome's most familiar landmarks struck him as changed, surrounded, as many of them were, by new roads and buildings. The ancient stones of his city seemed to have vanished under a tidal wave of cars and concrete. His surviving relatives were strangers, his old friends and colleagues dead or scattered. "I didn't even know how to pay for an espresso," he recalls. "I was a foreigner in my own land." He came back home to North Beach.

One evening not long ago, back from a losing day at Golden Gate, Giuseppe strolled into the reassuringly familiar premises of the Café Italia. Waggling his fingers in the air, he walked mincingly up to the bar in an exaggerated parody of a drag queen. "I want a coffee dark as a forest," he lisped, "as long as a cypress and as sweet as love." The bartender grinningly gave him the finger. "Is that a promise?" Giuseppe asked.

Later, over a glass of red wine, he regaled a friend with an account of how he had once thought of applying for a part-time job at the Italian cemetery, which is located in Colma, a small town a few miles south of the city. "I went there to see it," he said, "and all I could find were these headstones that praised the departed—beloved father, faithful wife, loving son, adored daughter. I looked at all those names there and I asked myself why it is that only the virtuous die. What happens to all the rogues, sluts, and imbeciles? Where do *they* go? Surely they are not immortal." He laughed. "Perhaps, like most of us, one day—poof!"—he snapped his fingers in the air—"perhaps they simply disappear."